Head Rig

STORY OF THE
WEST COAST LUMBER INDUSTRY

by ELLIS LUCIA

with introduction by
ARTHUR W. PRIAULX

OVERLAND WEST PRESS
PORTLAND, OREGON

other books by Ellis Lucia:

In hard cover:

The Saga of Ben Holladay

Klondike Kate

Tough Men, Tough Country

Soft cover:

The Big Blow

Don't Call It Or-E-Gawn

Wild Water

Included in anthologies:

Bits of Silver

Legends and Tales of the Old West

Head Rig, Story of the West Coast Lumber Industry
by Ellis Lucia
(c) 1965 by Ellis Lucia

First Edition

Published in cooperation with the West Coast Lumbermen's Association
Yeon Building, Portland, Oregon

Printed in the United States of America

Times-Litho-Print, Forest Grove, Oregon

Library of Congress Catalog Number: 65-28360

Published by:

Overland West Press, Post Office Box 11507, Portland, Oregon 97211

gift 01/01

In Memory of

ARTHUR W. PRIAULX

who left his blaze

on the West's great forests

Foreword

When it became apparent that the West Coast Lumbermen's Association would transfer its responsibilities of more than half a century to a broader regional organization, we felt there was an important story to tell about this leading trade association and its many accomplishments for the lumber industry and the people of America.

We believed that our story should be detailed in some permanent form, and others outside the realm of WCLA, including authors and historians, were in hearty agreement. What was needed was a full-blown history of the West Coast Lumbermen's Association and the industry it represented, to become a part of the permanent record on the historical shelves in the Pacific Northwest and throughout the country.

However, we wanted more than an internal kind of book that would satisfy only a few egos and generally be read by no one. Like the industry, it should be lively and have public appeal, in addition to telling an accurate story. It was also quickly recognized that in portraying the story of WCLA, the author must tell the story of Northwest lumbering, since each was so much a part of the other.

As one of its final actions, the WCLA board of trustees in 1964 voted to commission Arthur W. Priaulx, our capable publicity director, to write such a book. Mr. Priaulx had a background of some twenty-five years with the association and almost a lifetime in the lumber country of the Pacific Northwest. He had sawdust in his shoes, and had seen many of the accomplishments come to pass and been a part of them. To assist him in the tremendous research task, we assigned Miss Ann Nordstrom who has been a loyal staff member of WCLA for forty-five years and served in key positions, among them as private secretary of Colonel Greeley.

Mr. Priaulx swung into the project with all the excitement and enthusiasm that were characteristic of him. He made progress organizing and outlining the material, and in roughing out the introduction and the first chapters. Then in November 1964 he passed on. One of Art's last concerns was for the book, which he felt most strongly should be completed.

The project was stymied for many weeks, while we searched for the right person to take over the work. We finally approached Ellis Lucia, author of a number of lively historical non-fiction books on the West, plus hundreds of magazine and newspaper articles, and with a broad background on the Pacific Northwest and its people.

Mr. Lucia proved to be a "natural" — not only did he enjoy writing about colorful people and events, but he had been a personal friend of Art Priaulx and was many times assisted by Art during his career. Miss Nordstrom agreed to remain as researcher and adviser, and Mr. Lucia tells me that her services and vast knowledge of the industry and the people in WCLA have been invaluable to him.

This then is our story, as seen through the eyes of Ellis Lucia, to whom we gave a free hand in its telling. It is a profile of a huge and robust industry, of the wonderful, exciting years of one of the greatest trade associations of them all, and of the people who made it great.

G. CLEVELAND EDGETT
Executive Vice President
West Coast Lumbermen's Association

Contents

Introduction

The year was 1827, and the scene so remote that scarcely two hundred venturesome trappers of the North West and Hudson's Bay companies knew its whereabouts. It was two thousand miles from the nearest civilization which lay along the Mississippi River.

It was late in October and a drizzle of rain was falling. The leaden skies cast their dark shadows on the wide and rolling Columbia River to turn its waters to the same leaden gray color.

There was an urgency in the air as there had been at stockaded Fort Vancouver since spring, when the odd events were first set in motion. Now, six miles east of the Hudson's Bay Company fort, in a small gorge along the banks of the Columbia River, a strange hewn frame of logs stood beside the small water-filled stream which helped swell the Columbia a hundred feet away.

All was hustle and bustle. Some twenty dark-skinned Sandwich Islanders were working to fit machinery into the frame. A handful of white men, workers at the fort, in English gentlemen's garb stood off to one side watching proceedings. Above the mill, for mill it was, were two dozen local Indians, intent on the goings-on below them. They were puzzled with the white man's enterprise. They thought it might be some strange workings of God.

These thoughts may have been prompted by the presence at the creekside of a man so forceful in appearance, so domineering and overpowering that all knew that he was in charge as he watched intently each move of the skilled Sandwich Islanders. He was dressed in black habiliments resembling the clergy, yet there was none of the clerical about this man. His straggling gray hair covered with a flat beaver skin hat was a trademark. He was the boss man and make no mistake.

Dr. John McLoughlin strolled about the scene of activity as though he were king; and a king he was in truth, for as chief factor of Hudson's Bay's Fort Vancouver he ruled the vast western part of what was to become, thirty years and more later, the states of Oregon and Washington, Idaho and Montana, and British Columbia Province. He had the power of life and death over white man and Indian, a power he seldom used. He was a dreamer, but far better educated than the average Briton or American.

One of McLoughlin's biggest dreams was soon to be tested. For several years, he had been troubled with the gradual disappearance of the beaver, otter, and other valuable furred animals, whose hides had brought men half way around the world to seek them out of their watery highways and bring their pelts to market.

Dr. McLoughlin, in his lonely walks about the stockade, often reviewed the future of his company, in which he had a huge stake, and decided that some new commodity other than furs must provide the main trading goods. There had been no exploration for metals, to determine if there might be gold or silver about. There was no knowledge of the existence of even the baser metals.

One great natural resource abounded; but it was so close and in such vast abundance that even the great McLoughlin took several years to discover its potential. It was the timber which grew down to the water's edge and so thick that man made the rivers his highways, and kept out of the brush and tall trees.

The furs will soon be gone for all practical economic purposes, so timber it shall be. In one of his frequent letters to London and Montreal headquarters in 1825-26, he asked for machinery with which to build a sawmill to be powered by water.

In due time, in the spring of 1827, the metal parts for the muley, up-and-down sawmill reached Fort Vancouver, shipped from England as soon as Dr. McLoughlin's letter had arrived. Overland came R. W. Crate, a millwright, who promptly set to work designing the mill and with the help of his twenty Sandwich Islanders, spent the summer building the plant. A 6x6 inch crank shaft powered the mill, which consisted of an upright saw. A flume above turned water from the small stream to power the waterwheel.

It was getting late in the day when Crate signaled that all was in readiness and Dr. McLoughlin ceased his endless pacing and moved down beside the mill. A Sandwich Islander rolled a thirty-inch log onto the crude mill carriage, fastened it with primitive iron dogs; another Islander shoved ahead on the handle which started water down the flume. Slowly the mill wheels turned and the muley saw bit into the log with a shrill whine which sent the band of Indians running to the nearby hills.

Slab after slab of beautiful yellow fir lumber fell away from the saw onto crude rollways. The mill could cut about 3,000 feet of lumber a day with a crew of twenty Islanders, Dr. McLoughlin soon discovered. For nearly two years the output of the sawmill was used around the fort to build needed housing for men and animals.

Thus, the squeal of the saw and the shrill, terror-filled screams of the Indians fittingly heralded the start of an industry that one day would reach $2.5 billion in value for each year.

Dr. McLoughlin had taken destiny by the forelock. He was brave enough to shoulder responsibility for his action. But he wanted income for his fort and so, within less than two years, he was shipping lumber from the crude mill upstream from the fort. A wharf had been built to make it easier to load lumber. In 1829, Dr. McLoughlin shipped the first cargo of lumber from his sawmill to the Hawaiian Islands and got $80 per thousand, which must have pleased his Scotch-Irish heart. It made his dream come true, but it was just the start. By 1833 a 50,000-foot parcel of yellow Douglas fir was shipped to China. The mill output for a number of years was sold either in China or the Islands and brought in much cash to offset the drop in fur revenue.

Thus, in this inauspicious way, a vast commercial empire was launched, which those 1827 participants could scarcely dream would happen. Of this tiny band of pioneers, probably only Dr. McLoughlin could envision the future. And it is not to be doubted that he did foresee the great trade that would develop around the vast stands of prime timber which everywhere reached down to the water's edge.

A brief look at Dr. McLoughlin himself is in order. He was born at Parish La Riviere du Loup, Canada, a few miles from Quebec, on October 19, 1784. He got the beginnings of his education in Canada and then was sent on to Scotland and Paris. He was fluent in French and English, and at sixteen years of age had considerable knowledge of medicine. He was bold and resourceful, and took a job as physician with the North West Company and served in several posts when he was only nineteen. He entered service with the Hudson's Bay Company in 1824 after peace had been declared between the North West Company and the rival Hudson's Bay Company.

Dr. McLoughlin first introduced steam navigation on the West Coast when he brought the sidewheeler *Beaver* out from the Thames in 1835. McLoughlin is credited with giving the name of "Oregon pine" to the famed Douglas fir, a name which still is used in the export industry.

His simple muley sawmill was the grandfather of all the thousands of sawmills, big and little, which have subsequently been built in the great Douglas fir region and, for good measure, you could include the sawmills of the great western pineries and throughout the redwood region.

We, of this generation, owe a salute to the famed Dr. John McLoughlin, trader, trapper, industrialist, and leader of men; and we owe a long toot of the whistle to the "little giant" muley rig which started chewing into the impenetrable forests of the Pacific Northwest.

—ARTHUR W. PRIAULX,
Portland, Oregon. 1964

Part I
The
ROARING
YEARS

Chapter I

Axe-Burying at Willapa Bay

IN the dog days of August, in the yesteryears just past, and leading to the coming of autumn, a gray-blue smoke pall often enshrouded vast sections of the deeply forested Pacific Northwest, from the towering Cascade Mountains to the sundown sea.

This blue veil hung silently above the land, blurring the graceful outlines of the tall Douglas firs and giving the blue sky a faded, washed-out appearance. If the summer days were long and hot and windless, and there had been no rain for some time, the veil grew heavier, surrounding the sawmill towns and logging villages and giving off a pungent fragrance of forest campfires on a summer night, and of something on the move. The woods were crackling dry, the streams low, their trout listless, and the wild things bedding down through the heat of day. Logging operations closed, except for the hoot owl shifts, and the sawmills ran at a slow pace awaiting a cooling rain, a fog, and a rising humidity. And in the towns, too, there came the zing of power saws biting into the slabwood piled high along the curbings of the neighborhoods. Autumn was definitely on the way.

This pleasant haze from the deep woods has long been a part of living in the Pacific Northwest, although now it is nowhere as pronounced as it once was. Neither was it always a sign of great disaster, although the casual visitor to this land of giants might inquire, "Is there a forest fire somewhere?" More likely, its silent arrival at this particular time of year was an annual reminder of something generally accepted and forgotten even by the natives themselves, the Pacific Northwest's traditional and long its foremost industry—lumbering.

The smoke pall rose from the cone-shaped burners of countless thousands of sawmills scattered everywhere throughout the region, from a farmer clearing a stumpland section and from the first fall slashing fires, if there had been a good rain. Never in my memory was this haze looked upon in the same attitude as the choking carbon monoxide which plagues our modern cities, although I suppose it could be classified as "industrial smog." Instead, living in a lumber town of what better name than "Forest Grove," it seemed a welcome sign that the mills were running, the loggers at work in the woods, that all was right with the world. Now it is a fading thing, for, in this modern age, waste and forest fire disaster have been curtailed to the place where even the great burners which served as landmarks of this sprawling sawmill country have largely vanished from the scene.

It was on such a day, in late August of 1911, that a great gathering of raw-boned lumbermen boarded a westbound train headed for Willapa Bay and the sawmill town of Raymond on the southern coast of Washington. They represented a vast, wealthy empire of big trees and big men, but currently in a time of crisis. The roaring hell-for-leather years were about done, as they were for all pioneers, but what the future held no one could forecast with any degree of certainty. Yet as the blowing steam train thundered through the night, amid the dense forests, it seemed that the lumbermen were rapidly approaching a major crossroads and that what took place in Raymond would be of lasting importance, not only to themselves but for all this great timber country which stretched from British Columbia deep into coastal California and to the distant mountains.

Indians and pioneers looked upon the dense forests as a plagued nuisance. The redmen purposely started forest fires—they had done so for centuries—to open up the country for better hunting. The early explorers saw much evidence of these holocausts which rampaged unbridled for many miles, not dying until the heavy rains arrived. The settler found the trees handy for his simple cabin, his furniture, his barns, lean-tos and fences, and to establish the first settlements. All were fashioned of rough logs, for this did double duty since it cleared the land so you could go to farming if you could get the blasted stumps out.

If there were thoughts of lumber, it was a sometime thing; there was no time or energy for being so high-toned. With all those trees around, the first house of lumber in Portland—called "Stumptown" because the pesky stumps were everywhere so they had to be whitewashed to see at night—was a prefabricated job, dismantled in far-off Maine and shipped 'round the Horn. So, cursing as he swung his axe, the pioneer felled the timber for his wood supply, cut a few rough boards here and there, grubbed and burned the stumps, and could see little of lasting value in the big trees. Why, one man took them so for granted that when he went seeking gold in California, he returned with Sequoia cones rather than nuggets and planted the seeds to beautify the country. No doubt about it, the native trees were in the way.

A few men of vision, taking a cue from Dr. McLoughlin, felt differently about the trees. They erected the first flimsy sawmills and cut rough boards of many sizes and but a single grade. The idea spread. Huge cities of today—Seattle, Tacoma, Portland—and most of the smaller ones have their foundations set deep in sawdust and were nourished by the head rig biting into logs so large that a man could scarcely turn them for the next cut.

Every village, every town, every river, bay and inlet had its
sawmill, and more than likely a dozen of them. One large company still boasts of its "Main Street Yards." The mills sprang up
by the thousands across the wild frontier and in the ensuing decades, built the country, for the people who settled here came
to depend upon this logging-lumbering business which grew to be
as large as any this nation would know. In this region there
were great mills, the largest in the world, average mills, lesser
mills, specialty mills, small mills, tiny mills, gyppo mills, portable
mills that were here today, over yonder hill tomorrow, and all
dedicated to one thing—getting out the timber. Even in the modern
Northwest, with its cloverleafed freeways and tall buildings and
eager population, the great log booms, the whine of the head
rig, the clatter of the green chains, the scream of the planer,
the thunder of the snorting diesel trucks arriving at the log dumps,
the oh-so-sweet smell of freshly cut lumber, are never far away.
This is a way of life and if the pioneer log cabin is an accepted
symbol of the frontier past, the sawmill cannot be far behind . . .

In August's dog days of 1911, the Pacific Northwest was observing a full century of growth since the first American outpost,
a strong stockade of hefty timbers, was raised on a knoll near
the mouth of the Columbia River by the men of tycoon John
Jacob Astor. Had Astor been of a later generation, he might have
built a sawmill; but the New Yorker, far removed from this un-
settled coast, knew only the wealth of the fur traffic of the Pacific
Northwest empire, which was also being strongly claimed by the
British. Now all roads led again to Astoria where banners were
flying, bands playing, high-toned speeches were being made, and
the Pacific Coast track and field championships were being held
"before a huge centennial crowd." Few paid even passing attention
to what was happening to the north on Willapa Bay.

The lumbermen were beginning to arrive while forest fires
burned in both Oregon and Washington, a sight which sickened
the hearts of the timber people as it did the unsympathetic
public. There was a bad one threatening the town of Chehalis, and
in Oregon, a raging conflagration was out of control in Linn
County where flames leaped a river and drove out the brave fire
fighters. East of Portland, in the Estacada country, seven hundred
men, including quick recruits from Portland's skid road district,
were on the fire lines.[1] Good timber was going up in smoke and
it was a sorry thing, but with it the old ways were dying, although
it would still be a long while before this simple fact was fully
realized.

Near to seven o'clock on Friday morning, August 25, the special
train of seven coaches plus sleepers and dining car snorted to a

The tall, stately trees of the north Pacific Coast, in thick forests stretching seemingly forever, excited early lumbermen, although farm-bent pioneers found the timber a plagued nuisance which stood in the way of their plows.

halt before the Raymond depot. Hundreds of lumbermen swarmed over the platform, having come from the broad region of Washington, Oregon and British Columbia, to be greeted by a heavy set man with a ruddy complexion and wearing a jolly smile and a high collar, the fashion of the time. Everett G. Griggs of Tacoma, a powerful figure in the industry, had arranged this affair and at times it was touch-and-go. But Griggs took things in stride and now with intense satisfaction cast his eyes over the milling crowd which represented at least two hundred sawmills, large and small, of the Douglas fir region. Among them were many men of power, Paul Bunyans if you will, of lumber manufacturing and possessing the wealth of untold millions. Indeed, a newspaper reporter observed that the eleven leaders alone represented the combined wealth of $100,000,000.

These tycoons in overalls had not come to Raymond "to get their teeth fixed," as the loggers said when going to town for a blow-out. They were here to bury the hatchet—at least Griggs hoped so—in a peace conference that would bring about the dawn of a new age for the floundering lumber industry. Griggs and the other leaders hoped it would result in a permanent combining of interests and objectives into one large organization which would serve the common needs and hopes of a very large, scattered and exceedingly independent industry. It was high time, too, yet it could be made to work, as had been done successfully during the past decade through Griggs' Pacific Coast Lumber Manufacturers Association of Puget Sound mills.

This was a prime topic of conversation as the lumbermen, all rugged individualists, boarded the steamer *Reliable* for what was a softening-up tour of the bay. Northwest lumber had gone through many rough times in recent years, with strikes, panics, a sagging market, jumbled prices, a railroad blockade, too many forest fires such as the Yacolt Burn, and growing criticism from press and public against its free-wheeling methods of operation. What was equally bad, the lumbermen had been fighting among themselves, in and out of their haphazard organizations, yet through it all the Pacific Coast association headed by Griggs had time and again proved there was something of value in hanging together rather than hanging separately. But how do you get hundreds, perhaps even thousands, of bull-headed, singlefooted, loud-mouthed, red-necked, outspoken, opinionated, and downright stubborn mill owners and managers to quit going off in all directions and agree on anything? To bring them under a single roof was an achievement in itself, as Major Griggs well knew. He had worked long with patience, tact and diligence for this particular day, but he still wasn't sure that it wouldn't all blow up in his face, like a forest fire jumping its lines and crowning through the tree tops.

By mid-morning the delegates were back ashore, crowding into the Commercial Club rooms to get to the business at hand. Major Griggs rapped a board of fir lumber serving as gavel, bringing the loud-talking delegation to attention. They were willing to hear him, for Griggs had long held their respect, but some of them demonstrated with folded arms their doubt and cynicism at what was being proposed—the combining of the three existing lumber associations which held little mother's love for each other into a single unit. Odds were it would never work for very long. They considered the high-toned bylaws and articles of incorporation which Griggs assured them were "flexible" to cover "many matters of concern to the association without conflict with United States laws."[2] The industry, it was maintained, needed three associations like it needed more knotholes. Only through this kind of merger could they hope to survive and grow, and find the strength they desired in these troublesome and rapidly changing times. Yet there were many among the Raymond lumbermen who still looked longingly back over their broad shoulders to the roaring past, when they did as they pleased and answered to no one, and without the pressures and government interference that they now faced. Those were the Good Old Days!

During the afternoon, they heard a speaker from the State

Industrial Insurance Commission. But they were most impressed by a proposal that the new organization establish a selling agency for publicizing and marketing Northwest lumber. This sounded good, for it directly affected their pocketbooks, these companies being tucked off as they were in the far corner of the land, a terrible distance from the leading markets, with the railroads against them and stiff competition from the other timber areas to the east, most of all in the Deep South.

Sometime during this eventful day, Major Griggs, W. C. Yeomans of Pe Ell, Washington, and L. J. Wentworth of Portland affixed their signatures to the articles of incorporation before Martin C. Welsh, notary public. This was the merger, the signing of the peace, for Griggs represented the Pacific Coast Lumber Manufacturers Association; Yeomans, the Southwest Washington Lumber Manufacturers Association; and Wentworth, the Oregon and Washington Lumber Manufacturers Association, primarily Oregon mills. It was indeed an achievement, for there had been much bitterness between Oregon and Washington wood interests since the lumber blockade of 1907 when the Oregon mill owners had sided with the railroads. That had been pretty hard to stomach for the Washington lumbermen and was still not entirely forgotten.

A name was agreed upon—the West Coast Lumber Manufacturers Association. Four years later, when there was some reorganization, the name was shortened to the "West Coast Lumbermen's Association." This was the name that rang as true as a logger's axe down across half a century as one of the largest, busiest and most influential organizations of its kind, known the world over. WCLA, as the association came to be known most everywhere,[3] was sometimes called the "lumbermen's Chamber of Commerce," although it grew into much more than that.

At the outset, to be sure, its objectives were purely selfish ones—to battle the railroads over shipping costs, to establish sound grading rules and standards, to make some sense out of lumber prices, to deal with federal, state and local governments on taxation, regulations and all matters affecting the industry, to give the industry a look at itself and generally be a watchdog over the world of lumber, and to promote and sell lumber products manufactured from the raw trees to an ever-expanding market.

But over the decades, the West Coast Lumbermen's Association became something unique even among lumber amalgamations. It had a far-reaching impact on American thought, culture, institutions and patterns of living, following not only the sawdust trails but the side trails through unknown forests to demonstrate that lumbermen weren't destructive monsters, but that America's first industry, dating from Jamestown, was an important segment of the American saga and certainly that of the great West.

—WCLA files
Sawmills large and small became the leading industry of the Pacific Northwest from frontier times. It was huge and thriving when the lumbermen met in 1911 at Willapa Bay.

Somehow, through its many facets, the West Coast Lumbermen's Association developed a combination that worked extremely well, so that when WCLA closed up shop in 1964 to become merged into a new organization, people found it difficult to accept, for its banner had long waved on a variety of fronts throughout the world.

But in 1911 the prominent lumbermen in session at Raymond had no inkling of what was to come, even men of vision like Major Griggs. The articles of incorporation helped point the way, but the most significant milestone was found at the end of the second article, concerning the association's interest in making studies on the "cultivation, protection and conservation of forests."[4]

A dollar a share financed the new association and there were a thousand shares of stock purchased to get the show on the road. Things had shaped up rather well and that evening the lumbermen celebrated with a thundering whing-ding in the true tradition of this rugged timber country, setting the fashion for things to come, for their blowouts became legion. Then they boarded the train at midnight and left Raymond. The historic meeting was over.

A few days later the articles of incorporation were filed in Washington State and the board of trustees gathered at Centralia which had been selected as the association's headquarters and central offices, at least for now. Centralia was a compromise, halfway between Puget Sound and the Portland area. Oregon lumbermen didn't want the control to become too firmly entrenched in the Seattle area.

There were eight trustees in addition to Griggs, Yeomans and

Wentworth—Richard Alexander of Vancouver, British Columbia; J.H. Bloedel, Bellingham, Washington; W. H. Boner, Everett; E. G. Ames, Seattle; W. B. Mack, Aberdeen; Ralph H. Burnside, Raymond; A. C. Dixon, Eugene, Oregon; and G. B. McLeod, Astoria. Major Griggs was elected president and Wentworth, vice president. Other officers were Thorpe Babcock, whom Griggs brought from the old Pacific Coast association to be hired as secretary; C. S. Gilchrist, Centralia, treasurer; W. C. Miles, Globe, Washington, mnager; and J. N. Teal, Portland, retained as counselor.

Major Griggs couldn't help expressing his happiness at the way things were going. As president of the Pacific Coast association for the better part of ten years, he had guided that group through some mighty stormy times. He could only hope that the members would be patient and give the new trade association a chance to see what it could do. Victor Beckman, for years the Pacific Coast association's permanent secretary, had also worked hard for this kind of thing, but Beckman was unfortunately out of it now. . .

Since before the turn of the century there had been a growing trend toward some sort of integration of interests among timber holders, loggers and lumbermen of the Douglas fir belt. Most of the attempts had been short-lived, like the Lumber Manufacturers Association of the Northwest, organized in 1891 in Seattle as the first lumber association anywhere in the West. It got off to a rousing start, but died two years later during the depression of 1893. A loggers' organization known as the Puget Sound Timbermen's Association came into being late in 1895, followed closely by the Seattle Lumber Exchange in 1896. This was soon changed in name to the "Washington Lumber Exchange" for the purpose of covering the state. But again, these groups broke up in 1897, for it was a hard thing to get independent lumbermen to sacrifice for the good of all.

For a brief time, the shingle men had a strong association but, like the others, it faded into history. Undaunted, the small lumber plants of southwestern Washington formed their own trade group in 1899. The large mills around Puget Sound did likewise in 1901 and so did a group in Oregon where lumbering was still a comparatively modest industry in contrast to what had happened in the Evergreen State where big timber interests, faced with depleted forest reserves in the Lake States, invaded the Pacific Northwest with their huge financial backlogs, their spinning head rigs, and the know-how of generations. The latest Oregon association soon gave up, but was replaced in 1905 by another organization calling itself the Oregon and Washington Lumber Manufacturers Association, also the Oregon and Columbia River, and formed that May at the famed Portland Hotel, electing Philip Buehner of the Buehner Lumber Company, North Bend, its first president. It seemed like good timing, for the talk of this moment was the Lewis and

Clark Centennial Exposition which had as one of its leading attractions the golderndest log cabin ever built, of stupendous size from the biggest timbers found in the Northwest region. Loggers and lumbermen had pitted their voluntary skills and muscle to raise it with pride as a demonstration of the greatness of their industry.[5]

The region's lumber industry, something of a helter-skelter thing since pioneer times, was suddenly mushrooming. The coming of the transcontinental railroads had vastly altered the marketing picture, although California where the lumber schooners had plied for years continued to be the industry's main outlet. But now there were prospects of further potential in the East with the opening soon of the Panama Canal and it was once again apparent that concerted action was needed for more equitable freight rates and some standardization of lumber grades, for pioneer lumbermen were notoriously sloppy in their cutting. The Pacific Coast Lumber Manufacturers Association, the most stable of the organizations and the most influential, grew out of the need to negotiate freight rates with the railroads. By the end of the decade it was increasingly certain that things were happening in the industry with which no single mill owner could cope, no matter how rough and tumble he might be.

Trouble was, the various associations were often at war with each other. At times things became as heated as among hobnailed loggers tying into each other in the waterfront saloons of Aberdeen, Portland and Seattle. It took strong personalities like Major Griggs to keep matters in line when someone broke down the barriers and things were falling apart. Puget Sound operators found they were often being undercut by small mills in the south. Oregon lumbermen, characteristically independent, were regular mavericks and non-conformists. While the lumbermen of Puget Sound, where the Northwest industry was truly born, managed to reach a rather stable agreement with the Southwest Washington association, they got virtually nowhere with the Oregonians who considered them arch enemies. Well, if the Oregon mills wanted it that way, it was damned unfortunate, Griggs felt, but he advised members of his own association to cooperate with the price list, transportation and grading committees which he reminded "after all are the main features of association work with the majority of the mills."

"We must all sooner or later appreciate," Major Griggs emphasized, "that the mills of the Pacific Coast Lumber Manufacturers Association are allied to further the interests of a common product, and by allying the competition among ourselves unite to push our Pacific Coast woods into an ever-widening territory."[8]

Griggs pointed to a graphic demonstration following one heated freight battle with the railroads, involving the several associations all working together. The favorable decision, he observed, was a "great thing from the fact that we stood together. Victory would have been impossible otherwise. . . The dynamic force of associated effort will jar even a railroad man."[7]

Thus under his wise stewardship and the steady hand of Victor Beckman, the Pacific Coast association continued to expand and so did its power and influence. By 1908 its membership, originally eighteen, had reached an astounding 268 members. This frightened the other associations, especially the Oregon mavericks, for there was little doubt now where the strength of the industry was located.

And by 1910 the Northwest timber industry was of momentous size and potential. Washington led the nation in lumbering, cutting well over three billion board feet a year. Oregon was still in the raw stages, but was seventeenth on the list.[8] There were 1,263 sawmills in Washington and a payroll of 47,447, while 713 mills in Oregon directly employed 16,833.

It was one thing to produce this lumber, quite another to get it to market. Under the circumstances, it made little sense and was of far less an advantage to continue the war. The fighting factions at long last began listening to Major Griggs and decided upon the peace meeting at Raymond where they could once and for all bury the axe. They had come a long distance from the wild frontier which had once molded their future.

NOTES TO CHAPTER I

1. *The Morning Oregonian*, September 1, 1911.
2. *The Morning Oregonian*, August 26, 1911.
3. We shall often in this book refer to the West Coast Lumbermen's Association by the letters WCLA, by which it was widely known and recognized. The association was also known throughout the industry as "The West Coast."
4. Record book, West Coast Lumber Manufacturers Association.
5. The historic Forestry Building stood for half a century as a Portland landmark. It was burned to the ground in the summer of 1964, the fire taking with it many mementoes of Northwest logging and lumbering history.
6. *The Lumber Industry Part IV*, U. S. Printing Office, 1914.
7. *Pacific Northwest Quarterly*, University of Washington, October, 1950.
8. 1910 Census Report.

Chapter II
Sawdust in the Wilderness

THE Pacific Coast's lumber industry, which by the turn of the
century had grown to tremendous size and wealth, had its roots
far back in the raw days of the frontier. Its tradition was a roaring
one. The logger and the sawmill man had as much to do with
taming the West as did the cowpoke, the rancher and the miner,
although they have never been so romanticized. Gun-slinging sparks
the imagination much more than axe-slinging.

The lumberman thrived amid the tall timber and the cattleman
in the rich grasslands of the open cow country, but they had things
in common in the lives they led on the raw frontier. Like the cowboy, the logger was rugged, hard-living, independent as all get out,
and something of a fiddlefoot.

The sawmill man can be likened to the rancher and the cattle
baron. He was often a man of wealth and power, who came up the
hard way and was also as tough as nails. He built the mills, hired
men to run the saws, worked in sweat beside them, and turned
raw logs into lumber to raise the towns, the homes, the barns,
the business houses, the industries, the steamboats, the windjammers and the railroads, and to supply the vast and varied needs
of the wild frontier.

There were lumber tycoons and cattle barons who owned the
towns, made the laws and ruled with iron fists over the frontier
empires they created. There were some great empires, too, for timber was the staff of life from the far Marias to the Mother Lode.
Every area had its sawmills—they came on the heels of the first
settlers and traders—for you couldn't do much without lumber
whether you were Johnny Studebaker building wheelbarrows in the
Sierra gold camps, which made him a fortune when he turned to
wagon-making, or the engineers of the Silver Kings, hauling massive
timbers up Sun Mountain to shore the sagging shafts and tunnels
so they could get out the treasure of the great Comstock Lode. If
there were no sawmill handy and no trees, you had to drag the
lumber in as Cattleman Pete French did for his empire on the
Donner und Blitzen River of southcentral Oregon, several hundred
miles from the Blue Mountains and along the hot, dusty trails of
the Nevada wasteland, clean from California, to build his famous
White House in the middle of nowhere. Lumbering was the West's
basic industry, as it had always been on the American frontier.

A sawmill touched off the greatest of all the westward migra-
tions. One day in 1847 a crew of men bossed by John Marshall,
a millwright from Oregon City, was erecting a small mill at what
today is Coloma in the Sierra Nevada foothills. The mill was for
Captain John Sutter who had a fort and ranch in the valley. It
would be the fourth built in Spanish California, the others at Bo-
dega Bay, near Sonoma, and at San Mateo. Sutter's mill was destined for more lasting fame. As the plant neared completion Marshall spotted something yellow in the millrace. From that moment
forward, everything was changed, all because old Captain Sutter
wanted a sawmill.

News of the gold strike spread on the four winds and most
everyone was soon bound for Californy with the glint of fortune
in his eyes. Farmers and townsfolk of the Pacific Northwest abandoned whatever they were doing to seek a treasure in the south,
unable to see the coin to be made at home supplying the thousands
who were scratching in the creekbeds of the gold country. The
miners needed to be fed, which the Oregon farmer could do; and
there was call for many other things, foremost of which was lumber, to be had in the remote Oregon country of any size and
dimension. Suddenly the flimsy sawmills took on a new importance
and the way was pointed for a permanent market of Northwest
timber in California.

The ship that broke the news of the great gold strike at Oregon
City brought a demand for lumber of any kind, at any price. The
poorest sticks went for $60 a thousand feet, ship's side, and good
clear stuff, $90 per thousand. That jolted the few sawmill opera-
tors who had lazily enjoyed a purely local industry. Water-powered
sawmills were few in Oregon since that first one of Dr. McLoughlin's and the mill built from some of the same machinery by Dr.
Marcus Whitman near his Walla Walla mission in 1836.

The pioneer mills, only about thirty in all, were crude affairs,
slow up-and-down muleys, producing a scant million board feet a
year for the settlers. Lumber was mighty scarce and often hand-cut.
Ewing Young, the trapper-explorer, erected a small mill along
Chehalem Creek in 1837, the first in the Willamette Valley; while
in 1844 Henry Hunt took mill irons he'd brought by wagon
train across the plains on a raft to the lower Columbia and raised
a plant at Cathlamet Point where he shipped rough cut lumber
to the Sandwich Islands in probably the territory's first such commercial effort of foreign export since McLoughlin had tried it. Members of Jason Lee's mission had a mill going at Salem and soon a
second at the Willamette Falls, which they sold to George Aber-
nathy and Alanson Beers in 1846. Small mills were being operated
for local trade at Eugene, Coos Bay and other scattered coastal
places, and along the Columbia River.[1]

The Yankee axes came west and millwrights were in demand

—Washington State Historical Society
The first sawmill in the Pacific Northwest cut lumber in 1827 by water power near Camas under supervision of Dr. John McLoughlin.

as more sawmills sprang up to supply the feverish needs of the gold rush. Oregonians were anxious to cash in on the utterly fantastic prices being paid for lumber in San Francisco and Sacramento, now climbing to $100 and $120 a thousand board feet compared to $30 being offered locally. And timber land was selling for $2.00 an acre. Suddenly and unbelievably, the Oregonians were sitting on a fortune, with only scant competition. Lumber rather than salmon, grain or minerals was destined to become economic monarch of the Northwest.

"There are many unoccupied mill sites in the country," suggested the *Oregon Spectator,* "where a mill could be stocked with logs for a year without clearing off more ground than would be required for the convenient use of the mill.[2]

Colonel William R. King had ambitions in this direction at the budding town of Portland, where a whipsaw plant was established in 1847 near the Indian campground at the foot of Washington Street. But King's mill burned down before he could really get it going. The following year W. P. Abrams, a millwright from New Hampshire, arrived in Portland at the inducement of the ambitious Stephen Coffin who was promoting the town where he had heavy land interests and was building a plank road to the Tualatin Valley. Coffin wanted a steam sawmill, so he teamed with Cyrus A. Reed, sign painter, landscape artist and school teacher who yearned to be a sawmill man, too.

The mill was to be erected at the foot of Jefferson Street, near the spot where Portland's first log cabin was raised. It would measure up to this big country, forty by eighty feet in size and of sixteen-inch squared timbers hewn from the giant firs alongside the mill site. It took six months to complete the project and the partners found themselves in the rather ridiculous position of having designed a plant too big to be fitted together by all the men in Portland, who simply couldn't lift the huge timbers into position.

Coffin went to Oregon City seeking more men of muscle. Meanwhile, Reed designed a derrick on a one hundred dollar bet that it would work and with block, tackle and much grunting, groaning, huffing and puffing, they finally got things into place.

Soon logs were being dragged toward the river bank along what would become Portland's streets and the shrill whistle of the mill echoed against the hills, scaring the devil out of the local Indians. The mill was well equipped with twin boilers, two flues each, a plucky engine, the head rig an old-fashioned sash saw, two circular saws for edging, and a cut-off for small lumber. The mill could turn out about 5,000 feet a day (later this was raised to 10,000 feet), but for the first week Abrams had to operate it largely by himself while he trained unskilled help. Abrams, Reed & Company came into being, with Coffin remaining a silent partner. Shortly they were joined by John Gates of San Francisco who was hired as an engineer and became widely respected for his talent of tinkering and invention. The great mill had a brief but happy life, burning three years later in what was looked upon as a calamity of full-blown proportions for the budding metropolis, although by then there was a second steam mill and others would soon be spewing out lumber.[3]

Things were stirring, too, around the waterway named for Lieutenant Peter Puget who had arrived there in 1792, the year that Robert Gray found the Columbia River. On this massive inland sea the fat trees marched right down to the water's edge and had long been known to Spanish and British sea captains and other roamers of the unknown world. They came seeking towering timbers as tall masts for their sailing vessels. Captain John Meares, the British fur trader, was among them. In 1788 the bold Meares left Puget Sound with a cargo of fine ship spars, bound for China. But he ran into a heavy storm and had to jettison the load, which abruptly ended the first attempt at foreign lumber export.

There were few pioneers and no settlements around Puget Sound, for the Hudson's Bay Company at Fort Vancouver discouraged any American settling north of the Columbia River, the British still holding hopes for establishing the international boundary at the river. Any sizable number of Americans on the north side would weaken their position. Now in 1844 the Americans were pushing in increasing numbers across the plains to settle in the Willamette Valley, a situation which was pressing against the barriers to go north.

Among those captivated with the Pacific Northwest was George Washington Bush who had visited the Oregon Country on the payroll of the Hudson's Bay Company as a voyageur in the fur trade. Bush gave up the life, returning east to move from Pennsylvania to Missouri where he became successful in cattle trading and farming, for which he seemed to have a particular talent. He had acquired a good education among the Quakers of Pennsylvania and was a man of some means, but Bush had one thing in his disfavor. He was a Negro, married to a white woman.[4]

Born in Louisiana in 1791, Bush was the son of loyal servants to a wealthy shipping magnate who later took them to Tennessee. Bush's parents cared for the elderly couple in their declining years and were willed what remained of the man's fortune. The Bush family moved to Pennsylvania where George received his schooling and later served with General Andrew Jackson in the Battle of New Orleans.

When Missouri passed a law making it illegal for free Negroes to live in the state, Bush who was seeking happiness, freedom and dignity for his growing family remembered the Oregon Country, part of which might become British and where slavery wouldn't be permitted. Among his closest friends was Michael T. Simmons, a thirty-year-old illiterate army colonel who had seven youngsters and also wanted to go to Oregon. Using Bush's money and Simmons' authority to command, they organized a wagon train in 1844, Bush bringing along nursery trees, seeds, farm implements and herds of stock. It was a spring of heavy rains and the train was often in trouble. Bush loaned teams, provisions and money from his own pocket to the others to see them through. He was considered "the wealthiest man to migrate to the Oregon Territory" at that time.

But Bush's arrival was an upsetting thing in this raw land, even though it was planned to locate north of the Columbia. Under a sweeping Oregon law, passed by the new Provisional Government, no person of Negro blood could settle upon or own land, no Negro slaves could be imported, and all Negroes and mulattoes were banished under penalty of arrest and flogging "once every six months until he or she shall quit the territory." Bush wanted to farm and to build an independent life for himself and his three sons. He had loyal support among people of the wagon train, especially outspoken Mike Simmons who despite his lack of formal education was a staunch proponent of human rights. The emigrants registered shock at the anti-Negro law, but there was continued pressure among people of the Willamette Valley to remove Bush before he became too firmly entrenched there.

Meanwhile, bearded, rangy six-foot Mike Simmons made an exploratory canoe trip up the Cowlitz to Puget Sound to look around. He continued to hammer away at McLoughlin, who knew the miseries of race prejudice, and gradually the White-Haired Eagle began to yield. It was suggested that if Bush located to the north, he wouldn't likely be bothered by the sheriff of the Provisional Government. Dr. McLoughlin was kept even busier by the inpouring American emigrants and by the following October, 1845, the persistent Simmons was headed north with his party of thirty-two men, women and children to settle on Puget Sound. Tucked inside his shirt was a letter from McLoughlin to the superintendent of the agricultural company at Nisqually, where one day there would be a great tree nursery, directing his full cooperation with the Americans. It was the first definite breach of the line held by the British.

Bush and his family soon followed, working quietly from the upper landing of the Cowlitz River over a thin trail in dense forests where no wagon could roll. They pushed across the rugged land with packs on their backs, dragging heavily loaded wooden sleds and driving the nervous stock animals forward, finally reaching the Sound at a site to be known as Tumwater. Simmons had taken a claim near the falls which held promise for some kind of mill, while Bush staked out land on the adjacent prairie, with room for the livestock he had brought along. In quick order he and his sons were bending their energies to the farm and George was demonstrating his characteristic drive and ambition. Within brief years, his farm was the best of the region and often a major source for grain, vegetables and fruits, for he seemed able to grow things in abundance when other men failed.

In the summer of 1847, at the foot of Tumwater Falls, Bush and Simmons built a combination grist and saw mill of water power where timber rafts and small vessels could work the high tide at a place called New Market. The mill, financed by Bush and with Simmons' know-how, and using discarded machinery from the Hudson's Bay mill, which really got around, was the first of hundreds to come to Puget Sound in a trade that became world-wide. But for now this was purely of local benefit and the early ventures proved luckless indeed. Floods washed out the first mill and when it was rebuilt a second deluge pushed it so out of kilter that it couldn't be repaired. Finally, there was a workable plant and within three years, with the gold rush stimulating things along the coast, the brig *Orbit* called at Tumwater to export the first cargo of lumber, hand-made shingles and piling, and leaving supplies for a small settlers' store. Simmons later organized the Puget Sound Milling Company and brought in other partners, among them Edmund Sylvester, Antonio Rabbeson and B. F. Shaw. The mill which gained a capacity of one hundred feet an hour was then sold for $35,000 to Captain Clanrick Crosby of California, ancestor of a man nicknamed "Bing" who first exercised his vocal chords as a youth in the timbered Northwest lumber camps and became one of the most famous entertainers of his time.

When the boundary matter was settled with the British, Oregon law extended north of the Columbia and thus the cruel anti-Negro act followed Bush into his new and happy home. But Simmons was now justice of the peace and a man of growing influence in the territory. Big Mike went to Oregon City where he pleaded Bush's case so eloquently and sincerely that he succeeded in having a special act passed to remove the man's racial disability, although Bush still had no permanent claim to his holdings under the Donation Land Claim Act.

Bush continued to grow in stature and respectability in the eyes of the settlers. His home at Bush Prairie was a hospitable station on the way to the Sound. He supplied nursery stock and seed to many of the new farms. During the winter of 1852, a severe one when famine was a reality, Bush was the only man on the Sound with a good supply of surplus wheat. Seattle speculators offered him high prices, but George refused to profit on the misfortunes of others and instead apportioned out his supply fairly and with charity to his neighbors.

The neighbors didn't forget. The Washington Territory had no sooner been created in April 1853 than Simmons and other friends were pounding on the legislative door, demanding a resolution to Congress granting Bush permanent possession of the land he had occupied and developed for ten years. The legislature complied, the memorial reading that "he had contributed much toward the settlement of the territory, the suffering and needy never having applied to him in vain for succor and assistance. . ." Two years later Congress passed a special act giving Bush full title to his land.

Bush and Simmons hadn't been too long in the sawmill business when others were latching onto the idea, although there were scantly more than a hundred settlers on the entire Sound. In Gallagher's Gulch at a place called Chebaulip, Swedish-born Nicholas Delin got a water-powered mill operating from a ten-foot dam, but "none too well," by the end of 1852 at what became Commencement Bay. Delin interested Simmons and another pioneer, Smith Hayes, in developing the mill. The following year Captain Lafayette Balch came calling, taking a full cargo to fire-ridden San Francisco where lumber was selling for a whopping $500 per thousand. Tacoma's lumber trade was on the way! But it wasn't much of a saw and many days couldn't keep up with the supply Pete Anderson and Steve Judson, local settlers who were doing the logging, could haul to the landing. Three years later, the Indians drove them out.

There was the sound of a saw at the small upright mill built by James McAllister near the mouth of the Nisqually, also cutting boards to rebuild San Francisco from its latest holocaust. That place seemed to have more trouble with fire than anything short of the devil's domain, but it was a fortunate thing for the pioneer lumbermen. A circular mill was set up by J. J. Felt at Appletree Cove and moved two years later by George Meigs to Port Madison; and Henry Roeder, a Great Lakes ships' captain, and one Russell Peabody canoed from Port Townsend to Bellingham Bay to go into sawmilling in 1853. They smoked the peace pipe with Chief

Chawitzit and his Lummi Indians who worked in the mill. Indians were the original sawmill hands around Puget Sound.

Everyone wanted to mine timber, but the problem was finding good water power and stout machinery to bite through this heavy stuff. Midway up the Sound a town was in the making in 1851 and its founders agreed to call it "Seattle" for a local Indian chief and without the need of any coin-flipping such as named Portland. Now the five founders—Arthur and David Denny, Dr. David Maynard, William Bell and Carson Boren—were hacking at the timber, trying to get elbow room and growing more discouraged by the moment. The brig *Leonesa* arrived that winter and took away a load of piling for San Francisco wharves, 13,458 feet cut in three weeks by axes and hand spikes. Then millright Henry Yesler, a native of Maryland, wandered upon the scene, curious to learn what was going on. He wanted to build a sawmill, he said, a steam-powered plant like the one erected in Portland a couple of years earlier. Made much more sense than these crude hand and water-powered jobs.

Seattle's founders were jubilant, already seeing the potentialities of such a mill falling into their laps, insuring success of the new town. Yesler liked one particular site, so they obligingly moved Dr. Maynard's salmon salting enterprise to accommodate him, fearing Yesler might get away since he was also studying other locations for his mill, being an old hand who had cut boards in Oregon before getting the gold fever. Satisfied, Yesler headed for San Francisco to buy machinery. That ship's captain who'd told him about the Sound was dead right, for the deep water did indeed run right to the shore and with the skyrocket prices being paid in the Bay, Yesler felt his future was bright. Puget Sound was natural lumbering country.

The builders of Seattle were more than kind to Yesler, presenting him with a shovel-shaped timber claim of three hundred twenty acres extending back up the hill from the water's edge, and all heavily forested. The shape of the claim would provide him with permanent access to the forested hillside, the logs to be dragged to the mill by huge oxen and giving him a raw supply for years to come. Yesler erected a huge cookhouse for his sawmill and logging crews that became a landmark, the town's nearest approach to a hotel, while outside hung a huge circular saw used as a dinner gong and for signaling starting and quitting time at the mill. The village sure enough had its first industry and its first payroll.

A quarter century earlier, a world away in East Machias, Maine, a newspaper article written by the principal of the town's Washington Academy had attracted the attention of the Pope and Talbot families, who had been felling trees and shipping Maine lumber for eighty years. Referring to the remote Northwest, the article stated that "large trees grow close to the water's edge,

so that the common method of mooring a vessel is to cast an
anchor from her bow and carry a hawser from her stern to a
tree on shore. Vancouver states that as good ships' timber as the
world affords may be found up the Straits of Juan de Fuca."[5]

The Popes and Talbots were intrigued with the Pacific Northwest and its timber long before gold uncorked everything. Now
Andrew Jackson Pope and Frederic Talbot, on the West Coast, were
drawn to Puget Sound by the spectacular timbers they'd seen in
San Francisco Bay, a network of gigantic piers stretching
far across the water. There was much speculation where the
giant timbers came from. Perhaps some of them were from Alki
where oxen were introduced to move the biggest stuff these early
lumbermen had ever seen and even now could hardly believe
existed. In San Francisco ships' captains and others engaged in
such enterprise were mighty secretive, but Pope and Talbot had a
hunch they knew. There seemed only one logical place where everything was just right for cutting, handling and loading such immense
stuff—Puget Sound, where the trees could be felled directly into
deep water by villagers and a ship's crew.

Wise old Lafayette Balch, who had made some trips up the
coast, teamed with Pope and Talbot in the selling of his lumber
cargoes, although the partners sometimes felt Skipper Balch was a
liar about the forests he'd seen to the north. Other seadogs were
also tapping the green bonanza. The *G. W. Kendall* came to Puget
Sound seeking ice, her owners reasoning the place was on the same
latitude with Newfoundland. Instead, she returned to San Francisco with piling. The demand for lumber grew even greater. What
the Bay needed was good common lumber for about $25. At cur-
rent prices, lumber for a five-room house would run to $2,000. The
problem with eastern lumber was the matter of transportation costs
which allowed for a "decent profit." Pope wrote eastern relatives
in 1850 that lumber from Back East, even at these high prices,
couldn't be sold in San Francisco for gain when the freight was "four
times the cost."[6] Main was too far off to serve as a woodbox.
Years later, West Coast lumbermen would be faced with the same
trouble, only in reverse.

Pope knew for certain where lumber could be had, in the
giant redwood country of northern California where a single tree
contained 200,000 to 300,000 feet of lumber, more than a vessel
could hold; and farther north, where "Oregon could supply this
state with all but pine boards." But though the pioneers were poor
and villages could use the money, the mills were makeshift and
pokey. An entire town might go to producing boards by handsaw,
but it was slow, tough, back-breaking work which brought the
cursing complaint "If blisters were sold by the board foot, I'd buy
gold mines. . ."

Now Captain William Talbot, his sights on the green bonanza,

loaded his brig *Oriental* with Maine lumber for the California mines
and took the long haul around Cape Horn to join his brother and
partner on the Golden Shore. The men planned to rebuild San
Francisco of "Oregon pine" and to erect a mill to turn out the
sticks in quantity, rather than the chaotic way things were being
done in the Columbia River and on the Sound. An agreement
was signed with Captain J. P. Keller for construction and operation
of "a steam sawmill for manufacturing lumber in Oregon in the
vicinity of Puget Sound." To make ready, they peddled the
Oriental since she didn't suit their plans anyway. And they sent
back for their own millwright, E. S. Brown, who met on shipboard
one Cyrus Walker who claimed also to be a millwright and would
loom large in the future of the lumber industry in Washington.

In June 1853 Captain Talbot, with Walker aboard, reached
Puget Sound. The men were awe-struck by the sight, for everywhere they looked they saw timber . . . timber . . . timber . . .
on a monumental scale reaching more than two hundred feet into
the damp sky—Douglas fir, Sitka spruce, western hemlock, red
cedar, grand fir . . . The unbelievable virgin trees stretched
forever into the distance, as thick as grass, ripe and ready for
cutting. The giant firs were straight and tall, and free of limbs
for at least a hundred wonderful feet above the ground. It was
an El Dorado the likes of which these Yankee lumbermen had
never imagined existed in all the world.

Trying to restrain an inner excitement from overwhelming
him, Captain Talbot began cautiously looking for the right place to
locate. He had virtually the entire Sound to choose from, although
he felt he was none too soon for there were some flimsy water-
powered sawmills and Henry Yesler's steam job ahead of him,
Yesler having started sawing boards in March of that year. Dropping
the *Junius Pringle's* anchor at Discovery Bay, Talbot began
probing the Sound in a longboat and a canoe obtained from the
Indians, with Walker skippering the latter. The timber cruisers
touched several places destined to play heavy roles in the Sound's
future industry, among them Port Townsend with its scattered cab-
ins and the hotel of Alfred A. Plummer, founder of the place;
and Port Ludlow where Captain William Sayward, another brawny
Maine lumberman, had his saw installed and was beginning to
harvest timber on a spot which, Talbot observed with envy, was a
"marvelous site."

The two boats cruised further along the east side of Hood
Canal to a place the Indians called poetically "Teekalet" or
"Brightness of the Noonday Sun" because of the brilliance of its
sandy shore. There was an attraction here; the peninsula jutting
into the bay appealed to them, so they charted the course to the
channel, took high and low tide soundings, and cruised the timber.
Talbot felt it was the best site yet, but he continued south to Apple-

tree Cove where Felt had opened his mill, while Walker inspected the possibilities of Vashon Island. Then they returned to Teekalet which would become known as Port Gamble.

The men built a bunkhouse, cookhouse and store of eastern lumber brought aboard the *Pringle*. Leaving a crew of ten men, Captain Talbot took the ship to Seattle for a cargo of piling and lumber from Yesler's busy mill. He found the place booming with enthusiasm, for in this year of years, Seattle had gotten not only the Sound's first steam sawmill, but the first American steamer had called, the first post office was established, the first marriage performed and, best of all, the Washington Territory was created and given its first governor, Isaac I. Stevens. There would soon be four steam sawmills in production at Seattle, Alki, Appletree Cove and Port Gamble, and within the decade some twenty mills would be built here, producing 85,000 board feet daily. The prospects caused the Olympia *Columbia*, the territory's lone newspaper, to cheer industry foward by observing:

"The enterprising inhabitants . . . seem determined that their full, high and important destiny shall be achieved as soon as possible. Success attend them."

Captain Keller arrived shortly with his wife and daughter. The

—Oregon Historical Society
Logging camps and sawmills sprang up in growing numbers throughout the Douglas fir region, pioneered by men like Henry Yesler (inset) of Seattle.

mill machinery, engines, boilers and store supplies were somehow all lashed aboard. He passed Talbot's ship, heading south, near Port Townsend and got the news. Keller lost no time getting the gear unloaded and installed in the unpretentious shell of the new mill, its size only 45 by 70 feet. Within a week the little muley saw was ready to tackle the first logs of the Puget Mill Company. The initial boards were cut to enclose the mill itself as protection against the chilling autumn winds, not much of a task considering the size of the place. At first it went slowly, only a painful 2,000 board feet a day, but the following January better machinery arrived. A sash saw and live gang saw replaced the muley. The sash, similar to a buck saw, cut the logs a slice at a time, while the live gang was a series of vertical blades set side by side in a frame and capable of cutting an entire log in a single run of the carriage. Production shot up to 15,000 board feet daily—these Yankees had the know-how—with Sundays and holidays excluded when the mill didn't operate.

It was a good year for the pioneer mill, for the little lumber schooners were drawn to Teekalet as to a magnet, loading 3,673,797 board feet plus 64,000 shingles, 42,103 feet of piling, 223 masts and spars, 2,000 gallons of dogfish oil and 71 barrels of salted salmon, just for good measure. Foreign lumber shipments totaled 1,468,912 board feet and this was considered of great significance, too. The mill showed a gross business of $70,999 and was capitalized at $30,000.

There was need for a fourth partner and the men found an eager one in Charles Foster from their home area in Maine, a shipbuilding partner of Captain Keller and relative by marriage to Captain Talbot, thus keeping things pretty much in the family. The second year the mill earned $20,000 and its properties were valued at $100,000; and by 1857 the plant was spewing 25,000 feet daily, excluding spars, masts, piling, pickets, lath and shingles— almost 8,000,000 board feet for the year. These were figures to swell Foster's pride when he gave them openly to the editor of the *Puget Sound Herald* at Steilacoom, something many mill operators were unwilling to do.

If there was gold in the hills, there was gold in the forests, too, but not all went as smoothly as anticipated. The Northwest Indian tribes were restless and under Yakima Chief Kamiakin were organizing a master plan to drive the white man from the territory. The bold maneuver incorporated attacks on Seattle and Portland, and capture of the crucial Cascade Portage gateway of the Columbia River, key to the Inland Empire. Some 1,500 Yakima and Klickitat warriors filtered into the Puget Sound area, the garrisons at Steilacoom and Vancouver were alerted, and the war sloop *Decatur* ordered north. In January 1856 Seattle was attacked, two men killed and much property destroyed. The town prepared for a long siege which lasted only a day. Then in March the Yakimas and Klickitats, teamed with local tribes, swept down upon the Cascade village with its blockhouse, trading store, sawmill and portage railroad deep in the Columbia Gorge. For several frightening, bloody days the Indians kept the community's men, women and children bottled up in the general store and soldiers trapped in the blockhouse. Volunteers were raised in Portland and with troops from Fort Vancouver, rushed by steamboat up the river, driving off the attackers and capturing the leaders who were hanged, which the settlers hoped would end hostilities.

But the Indians stayed threatening throughout the year. When Seattle was attacked, people at Port Gamble felt reasonably safe although only thirty miles away, since the menacing redmen were without a canoe fleet and essentially immobilized. But late in the year, the northern tribes of the Queen Charlotte and Alexander archipelagoes, warriors for many generations, became restless and decided to take full advantage of the warlike atmosphere in the south to pillage and plunder the white settlements.

In late November a war party of Haidas in seven huge black canoes, each carrying twenty-five to thirty warriors, swept the Sound at great speed toward Port Gamble, hoping for a sneak attack. The Indians pulled up on the far side of the cove and were spotted. The mill's shrill whistle blew a frantic alarm and the men dropped their tools, scrambling for a makeshift blockhouse of heavy rough planks built by order of Captain Keller who had a hunch something like this might happen. Crouched there, they waited for the attack, with the full-blown Keller in command, Cyrus Walker his second, and a fair supply of arms—thirty good rifles, some Colt swivels, and plenty of black powder and lead.

At Steilacoom, Captain Balch who was storekeeping there heard the news and decided that this was a job for the U. S. Navy, so he dispatched word to the warship *Massachusetts* which was patroling the lower Sound searching for marauders and troublemakers. Next day the warship hove into sight and lobbed cannon balls at the war canoes. The sailors executed a landing. There was spasmodic fighting, for the braves hadn't quite counted on this and began to scatter, but not before the first U. S. Navy man to die in a Pacific conflict was killed when curiosity got the best of him and he peeked over a protective log at a warrior he'd just killed, or thought he had. The Indians were shortly driven off, the mill was safe, and now the "war" was over, leaving behind only a collection of tall tales and a cannon ball found buried deep in a log some years later.

It wasn't long before the ambitious Puget Mill partners were planning a second plant farther out on the spit and beyond the reach of forest fires which seemed to be growing in number, for the Sound was taking on the appearance of a flourishing lumber community. There had been fires for years from Indians, settlers and lightning, and as early as 1835 the Hudson's Bay factor at Nisqually had recorded in his journal: "The country around us is all on fire and smoke is so great that we are in a measure protected from the excessive heat . . . The weather is gloomy from the smoke around us . . . "

The new mill was an ambitious project and a milestone, to be one of the biggest in the West. It was a circular type, 55 feet wide and 250 feet long, with a 124-foot carriage that pushed the massive logs through the blades and permitted the cutting of ships planking sixty feet in length and able to shape spars on the head rig, where they had previously been hand-hewn. Engines and boilers for the mill cost the partners $4,500 and there was an additional $2,000 outlay for the planer. But the greatest innovation of all, clear from Maine, placed the Puget Mill Company far ahead of any other on the Sound. The double head rig was equipped with two circular saws, fifty-six inches in diameter, with twenty-four teeth, and able to handle logs eight to nine feet across. If logs came any larger, dynamite was used to reduce them to proper size.

The twin plants could now produce 70,000 board feet a day. To handle this capacity, other· changes were necessary. More men were needed; local Indians did much of the common labor, but tribal customs interfered with production (as "tribal customs" of the free-wheeling loggers would also do in later decades) during the salmon fishing and hunting seasons, or when another tribe invited them for a celebration. Skilled workers were imported from New England and others came north from the gold fields where their luck had petered out, the dreams of quick wealth were gone, and they were back on wages.

The men were paid $30 a month for a six-day week, 11½-hour day. Pope and Talbot had no regular pay days for the mills and camps. You could draw your pay each night in hard silver or if you wished "leave it lay" till you quit or were fired. This became permanent policy, adhered to for many decades and three generations of loggers, Indian and white, and even the Chinese cooks who worked the Puget Mill operations. When at long last the company introduced a monthly paying system by check, old-timers roared their displeasure. One veteran, goes the yarn, demanded what he had coming in hard cash. The teller meekly counted it out and with a small wheelbarrow, the lumberjack wheeled 8,000 silver dollars aboard a Seattle-bound boat, then guided his treasure up the street and into the bank.

Now with better crews, the Puget Mill could do its own logging and was no longer forced to depend upon the surrounding unpredictable settlers to supply timber from their land clearings. The appetite of the mills was that of a growing boy. Teams of

loggers fanned out to cut trees along the water's edge and
roll them by some manner requiring much muscle and an equivalent
amount of cursing into the Sound where men could pole them to
the mill or guide them from rowboats. Handling the logs in the
water was troublesome, so a steam tugboat, the *Resolute,* was
brought from San Francisco. Her arrival set a pattern for
logging on the Sound and elsewhere in the Northwest that was
unique in the world to cope with the combined problems of hard-
to-handle logs, the lack of good roads, and broad and inviting deep
water highways.

The *Resolute* marked a drastic change that other sawmill men
would take to heart, but she was only in service a year when she
tangled with a Pacific Mail steamer, the *Northerner,* putting a crimp
in the larger vessel's proud paddlewheel and unsettling her dignity.
The Pacific Mail owners filed suit, even in this far-off wilderness
which was already becoming too crowded, but the Puget Mill Company had no attorney. Christopher Hewitt stepped forward; he was
an ex-lawyer from Illinois who was acquainted with another lawyer-
lumberjack named Abraham Lincoln. Hewitt was currently earning
his keep carving yokes for the skid road bull teams. For three years
Hewitt carried on a determined but effective fight against the steamship line, taking the matter clear to the United States Supreme
Court where he won the case with a brief so impressive that one
of the justices called its attention to President Lincoln, who
remembered his fellow member of the bar in Illinois and appointed
Hewitt chief justice of the Washington Territory.

The luckless *Resolute* kept on hauling logs around the Sound
to feed the Port Gamble mills for another decade, but finally reached
an inglorious end on a bright summer afternoon while towing a
long boom of logs for her skipper, hard against the current. Suddenly her boilers parted with a ka-boom that shivered the tall
timber, sending her master, Johnny Guidon, and the mate flying
head over teakettle through the air and killing four of the crew.
Guidon was scalded badly, a chunk of boiler plate smashed his
leg, and he was roaring mad from all this inconvenience, but he
and the mate clung desperately to some wreckage until an Indian
picked them up and took them to Olympia. Guidon then sent word
to his bosses: "*Resolute blow up boom gone to hell and I'm at the
Pacific Hotel.*"

It was just one of those things, so when he had his sea legs
back, Guidon was assigned the *Politkofsky.* The *Polly* was an impossible sidewheeler, built by the Russians at Sitka and a fringe
benefit for Uncle Sam in the purchase of Alaska. She was something
of a problem, so the U. S. government gladly sold her to a private
firm which took her south for refurbishing. When she arrived at
Victoria, a newspaper editor commented in horror, "She looks as if
she had been thrown together after dark by an Indian ship carpen-

ter with stone tools." Nevertheless the *Polly* was plenty game and lasted until the Klondike gold rush.

The Puget Mill had shared its first tug with another company. This arrangement proved inefficient, so the owners acquired a new one all to themselves, the *Cyrus Walker* built in San Francisco of choice Douglas fir from Port Gamble and named for one of their budding executives. She was a fine vessel, 128 feet long, with two huge paddlewheels and more power than any other tug on the West Coast. There were others, among them the *Goliah* which was built specifically for towing windjammers from Cape Flattery where they often encountered adverse blowy conditions.

By 1860 there were thirty-two sawmills in Washington, with twenty-five of them on the Sound. Sailing vessels were arriving at Puget Sound in ever increasing number—schooners, barkentines, brigantines, a strange and motley collection of vessels, large and small, which crowded to the docks to take on the much-desired output of the screaming mills and haul it to California and across the Pacific. There were no roads, no railroads, no other way to do it, but the Popes and Talbots were taskmasters at this, for the deeply imbedded heritage of the Maine families was not only lumber manufacturing but getting it to market in good and profitable order. If you didn't have sufficient bottoms, you couldn't move the sticks, money and time were lost, and the mills had to shut down, as happened from lack of railroad freight cars to later generations of sawmill men.

Mill operators, anxious to move the stuff from their docks, buried a windjammer to the water line until the skipper bellowed a protest, shaking a gnarled fist.

"What in damnation you tryin' to do? Sink me?"

"Hell," retorted the mill men, "it's only lumber. You never saw lumber sink, did ya?"

Sometimes the cargo was a far cry from lumber, since passengers unwilling to await the monthly coastal steamer boarded the lumber schooners to travel to and from Puget Sound and San Francisco. But the most memorable passenger list of all came in 1864 when Asa Mercer, a young and ambitious Seattle-ite, arrived in San Francisco with a party of unhappy young women in tow, escorted by him around Cape Horn to become wives for the lonely males, as Mercer viewed them, of the remote Seattle lumbering community. Mercer who was somewhat of a dreamer had made a deal with Big Ben Holladay, the stagecoach king and steamship monarch, to use the steamer *Continental* which Holladay wanted to bring to the West Coast.

The voyage had been a miserable one and by now the girls were infuriated with Mercer, who was desperate and down to his last nickel. Holladay refused to take the women north and wanted them off his ship. Mercer was at a loss what to do, since his charges would likely scatter if allowed to remain long in this wicked metropolis. The girls weren't of a mind to stay, either, so passage was finally arranged for eleven of the group on Pope & Talbot's good lumber ship *Torrent*, outward bound for Port Gamble. When the *Torrent* reached Port Gamble, the mill hands nearly fell into the head saws at the fetching sight; but, shucks, the girls were destined for Seattle, so they were taken by the sloop *Kidder* across the Sound where they received a rousing welcome and were soon married, assuring the settled future of this saw-milling center.

It was certainly a distinct advantage to locate a sawmill on a deep waterway where there could be a proper port, as Seattle had uniquely discovered, although not every sawmill village could expect shipments of women. Mills were springing up on the Oregon and Washington coasts at Coos Bay, Willapa Bay, Gardiner, Tilla-mook, Astoria, along the Umpqua, and at smaller inlets where brigs and barks could come. The Columbia and Willamette rivers were ideal and a growing fleet of sternwheelers and barges was moving saw logs and cut lumber to Portland under the wise guidance of Captain John Ainsworth, one of the greatest steamboat men of them all, and his huge Oregon Steam Navigation Company.

More ocean-going bottoms were wanted and it was happily dis-covered that Douglas fir was ideal for their construction, since this wood didn't possess the corroding acid of oak when iron fixings were imbedded into it. It also had sufficient pitch to hold the metal fastenings with far greater tenacity. In the 1870's the Marine Board of Underwriters endorsed Douglas fir for these qualities and the shipbuilding industry received a sudden shot in its portside. Many lumber companies got into the business to a greater extent, not only to construct vessels for their own use but for the general marine trade. Often new ships were put together alongside the saw-mill, then loaded with the mill's output and away they would go . . . They weren't average ships, but were of special design to suit the lumber trade's peculiar requirements, with yawning open holds to handle the ready cargoes rather than loading through portholes.

When business was booming, the docks bristled with masts as tall as the trees and rigging that appeared as a snarled mass, while the vessels took on their great loads of lumber, shingles, spars, pil-ing and after the iron horse came, railroad ties. Puget Sound spars became world-renowned, 80 to 100 feet in length with butts measur-ing 30 to 43 inches, and used by navies of not only the United States but England, France, Holland, Spain and Italy. Years later when the famed frigate *U.S.S. Constitution*, "Old Ironsides," was be-ing refurbished, the Pacific Northwest supplied her with new tall masts, the only place in the nation where they could be obtained.

The ports and sawmill areas, as we have seen, were closely

allied and when the vessels docked, the tough lumber towns swarmed with men of the sea. In the waterfront saloons, card rooms and clip joints, the sailors mingled with the lumberjacks and mill hands who had also just arrived in town to blow it off. In Seattle, Vancouver, Aberdeen, Portland or most any place where the logging skid roads had cleared the way, there sprang up a hell-for-leather kind of roaring whoopela existence the likes of which will never be seen again.

NOTES TO CHAPTER II

1. *Crow's Digest,* April 23, 1959: Oregon's Fabulous Lumber Past—Arthur W. Priaulx.
2. *Oregon Spectator,* February 22, 1849.
3. *Joseph Gaston, Portland, Its History and Its Builders; also Life of William P. Abrams,* by Seth L. Pope, original manuscript.
4. Some sources describe Bush as a "light-skinned Negro" or "a mulatto."
5. The article, hard to find, was "dug out of her attic" by Miss Marian Talbot for Stewart H. Holbrook in 1944.
6. *Time, Tide and Timber, a Century of Pope & Talbot*

Chapter III
A Rough and Ready Breed

A good crowd was gathered about a roaring fire in the lumber town of Maple Falls, Washington. In the background came the sound of axes as brawny loggers dragged huge boughs and knots out of the blackness.

All had come to see a fight between a tough lumberjack and a wild bear; and the fallers, buckers, bullwhackers and millmen were laying odds of fifty bucks that the bear would win as he had done before. The last logger to tangle with the bruin was badly clawed and lost an eye.

The challenger, called Timidy, was a giant of a man with great broad shoulders, powerful arms and the neck of a bull. He stood now, thick legs spread apart, pent-up and waiting while the bear's owner, who had $200 riding on his animal, prodded inside a shack with a long pole. There was a loud growl and the pole was struck so hard it knocked the man to the ground. Then the black bear, his eyes red with hate for the loggers who were forever teasing him, sauntered into the firelight's rim.

Timidy slapped the animal on his head, then leaped lightly aside. The bruin laid back his ears, growled and bared his long white teeth, constantly watching the nimble logger dancing like a boxer before him. Rearing to his hind legs, the bear came on. Timidy stood his ground, let the bear within swinging range and then landed a terrific blow to the animal's neck. The bruin staggered back, dropping to all fours, shook himself, then on hind legs again took a lightning slash which just grazed the woodsman. Timidy ducked and rammed his head full force into the bear's belly. He didn't jump back fast enough; the bear grabbed him, its sharp claws digging into his broad back, the teeth menacing his neck and head. The loggers yelled lustily.

Quickly the lumberjack pressed his spike-shod boots into the soft flesh of the bear's hind legs. Timidy's powerful fingers closed over the animal's windpipe. He squeezed in great force with hands that could handle massive timbers, ropes, cables, chains, peavies, sledges, heavy axes and all the rest. A gurgling sound came from the bear's throat. He went limp with a shudder and the crowd cheered as the "referee" counted to six, declaring Timidy the winner. Bets were paid off and all headed for the saloon, while the bear crawled sulkily back into his shed.

In this lusty Northwest wilderness, loggers and millmen hungered for entertainment. The remote logging camps and some of the mills were far back in the timber. The timber beasts, a class unto themselves, got to town only on holidays or when they quit—*"If you don't like it, mister, clear out; it's a free country"* —and by then they were half-crazed from the pent-up drives within them. Poker, rough and tumble contests at high climbing, chopping, log burling, axe-throwing and a good fight were the camps means of unwinding. The woods operations were filled with dangers and getting out the timber was an exceedingly rugged routine for long stretches of time. The tough loggers were mostly single migrants, moving from camp to camp, their only gear their calked boots, a blanket and the skills acquired by working the woods from Maine to the Lake States to the Southern pine region and clean across the continent.

When the holidays came, they headed out by train, flume or foot trail, their pockets bulging with season's pay and soon to be flat busted again, but what the hell? There was always another camp, another job, another season . . . The logging and sawmill owners often said they had three crews, one coming, one working and one going.

The skid roads derived their name from the district near Seattle's Pioneer Square which sprung up along Henry Yesler's original log hauling trail. These tenderloins were the lumber world's answer to San Francisco's Barbary Coast and what went on there became a pattern of a brawny life. The skid road was rough and wild, the hangout of the logger as was the trail town for the cowboy who also "blew 'er in" after many weeks on the dusty hot paths of a cattle drive halfway across the West to some remote railhead.

It wasn't hard to find, down by the waterfront and near the railroad depot, one to a half dozen streets that harbored the ultimate in reckless living and drew mostly single adventurers from the mines, the ranches, the construction projects, the fishing grounds, the river steamboats and the sailing ships. The logger dominated the scene in the Pacific Northwest and many of the lodging places, greasy spoons, saloons and dives took their names from his colorful lingo . . . "The High Lead," . . . "The Cookhouse" . . . "Saginaw Rooms". . .

The saloons and chippy joints got most of the celebrating logger's pay, for when he went on a spree there were no holds barred. The timber beasts worked hard and played hard, taking their coffee black and their whisky straight, and there was little they feared from their fellow men, having survived till now the dangers of getting out the logs.

The skid roads were paved with sawdust from the mills and the lowlands were filled in with the chips and shavings. Hustlers, pimps and sharpies prowled the planked streets. The name skid road didn't mean red light district, well not entirely; and neither did it mean the place for derelicts and the down-and-outers as it does today, although there were plenty of them.

Unlike the plush crystal palaces of the Comstock, the saloons of the lumber towns were rustic utilitarian abodes of massive bars and thick flooring to withstand, for a time at least, the steady flow of calked boots and the skull-smashing brawls that went on there. The logger went after his opponent with whatever vicious weapon was handy, scraping his face with boot nails and throwing him across the room with a force that broke the furniture if not the other lumberjack; and out of one such brawl came the famous lines, as a logger lifted his opponent high above his head:

"Don't waste him; kill the fiddler with him!"

Some of the drinking parlors were as legendary as the Long Branch of Dodge City, The Delta at Virginia City, the Umatilla House of the Columbia and the Bella Union of the Barbary Coast. Seattle's skid road was an important lumber social center and before the turn of the century, its most illustrious hangout was Our House, established by Joe Backer in what had been John Cort's first theater, a boxhouse. It was a place of distinction, the bar fronted by green tile, giant pillars flanking the huge mirrors and above them panels embossed with intricate carvings, while on the outside walls were gigantic false barrelheads, with a European tavern scene painted above. Each barrel carried the slogan: "Only straight whisky for Our House patrons." On the second floor was a large gambling hall of twenty-five games which operated as long as the customers stuck it out. Calks weren't allowed, an unusual thing for a place catering to loggers, but Joe Backer wanted only the better boys, not the roughnecks. Despite such a discouraging drawback, the place flourished as the grand palace of the skid road.[1]

There were Vancouver's Cordova Street and Aberdeen's Hume, but the lustiest and largest skid road of them all was in the old North End of Portland, which has long perpetuated a false legend of being sedate and conservative, only not exactly! Most everything north of Burnside to the depot was part of skid road, but Erickson's Saloon was the hub of the social life, about which Author Stewart Holbrook often waxed lyrical. Decades later, in the 1960's, Erickson's was still going strong, although a shadow of its former self. Holbrook would proudly take eastern guests of note to see this landmark of the glory days of lumbering. Among them was Bernard DeVoto, the noted Western historian, and Holbrook

and DeVoto were photographed in their derbies leaning against
the rustic bar. But no Portland newspaper would publish the picture, fearing to shock its readership with this visit of national men
of letters to skid road. It finally saw the light of day in Lucius
Beebe's flamboyant *Territorial Enterprise*, the Virginia City paper
of Mark Twain.

Erickson's was the most prominent drinking establishment of
its time, founded in the 1880's by August Erickson, a muscular
Russian Finn who caused the place to grow to a grand scale
reflecting the giant land and the giant industry it represented.
Loggers and lumbermen worked with big things and liked big
things, so Gus Erickson complied. The saloon's magnificence became
legendary, known everywhere across the world where the lumber
ships plied, with a massive meandering bar running 684 lineal feet
around much of the block and having five entrances. When loggers
were at a loss in describing something huge, they'd usually say,
"Bigger than Erickson's bar."

Sometimes the skid road prowlers didn't make Erickson's right
off, but were sidetracked by other attractions. While Erickson's
boasted the largest and longest bar in the world of timber, the
Palace House held unequivocable title as the biggest golderned
charm castle in the Northwest woods. This sprawling three-story
Portland building occupied a full block and housed cribs for over
one hundred depraved damsels, white girls on the second floor,
other shades on the third. Its massive size alone appealed to the
loggers and despite the tales of horrifying things that went on there,
the Palace House survived many a Portland reform movement until
1907.

There were other pleasure palaces of note. Liverpool Liz who
operated the Senate Saloon wore a four-pound necklace of dia-
monds and gold. Loggers didn't fear being rolled in Liz's place for
she had her own system. No sooner would a lumberjack, fresh from
the brush, wild-eyed and pockets bulging with pay that would
choke an ox, swagger through the doorway than Liz had him
pegged. He'd belly cockily to the bar, glance around and seeing
only a half dozen others, would order "drinks for the house." That
did it! The bartender pushed a button beneath the oaken counter
and down the stairs traipsed a score of gaysome dames giggling
and waving and calling for drinks. What appeared to be a cheap
round left the logger's bankroll considerably shrunken.

One of the most notorious of Portland's centers of female
pleasure was Nancy Boggs' so-called "floating hell hole," a whisky
scow which gave the Portland Police Department no minor trouble.
The barge had a saloon and dance floor with rooms above. If
there were a periodic police raid, Madame Boggs hoisted anchor
calmly and hovered safely offshore or floated to the opposite

bank, Portland being two towns in the 1880's. Thus, Nancy managed to float away from the law.

Her day of reckoning came when the authorities of both towns
got their heads together and staged a simultaneous raid against
Nancy's indelicate scow. She considered this damned unsporting.
Grabbing a hose, she poured boiling water and live steam on the
raiders, but the hawser had been cut so that Nancy found her
scow spinning out of control and outward bound on the spring
runoff. Her girls were diving overboard and facing ruination, Nancy
climbed into a rowboat and pulled angrily toward shore. She located a sympathetic steamboat captain who fired up his sternwheeler
and went chasing after the runaway scow. After a few cursing
hours, Nancy was anchored safely in mid-stream, back in business
again and thumbing her nose at the authorities, while the kind
river boat skipper had the run of the place. The boys in the skid
road saloons chortled over this, but concluded no self-respecting
lady saloonkeeper should be put through such an ordeal.

In the skid road atmosphere, the women had to be as rugged
as the men to survive and able to handle any woodsman who got
out of line. There were camp followers, too, who devised various
means of getting near this howling breed. The camps were off
limits, for the ladies disrupted the work, but where there's a will
there's a way. Up on Vancouver Island, the girls who had a place
down the road a piece from a logging camp took to selling magazines to meet the fellows. You had to buy a subscription or two,
it seemed, to be invited to the house parties. Hastily the lumberjacks were taking a wide assortment of reading material, including
such educational things as the *Ladies Home Journal* and the *Woman's Home Companion.*

In Seattle the hub of night life in the skid road area became
the boxhouse. This was a combination saloon, theater and dance
hall of a type that flourished in the cold Yukon at Dawson, which
by the way was named and staked out by a sawmill man, Joseph
LaDue, who saw the land go inside of two years for $50 a square
foot. In these traps proprietors, bartenders, waiters and a huge
stable of perfumed female entertainers, often of little talent, blend-
ed their abilities to fleece the customer of his last dime, rolling him
if necessary. But out of the Seattle boxhouses, which were in
quantity at the time of the Klondike Stampede, grew the theatrical
empires of John Considine and Alexander Pantages, two of the
most notable vaudeville kings of the Roaring Twenties. Thus the
lumber industry's skid road helped spawn one of the great entertainment eras of all time.[2]

The lumber towns, backed hard against the waterfronts, were
built on planks and piling and were of a rustic, helter-skelter design not unlike those of the great metal mines where thousands

Early day loggers were a rugged breed bringing out the timber giants. They "blew 'er in" along the wild skid roads of the lumber towns.

of men also labored. There might be half a hundred sawmills strung along the rivers and bays, one almost atop the other, their screaming and banging a constant din in the ears which only hurt when they all stopped dead silent as during a strike, or a fire. When the shifts changed, especially at night in places like Raymond, it sounded like a cattle stampede from the tromp-tromp of hundreds of men pounding in their calked boots along the hollow plank walks.

There were no basements in the skid road places and only the water beneath. Trap doors were installed along the saloon bars for the dual and handy purpose of filling out the crews of the lumber schooners and in ridding the place of unseemly characters and those who had the discourtesy not to pay their tabs. The Bucket of Blood Saloon in Everett, for one, squatted over the Snohomish River and had a trap door in the back room through which, it was said, many a nonpaying logger took the cure, his body later found in the bay.[3] Loggers risked their lives when they roamed the lumber ports, especially with a load on, but most took things as they came. Danger was their business, so what did it matter?

When the sailing vessels tied up, the crews often jumped ship. Not only was merchant seaman among the least-desired professions, with many of the ships being little more than floating holes of Hades, but the wages were lousy. Sailors got only $20 per month plus "slops" and tobacco, while they could make at least $25 in the woods and pull the pin anytime they liked.

Skippers of the great lumber fleet had difficulty filling out their crews. Shanghaiing or "crimping" became a flourishing trade in the lawless tenderloins where $35 to $50 a head was paid for a man and a crimper could do pretty well with hundreds of vessels calling each year. A lumberjack might be standing calmly at the bar, eyeing that pretty frill down at the end and unaware that the bartender was sizing him up. Suddenly he was plunging through a trap door, bound and gagged, and on his way to see the world. The girls, bartenders, waiters and pimps all teamed up to work a likely prospect over the trap. In places like Erickson's, this wasn't difficult with traps strung all along the bar.

Portland was the most notorious of the shanghai ports and of all its daring crimps, John "Bunco" Kelly was as highly skilled in the art as might be found.

"Nothing like some good sea air for a logger," Kelly boasted openly. Why some tough lumberjack didn't bash in Kelly's head was a source of amazement. The shrimp-size Kelly served neither ship's master nor logger, but outwitted both as he haunted the saloons and honky-tonks to ply his trade, charging $50 a head. The last face many an ocean-bound logger remembered was that of Mr. Kelly. Most lumberjacks swore if they ever got back, they'd nail Kelly's hide to a sawmill wall. Bunco figured the odds that they would cool down considerably from months of wind, sea and sky, and he was generally right. One timber beast declared thankfully that six months at sea cured his consumption.

So Kelly survived, although he was sent eventually to the Oregon Penitentiary where he was able to identify the body of Outlaw Harry Tracy and wrote a book about his thirteen years there. Bunco had no scruples and resorted to all sorts of trickery. Once when hard-pressed to fill out his order, Kelly wrapped a cigar store Indian in a tarpaulin and lugged it aboard, assuring the skipper that the big fellow was merely all likkered up and would make a top hand when he slept it off. The captain's face must have been something to behold when he discovered the ruse as he neared the Columbia bar. Certainly there was a puzzlement a few days later when a fishing crew hauled the wooden Indian up in their nets near Astoria.

Another time, so the story goes, a large number of lumberjacks on a spree near the Snug Harbor broke into an adjoining basement, thinking it part of the bistro. Instead it was a mortuary. There were barrels all around, a regular bonanza, and they tipped one up, downing a keg of formaldehyde. Shortly there were only corpses. Kelly viewed this windfall through a window and hiring every rig in sight, he got the corpses aboard an outgoing vessel and even shook down the captain for an extra two dollars each since "I got these guys stiff on me own money."

Port Townsend, the port of entry for Puget Sound, was another dangerous hangout for the crimping trade. Near the beach was a string of honky-tonks with trap doors leading to the beach where the crimps could lug their victims after pulverizing them with knockout drops. Up the street stood Limey Dirk's Sailors' Boardinghouse and opposite, the Pacific Hotel; and woe be unto any lumberjack who frequented either place, for Limey was the Bunco Kelly of Port Townsend.

Despite its evils, shanghaiing was an accepted part of the rough-and-tumble business of getting the boards to market. The crimps were allowed to exist, the law failed to crack down on them, and even the loggers and millmen found some enjoyment in the game of fox and hounds trying to escape a vacation at sea. People of respectability were even engaged in the racket, among them the Norwegian vice consul at Aberdeen, one of the rowdiest ports of them all. Only Indians working in the woods and the mills were safe from the crimps' snares, for the kidnappers feared trouble with the federal government if they messed with the redmen.

Billy Gohl, as ruthless a killer as ever walked a seaport, hung out in Aberdeen as agent for the Sailors' Union above the Grand Saloon at Heron and F, posing as a friend of all and an unofficial banker to keep a man's payroll safe from waterfront thieves and crimps. Gohl often lectured the sailors on the many evils of this wild hell hole. Billy had spent some time up in Alaska around Skagway and was something of a counterpart of the infamous Soapy Smith, even to the manner in which he operated with a gang of thugs to force a shakedown. Once Gohl and his gang boarded the ship *Fearless* to force off the crew, as he'd done many times. But the skipper stood his deck, roaring that the crew was satisfied. There was an exchange of shots and Gohl was scared off. The captain then filed charges and Gohl paid a $1,200 fine to keep the federal investigators off his back.

Gohl had good reason, for Aberdeen was being branded "the port of missing men," when hardly a month went by without a corpse being hauled from the Wishkah or Chehalis rivers. Often they were loggers. The lumbermen had no more use for Gohl than did the sea captains. One of the latter found a means of taking him down a few pegs. Privies hung from the rear of the riverside structures and Gohl had the bold audacity to have the Sailors' Union Hall outhouse painted a brilliant vermilion. The lumber schooner *Sophia Christenson* was headed down the Wishkah under tow, bound for Australia with a heavy cargo from the American Mill. Nearing the Union Hall, Skipper Michael McCarron simply couldn't resist. He swung the wheel so the ship's long jib boom clipped the outhouse as neatly as plucking chickens. Downstream they went with the seat of the old-fashioned two-holer swinging from the boomstick. The skipper was only disappointed that Gohl hadn't been inside.

But when the body of a logger, thought to have left the area for another job, was found floating in the Wishkah in the autumn of 1909, it upset this unruly lumber capital something awful. It was one thing to kill sailors, quite another to do in a man of lumber. By the end of that winter forty-three other dead loggers and sailors were floating down the river, discovered amid the log booms, bludgeoned or shot through the heart at close range, seemingly by someone they must have trusted. The people of Aberdeen hired an outside detective and the lengthy trail led to Gohl's hangout.

The lumber community was shocked, for many things now fell into place. Evidence indicated Gohl had killed far more than his bag of forty-three that winter and that the total might be well over a hundred, starting with footloose sailors whom he'd talked into leaving their pay for "safekeeping." Later he'd expanded to include robbing and murdering loggers and millmen, using a launch and small scow to transport his victims over the bar to drop them into the Pacific.

Gohl's own laziness was his downfall, for he began merely dumping his victims boldly into the river. Apparently he had operated his den of horror for years, for in later and calmer times crews laying watermains and sewer systems along the waterfront would dig into ground filled with human skeletons, causing workmen to comment, "Another of Gohl's catacombs." Gohl was sent to the state penitentiary at Walla Walla and later transferred to the insane asylum where he died twenty years later, by then long known as the "Mad Monster."[4]

By 1870 there were forty-two sawmills in Washington, most of them around Puget Sound, cutting 128,743,000 board feet and employing 474 men who along with the loggers survived on diets of native oysters from beds near the sawmills, consumed in such quantities that their bellies rose and fell with the tides.

Back in 1854, Joe Sherwood, a Yankee from Maine, invaded the Puget Sound country with sawmilling in mind. He was one of the pioneers, but Sherwood would mark his way in history in an unfortunate manner. He was the nearest thing to Paul Bunyan that anyone ever did see, standing seven inches beyond six feet, weighing three hundred solid pounds of muscle, and strong as a bull ox, too, rightfully earning the name of "The Hercules of Allyn." No man could out-chop or out-lick him. When one of his oxen took sick, Joe paired in the yoke along side the other animal just to keep in shape. The mill hands claimed Joe had to take it easy or the ox couldn't keep up. When an outsider challenged Joe in a contest to fell a big tree, Joe's trick was to let the sucker on a springboard seven feet above the ground get well ahead. Then Joe would high ball chips from ground level, falling tree, man and all.

Sherwood's talents as a millwright became widespread. In 1870 Enoch Willey asked him to build a mill at Oakland Bay. Sherwood framed the mill at his own plant at Allyn, built a giant water-wheel and then rafted the works to John's Creek.

But this strong man of sawmilling was destined to die violently. In 1873 Sherwood was muscling a log into his mill with the aid of a cantdog (a type of peavy) when the handle snapped, sending Joe into a spin which broke his neck. It was the first death by sawmill accident in the territory.[5]

By 1880 the industry was full blown and free from government interference, with a source of supply that seemingly stretched forever into the future. Only the best trees were harvested, ten-foot butts left as stumps and all the top section of the tree from the first branches becoming slashings to be burned along with the remaining trees and the new growth coming up.

When fire got out of control, it was to be regretted but not for long, for there were more sections to be had or swapped at $2.50 an acre. Under the Timber and Stone Act of 1878, you could stake claim on sixty timberland acres as an individual by merely signing the papers. One sawmill company paid ships' crews $5 each for filing on timber claims, then turning the title over to the company. The timber was mined as a mineral and by present-day standards, the waste was tremendous, not only in the woods but at the mills where thick saws cutting kerfs an inch wide had the chips and sawdust piled into mountains, more than the boiler fires could ever consume. The waste had to be hauled or dumped in any possible way, for paving streets of the towns if nothing else, and getting rid of the waste was a major headache for the mills.[6]

California companies with their own fleets of ships were financing more sawmills in the Northwest, assured of ready transportation for their output. The mills grew ever larger and Charles Hanson of San Francisco, coming north in the 1880's, built a whopper called the Tacoma Mill at Tacoma, able to turn out 150,000 board feet of lumber and 40,000 laths daily. Hanson set another milestone by buying up 30,000 acres of rich timberlands and employing four hundred men in getting out the logs, almost as many as were engaged in the entire industry fifteen years before. He had four vessels plying the high seas from Tacoma to foreign ports but he couldn't catch the Puget Mill Company which was steadily improving mills and equipment until the annual capacity reached 99,000,000 board feet—seventy five per cent of the state's cut in 1869. This fabulous outfit had also purchased 106,000 acres of timber and through its related Puget Sound Commercial Company had sixteen vessels now carrying lumber to market.[7]

Colonel Chauncey W. Griggs of St. Paul, Minnesota, a contractor and wholesale grocer in partnership with one James J. Hill, and several associates arrived to look things over, having heard much talk about Oregon timber and foreseeing a good opportunity with completion of Henry Villard's Northern Pacific railroad to the Northwest. At the Tacoma Hotel, the Civil War veteran met Henry Hewitt Jr. and Charles H. Jones and through them was able to swing a deal to buy 80,000 acres from the Northern Pacific, one of the region's largest single land purchases of timber and the first large-scale movement of lumbermen from the Lake States pine country to the Pacific Coast. It wasn't long before they organized the St. Paul & Tacoma Lumber Company which grew into one of the region's industrial giants by the time young Everett G. Griggs had completed his education at Yale and a year in Europe, and was ready to join his father's company as a time-keeper.

Cyrus Walker continued his rise in wealth and power. When Captain Keller died suddenly in 1862, he'd been offered a manager's position but refused, since he was expecting to move on. The Pope & Talbot partners then laid before him a choice tenth interest in the Puget Mill which had risen ten-fold in valuation from $30,000 to $300,000 in eight years. No man in his right mind could turn this down, so for the next half century Walker's booming voice was one to be heard in the Northwest lumber industry. He tied down matters even better by marrying the boss's daughter, Emily Foster Talbot, and gained a reputation for doing off-trail things within the industry. For one, he acquired but did not harvest stumpage immediately as did most operators, but bought logs from gyppos.[8] He put this land into his "ice chest" to await higher lumber prices, but oldtimers asserted that Walker simply couldn't bring himself to chop up those beautiful forests in the smashing practice of the times. If true, he was indeed ahead of his time, although a few others were also beginning to think about things.

In the tradition of the Silver Kings and cattle barons, Walker erected a startling mansion at Port Ludlow called *Admiralty Hall* and described as "the biggest damned cabin on the Sound." It was stoutly built of fine Douglas fir and red cedar and was as huge as the timber country, almost a block long and three stories high, with a cupola topside and a tall straight flagpole of Sitka spruce from which flew a massive American flag. This palace was surrounded by sprawling lawns, and shading maples, elms and cedars brought from Lebanon by windjammers 16,000 miles around Cape Horn. At the grounds' center stood a bronze cannon from the War of 1812 which was fired as a welcome to visiting notables

and on the Fourth of July. The bearded Walker, who was no
snob, was often found working alongside his men. This became
a characteristic of the industry, the only business of its kind where
you could find the millionaire owner in overalls and a pencil
behind his ear out in the yard, grading and handling his product
along with the boys.

Down in Oregon, Big Ben Holladay had turned lumberman to
lay his Oregon & California railroad. He and George W. Weidler
built a steam sawmill at the foot of Savier Street on the banks of
the Willamette which cut 50,000 feet daily and was considered
"the wonder of the ages," drawing the curious from near and far
and establishing this north end of Portland as a sawmilling district
long to be known as "Slabtown." Old Ben turned the mill's full
production to getting out the railroad ties, piling and bridge studding needed to thrust his railroad south along the east bank
and thus beat out his West Side opponents to win a federal railroad franchise, with its guaranteed rich timber resources. That sawmill, running day and night and Sundays too, did much to bring
Holladay the victory he needed so desperately, cutting the first
timber for a major railroading project in the Pacific Northwest and
good boards for Ben's East Side city as well as for his mansion
and hotel at Seaside.[9]

There was a fine steam sawmill in what became known as old
South Portland turning out boards as it would do in the same
location for more than a century. In 1859, the year Oregon entered the Union, young John Halsey Jones quit his logging job near
Clatskanie to go to sawmilling. He tramped the forests between
Salem and Portland seeking the right location and after seeing
much forest, he came upon one of the finest stands of cedar in the
region, west of Portland at a place known today as Cedar Mill.[10]

Young Johnny Jones teamed up with his father, Justus Jones,
a bushy-faced pioneer of the Oregon Trail in 1852. Father and
son built a dam and crude sawmill along what they named Cedar
Creek and acquired a small stand of cedar nearby. The mill was a
muley with the logs turned by hand. The pair first cut a few
trees, hauled the logs to the mill and then made boards. When
water of the pond was exhausted, the saw would stop and they'd
return to logging until the pond filled again.

Justus ran the mill while John, working with rugged oxen,
would load a two-wheel cart with lumber and make the long haul
to growing Portland down the planked Canyon Road. He'd try to
get away before dark to reach Portland by nightfall and then
next morning dispose of the load for cash or supplies, returning up
the steep canyon to start the process over again—log, saw, freight,
deliver and sell.

But the little plant did well and by the following year, 1860,

the Joneses came to Portland, purchasing three acres of James Ter-
williger's Donation Land Claim along the Willamette River near
Macadam Avenue. The deal was made for $500 and a crock of
whisky, as was the practice of the time. When a sale was con-
summated, the buyer and seller toasted each other.

At this place the Joneses erected a full-blown steam sawmill,
something to be proud of in those days and still to be boasted
on the company letterhead in 1881. Machinery was brought around
Cape Horn from New York, from where the Jones family came.
Part of it was packed across the Isthmus of Panama. When the
plant got started, it turned out 15,000 board feet of lumber a day,
although a day in 1860 was twelve to fourteen hours. But just
as they were getting under way, knots hit the head rig in a roaring
to-do between father and son. Johnny was headed to town for a
five-gallon can of oil for the machinery.

"What in tarnation for?" yelped the Old Man. Hadn't bacon
rinds always done the job? It took some tall explaining, but young
Johnny won his point and progress had come to the Jones Lumber
Company, for in yonder years the consumption of oil products
reached 5,000 gallons a month.

The men drove hand-made nails into their boots, then cut them
off for calks for lumberjacking. Logs were brought from across the
river in the Sellwood district, where there were good fir and hemlock stands. The crew did double duty as loggers and sawmill hands.
The plant would shut down and the entire crew move over the
Willamette, fell the trees, buck them and raft them up; then they'd
row the raft across the river, with two men in a rowboat hitched
to the forward end to serve as a guide. Reaching the Jones landing
with their raw product, the same all-'round crew would hang
up the axes and go to cutting lumber from the trees they had
logged.

There were early-day troubles with steamboats, public complaints, rampaging log rafts, log pirates, high ball competition, fires,
freezes and floods.

"It was a tough business," remembered white-haired Harry E.
Jenkins, long-time general manager who devoted his life to making
the historic sawmill run ever-better.

The thriving sawmill company survived many things. When
other plants were inundated by the great Portland flood of 1894
the Jones mill, on higher ground, was the only one in town able
to keep running. The lumber demand was immediate; all mills
sold what they had in the yards and could cut no more. The Jones
plant alone couldn't meet the emergency so up came every
plank in the Jones dock, bound for market, and then the wall
boards were yanked from the sheds to be hauled away.

In the big freeze of 1924, when the Willamette was tightly
frozen and Vernon R. Garrick drove his car across the river near

The gigantic seagoing log rafts of Simon Benson (inset) were legendary in the first decades of this century. Benson gave drinking fountains to Portland to keep loggers from saloons. It didn't work. . .

Sellwood, huge rafts of sawlogs held tightly in the ice. When the break-up came, the loss would be tremendous. The Jones people, with 650,000 board feet at its landing, acquired the services of a dynamite expert through the Portland Police Department. The residents complained over the explosions, but the dynamiter got the logs loose and Jones saved all but about 80,000 feet. The ice began breaking just upriver from Jones Lumber and the whirling cakes, picking up speed, ripped three big rafts loose from the Jones frontage and that of the Oregon Box Factory, pushing them downstream ahead of the pack. A runaway raft of valuable 24-inch "Jap squares" was fastened to the Jones landing for a brief time, then busted up in the ice. The raft was valued at about $5,000.

Old Justus Jones, who was born in 1812 while the United States and Great Britan were at war, died in 1890, but the descendants carried on the historic mill operation. The sawmill, sold in 1946, ceased production in 1962 and the planer the following year. Much of the mill and crane shed structures were destroyed by a fire in 1963 and two years later, the Fulton area was being developed into an industrial park, having become too valuable to continue as a lumber operation site.

Oregon's sawdust empire was expanding, although not as rapidly as in Washington. Some mighty big lumber tyees (Chinook jargon

for "chief") were coming to the Columbia empire, among them
John West, John Yeon and Simon Benson. West who was from
Quebec established quite an operation on the lower Columbia at
a place called Westport, with great skid roads far back into the
hills and one having a tunnel, perhaps the only bore in the history
of bull team logging. West liked doing things on a grand scale.
He raised towering trestles to span the ravines, shipped his first
cut clear to Sydney, Australia, and was claimed to have the loudest
bellowing bulls anywhere in the West.

Johnny Yeon was also a Canadian logging man who jumped
ship at Portland, arriving without a dime. By some manner or
means, he staked a timber claim and on borrowed capital bought some
bulls. Then Yeon went to work in the woods back of Cathlamet,
Washington, where he was a one-man operation—foreman, bull-
whacker, timekeeper, faller and bucker, and his own cook. Yeon
was not only tough but knew what he was about. Inside of two
decades he was one of the state's wealthiest men who erected one
of the city's first "skyscrapers," the fifteen-story Yeon Building
where, appropriately, much of this book is being written in the
last existing offices of the West Coast Lumbermen's Association.

But of them all, Simon Benson or Bergerson stood out as
a shaker of many trees. Like Yeon, Benson jumped ship at Portland
and eluded the likes of Bunco Kelly to stay awhile. Benson was a
big Norwegian from the Wisconsin woods and at the outset he was
a loner, driving his own bulls and himself at a hard pace, rising
at four in the morning and not quitting his duties till after midnight. But Benson enjoyed what he was doing and well knew
both timber and men, many of whom were Scandinavians like
himself. He understood the breed quite well, for he worked out
a plan for keeping his camps running over the Independence Day
bust when crews everywhere demonstrated their own independence
by getting roaring drunk. This was standing tradition and it took
three weeks for things to get back to full steam again, right in the
season when the lumber demand was at its height. So a couple of
weeks before the Fourth, Benson would bring a free barrel of
whisky to each camp. Generous of the boss man, thought the rugged Scandinavians who understood little English. They'd belly up
and the operation would shut down a couple of days while drunken
lumberjacks hung over the logs to dry. But come the Fourth, Benson's crews kept right on working, not champing at the bit to go
to town, calculating they'd had their summer drunk.

Benson grew into one of Portland's leading citizens. He built
a major hotel, The Benson, endowed a polytechnic school and,
as an early enthusiast for preservation of scenic beauty spots and
good roads, served as chairman of Oregon's first state highway commission. But a set of twenty bronze drinking fountains in the
downtown Portland area is the best-known monument to his

achievements. Benson expressed the hope that loggers would quench their thirst in these bubbling water fountains rather than in the saloons of skid road.[11]

Simon Benson, who was president of an early Columbia River lumber association, faced up to the transportation problems that bugged the industry, especially shipping by rail to California. By 1906 southern California was a mighty good place to peddle lumber products and Benson, who wanted to live in that sunny part of the world anyway, built a sawmill at San Diego, close to that major market. Northwest lumbermen thought he was full of knot holes, for shipping logs by water chopped away his profit and the railroads were impossible. Anyway you spelled it, there was an 1,100-mile haul from the Columbia. Undaunted, Simon decided to raft the logs down the coast. Lumbermen shook their heads sadly. But Benson was determined to eliminate the middleman and a raft that would withstand the pounding of the seas had been a dream of generations since Dr. James Tupper of Maine tried to take logs to England.

On the lower Columbia, Benson and his crew constructed an enormous cradle of planks and hefty timbers, cigar-shaped and sturdy as the day. He racked up the great logs like jackstraws, or such as is done with balls on a pool table, filling the cradle with 3,000,000 board feet. A floating crane placed the logs of various sizes with great care, the long ones being used for backbone strength against the waves and swells. The works was held together by one hundred seventy-five tons of heavy chain. When all was ready, the great cradle was removed, a deckload put aboard, towing lights to burn thirty days placed, a powerful sea-going tug hitched up, and down the coast went the awesome raft. Twenty days later the San Diego sawmill was cutting raw Oregon logs.

The Benson rafts, and there were many of them, became the largest things afloat, nearly one thousand feet long and fifty-two feet wide and containing upwards to 5,000,000 board feet of lumber. As late as 1942 Benson rafts were still being towed along the West Coast.

Benson's ingenuity spread in many directions. He was among the first to introduce steam equipment to the woods. From the 1880's things were changing drastically in the industry all along the West Coast. The skid road was a product of Northwest lumberjacking and as we have seen, the mills were held pretty much to good waterways. Now Sol G. Simpson, who came west as a railroad builder and was attracted to the timber, began logging with big dray horses he brought from railroading rather than the pokey oxen, something others including the cynical bullwhackers said couldn't be done. Simpson was of a type who didn't have "couldn't" in his vocabulary. But his horse logging didn't spread far beyond the heavy timber country of Mason County, Washington, where he would become a tyee lumberjack, for steam was invading the woods and would retire the animals.

Iron rails were being thrust back into the timber in many places to bring out the big stuff. Lumbermen would soon be rail-roaders, too. Simpson was hired to build the Puget Sound & Grays Harbor railroad, commonly called *The Blakely* because its terminus was the sawmills at Port Blakely. When the outfit went broke, Simpson took it over and formed the S. G. Simpson & Company, one of the greatest outfits of them all, supplying logs to many of the major mills around the Sound.

There must be an easier way to handle the big stuff and the lumbermen were trying to find it. No one knows for sure where and when the first steam donkeys were introduced to the woods, although it was long after steam came to the Northwest sawmills. Chances are, like Topsy, it just growed to meet the pressing de-mand for logs from the huge and hungry sawmills which were becoming speedier all the time as boss lumbermen from the Lake States moved to the Pacific Northwest. Some logger struck upon the idea to run wooden rails back into the woods and bring the logs out by carloads. Soon someone else, probably the Blackman brothers at Marysville, California, most authorities agree, brought in a small steam locomotive and the industry was shaken by change. With steam power on the railroads, it was only a matter of time before it was being tried in other ways for handling the logs.

One day in 1881, the Blakely Mill on Puget Sound ran out of logs, with a supply across the pond but no oxen. The father of Archie Binns, the noted author, hitched up a log to a steam pile driver winch and hauled it across. It worked and they got enough logs to keep the mill running, but the idea was dropped.[12]

That may or may not have been the first instance of using a donkey engine. Chances are there were other trial runs in the remote woods, for it wasn't too many years before the steam donkey made its debut and that changed things almost as drastic-ally as had the Sutter sawmill changed the West.

The loggers still moved logs along the rivers by current and sternwheeler, but there was another way of getting food for the mills as the timber lines receded ever farther into the back country where the mills couldn't easily follow. The lumbermen and log-ging operators built huge flumes stretching for many miles and as with the railroad trestles, these too were remarkable engineer-ing achievements. There were hundreds of miles of these flumes throughout the Douglas fir belt, skidding out billions of board feet of timber. The big logs came zooming down the flumes as on a toboggan run, miles an hour, to plunge wonderfully into the rivers and mill ponds, shooting sprays of water for hundreds of feet. These flumes ranged in length from a few hundred yards to twenty-two miles on the Moyie River of British Columbia, and across gullies, ravines and deep canyons from far back in rugged terrain. The grades varied sometimes to fifteen per cent like that of the Diamond Match Company on Big Creek, Idaho. In Skamania County near Underwood, there was a nine-mile flume one hundred feet high which cost $10,000 per mile to build. The Lewis flume of Oregon, near Eugene, was legion for its many crossings; in eight miles from the Lost Creek Valley to the roadside mill at Pengra, it crossed a state highway and the middle fork of the Willamette, passed other mills and for two miles was directly vulnerable to high wind, but it took a flood to knock it out.[13]

The historic Bridal Veil Lumber Company flume from Larch Mountain was legendary, too, for its steep descent, 1,200 feet in two miles down the bluffs into the Columbia Gorge where the mill was located. The V-shaped flume of 2x16 foot planks on trestles and over a high bridge carried lumber from the old Palmer sawmill down to the planing mill and handled timbers 16x16 and sixty feet long. Sometimes it took ten men half a day to break up a lumber jam, but the flume cost was nominal, only ten cents a thousand feet in the early days. When fire destroyed the Bridal Veil operation in 1937, the flume was put out of business and abandoned.

Daredevil loggers and lumbermen, with a whoop and a holler, rode the flumes at a hair-raising pace to town on Saturday night. It was nice and easy, oldtimers recalled, a real fun trip; and they'd save out the best cants during the week to carry them bobsled-like out of the brush to the bright lights. But the Bridal Veil flume wasn't much good for such antics, although a small dog once fell into it and rode a plank all the way to safety, as on a modern skate board. That encouraged some bold logger to make the attempt, but on the first bad pitch, he went sailing through the air and into the hospital.

That was the way it was in the glory days of lumbering in the Pacific Northwest.

NOTES TO CHAPTER III

1. According to James F. Stevens.
2. *Skid Road,* by Murray Morgan.
3. *The Roaring Land,* by Archie Binns.
4. Ibid: for more on Billy Gohl, see *The Last Wilderness* by Murray Morgan.
5. From *Big Skookum,* "100 years of logging in Mason County."
6. It hasn't been too many years since the problem was licked by the industry, and the great sawdust mountains have mostly disappeared. For years sawdust was a popular fuel for heating homes in the Pacific Northwest.

7. Lancaster Pollard, *History of the State of Washington.*

8. "Gyppos" are independent contractors, moving from place to place. The term is not at all derogatory.

9. The first railroad ties and pilings were cut at the Cascades in the Columbia Gorge, for the tiny river portage railroad. For details on the great railroad race up the Willamette River, see *The Saga of Ben Holladay.*

10. The story of the Jones Lumber Company is based on an article by Stewart H. Holbrook appearing in *The Oregonian,* April 15, 1934, and information supplied by Harry E. Jenkins, long the company general manager and member of the Jones family.

11. A few years ago the City of Portland was trying quietly to eliminate the Benson fountains, a Portland institution. An alert longshoreman, Francis Murnane, called the hand and saved them. Once when visiting Phoenix, Arizona, I met a young descendant of Simon Benson who said he always wanted to visit Portland "just to see the old man's fountains."

12. Detailed in *The Roaring Land.*

13. For the most authoritative account of Pacific Northwest flume logging, see "Fast Water Flumes" by Merlin Blais, Northwest Magazine section, *The Oregonian,* December 6-13, 1953.

Chapter IV
Keep an Eye on the Burner

IN the late summer of 1902 much of the Douglas fir region blew up in a series of forest fires that stretched from Lyman in northern Washington to the southern tip of the Willamette Valley, near Coburg and Eugene, and from the bustling coastal areas around Grays Harbor and Willapa Bay to the mighty Cascade Mountains.

An estimated 700,000 acres of beautiful virgin timber was afire all at once, creating a gigantic and choking smoke pall over the region and a strange gloom which caused ashes to fall on Tacoma, Grays Harbor, Vancouver, Portland and other great lumbering centers. The weather was hot and dry, the woods were explosive tinderboxes, and once a fire got started nothing this side of the devil could stop it.

Over one hundred ten fires in all were roaring their great destruction, the smoke billowing like an atomic cloud of a later time high into the atmosphere, the yellow flames leaping miles through the air, stripping and destroying forests that were centuries old, wiping out lumber camps and towns, ruining streams and ponds, creating destruction and black devastation on a massive scale. It was an untamed holocaust the likes of which the Pacific Northwest had never before witnessed and, thankfully, it would never happen to the same extent again.

Northeast of Vancouver, Washington, there was a tiny hamlet of fifteen buildings known as Yacolt, division point of the new Portland, Vancouver & Yakima railroad. The place was quickly evacuated, the people seeking the safety of a creek bed where they stayed throughout the night. But others weren't so lucky. Two families with six children, the youngest a baby, were traveling to Trout Lake for a picnic when the fire swooped down upon their big wagon. The charred bodies and skeleton of the wagon were found weeks later, less than one hundred yards from a creek where they might have been reasonably safe. Others died too— a Star Route mailman whose blackened body, clothing and skin burned away, was discovered against a log; a woman who tried to rescue her most cherished possession, her Singer sewing machine;

and several families who attempted to escape the savagery and failed. . . Thirty five persons died in the horrors of the "Yacolt Fire," named incongruously for the little town that somehow didn't burn except for house paint scorched by the heat.

The total loss from all the fires was set at $13,000,000; 12,000,000,000 board feet on 239,000 acres had been consumed by flames, three times the annual cut. There was a loss of 1,500,-000,000 board feet in the Columbia District alone, while unknown quantities of new growth were gone along with the creation of erosion problems in a land good for little else than growing timber. Only two future fires, the Tillamook of 1933 and Bandon in 1936, had equal dramatic impact on the industry and the general public.

The Yacolt Burn became a landmark of history, for it jolted both the lumbermen and the public because of the momentous size of the combined fires and the many tragic deaths involving children. Things couldn't go on like this, as men like Major Griggs and George Long well knew. The leading cause of destruction of Northwest timberlands was fire, and no matter how a fire started, the logging and lumbering industry was to blame in the public eyes. Certainly no timberman wanted to see his investment and source of supply go up in smoke anymore than did a farmer wish to see hail or fire destroy his wheat crop, or the fisherman want the salmon runs ruined.

The trouble lay largely with the free-wheeling boundaries in which the timber industry operated, the lack of adequate standards and controls, the slash burning and habitual use of fire by loggers, settlers, campers, hunters, hikers and trappers, just about everyone who entered the woods and had little consciousness of the dangers, particularly during the dry seasons. People built fires anywhere and left them, tossed cigarettes about freely, and because the forests were soggy wet for so many months, they couldn't believe that the woods would ever dry out during the brief summers. But the fact remained that the region's great timber source was being destroyed in a time when the lumber interests were coming to realize that the nation's tree supply was dwindling all too rapidly and that the last rich stands, comprising the greatest growing region of them all, were right here in the Pacific Northwest.

Action was forthcoming. Timber owners, not waiting for state laws, began creating their own fire patrols and protection organizations to reduce, if not completely eliminate, fire in the woods. Often they pooled their lands for the purpose of protection and financed the cost pro rata per acre to each owner. The year following the Yacolt Fire, the Washington legislature got busy and created a state forester and chief fire warden. The lumbermen who had worked for this kind of action observed that it was "about time." Two years later, this particular act was repealed and a state board of forest commissioners was formed with the power to appoint a state fire warden and deputies. Oregon created its first state forestry board in 1907.

As the private protection idea spread throughout Washington, Oregon, Idaho and California between 1902 and 1912, the organizations took the lead in developing sound fire codes, patrol laws, and pioneering techniques for better fire prevention and control methods which in turn were taken before state legislatures for adoption into laws of broader scope. Among these were compulsory patrols during dry weather, obligatory fire fighting equipment at all logging camps, closed burning seasons, compulsory slash disposal, snag falling and enforced shutdowns of logging operations when the humidity was dangerously low. Of great significance, too, was the first-hand experience the fire associations gave to timber owners in the spirit of cooperation and working together on common problems of the forest areas. This was something that hadn't happened before and a demonstration of what might be done on a great many fronts.

"These private protection associations took the lead in combatting forest fires and wrote a great deal of forest history," observed Colonel William B. Greeley who would one day become the popular and influential secretary-manager of the West Coast Lumbermen's Association. "It was here that industrial forestry began in the West."[1]

The industry in this decade following the turn of the century was in a state of flux. Great changes were in the wind. Efforts were being made to "sell" practical forestry to the rugged individualists of the timber country. By 1905 the National Lumber Manufacturers Association had teamed with the United States Forest Service in furthering this cause through the appointment of one hundred lumbermen and timber owners to raise an endowment fund of $150,000 to establish a chair of "applied forestry and practical lumbering" in the forestry school at Yale University.

Major Griggs, speaking at the annual meeting of the Pacific Coast Lumber Manufacturers Association in December 1905 in the Hotel Tacoma in Tacoma, reported on this movement:

"We are guarding a vast industry, representing 195,000,000,000 feet of timber, $60,000,000 in payroll, and affecting directly about 100,000 people. Our eastern competition is fast disappearing. In the east one third of the total output of three states was hemlock in 1904, a wood not considered a factor some years ago. Within five years that vast consumption will begin to draw its main supply from the coast, and with five or six competing transcontinentals and the prospective canal, I do not hesitate to admonish you to husband your resources. *Slab light, reduce the saw kerf, and keep your eye on the burner!*"[2]

The statements were profoundly significant for the time and

Major Everett G. Griggs, Tacoma lumberman, envisioned a region-wide organization
to deal with problems of lumber manufacture and marketing. He was first
president of WCLA.

place. Griggs was one of those who looked upon "timber as a crop" along with George Long, Frederick Weyerhaeuser and a few others, although one can well up a whale of an argument as to who first designated the big trees as something more than on a par with a mineral to be mined and when gone, it is gone . . .

"A lumberman after all," declared Major Griggs, "is a farmer cutting a crop of perpetual evergreens, and the intelligent application of diversified farming must apply to the markets we seek."[3]

"In some sections of our country," Griggs said further, "timber is the only crop that is developing the district, and population and transportation play a very important part in the value of the tree."[4]

George S. Long observed a few years later:

"With proper care and protection from fire, another crop will be ready for the lumbermen and the consumer by the time the present stand of mature timber is cut. Timber is a crop, and this crop can be renewed perpetually . . ." Long's speech at a lumbermen's meeting, where he also mentioned such things as "soil waste" and "waste in lumbering methods," was one of great impact. *The Timberman* reported that it was the general consensus following the talk that "without a doubt it was one of the most valuable addresses ever presented to a meeting of lumbermen."[5]

More changes were coming to the woods in this first decade of the 20th century. In 1901 an electric sawmill operated for six months at Tillamook Bay, until destroyed by fire. A new product called plywood was being exhibited to the public at the Lewis and Clark Fair of 1905 in Portland and in a few years the Douglas fir would be found to be an excellent production material for laminated woods. Hemlock which was long considered a "weed" and a menace would become the "Cinderella tree" of the Northwest after the discovery in 1909 of the sulphate process for the making of newsprint. Hemlock wouldn't work at first, but studies were intensified until it was learned how to take this wood apart and put it together again as paper and cellulose for many purposes. For the pulp and paper mills, it would be like finding an entirely new forest.

Things had been progressing steadily since Henry Villard drove that Golden Spike into the last Northern Pacific tie up in Montana in 1883, connecting Portland and all the Pacific Northwest to the East by rail. A few years later, in 1887, the line reached Seattle across Stampede Pass and the Southern Pacific that same year completed Ben Holladay's Oregon & California road over the rugged Siskiyou Mountains to the south. The Union Pacific was invading the Northwest, too, and lastly James J. Hill's Great Northern was laying track into the territory. The region had ceased its isolation from the rest of the nation. The rails provided a spirit of competition that had not been previously known by the shippers. Migration was far easier now, traveling by rail, and more people were coming to Washington and Oregon. This boosted the demand locally for lumber. Also millions of feet of ties, pilings, bracing and studding had gone from the region's mills for railroad construction.

But before 1905, shipments of general lumber to the East were nominal, although some products such as cedar shingles had found a good market there. The migrating Lake States lumbermen were conscious of the market in the East which they had long been supplying. There was a mighty demand for the Northwest's high quality shingles, huge timbers and top-grade construction lumber. But suddenly the lumbermen found no close friend in the railroads, the very systems that were built to open up the Northwest. The original rate on the Northern Pacific had been sixty cents per hundred pounds. Now freight rates were pushed ever higher. In the early years of the century the rate was $10 to $17 per thousand board feet of lumber, fifty cents per hundred pounds to Chicago, but by 1918 the rate had been increased to eighty cents per hundred. This trimmed Northwest lumber profits down to nothingness when competing with the low prices of the Great Lakes and southern producers, so that the matter of shipping rates became of prime concern to lumbermen in this "far corner."

The lumber interests had a hard time holding their own, for there was rank discrimination against producers west of the Rockies and rates were often set to the advantage of the eastern lumber producers, whose products rated second best alongside this wonderful Douglas fir lumber of quality. Even with the discouraging rates and the slim profits, the market in the East was so huge that shipments from the Northwest, at twenty-eight per cent in 1905, grew to fifty-five percent in 1910 and sixty-five percent by 1920.

The lumbermen were constantly at loggerheads with the railroaders, finding them equally rough and tumble, able to play a skull cracking game. The boss lumbermen thought they knew railroads—they had thousands of miles of them running deep into the timber. By 1917 along the Pacific Slope, there were 3,853 miles of logging railroads over which rolled 593 geared locomotives, 267 direct connected engines and 5,500 flat cars, on 8,000 sets of disconnected railroad tracks. At the peak of the glorious era of railroad logging and lumbering, there were 460 railroads, more than 6,700 miles of track and some 1,230 locomotives. But the timbermen who may have fancied themselves as "railroaders" understood only the mechanics of the Lima-Shays and Baldwins, the Heisler and the Climax. When they ran up against the big railroaders, they were playing with tough and daring gamblers for high stakes. It was a complicated three-cornered affair with the federal government involved and the vast timber holdings of the West in the pot. The play was not only huge but for keeps.

Crusty, bearded, rugged James Jerome Hill was one of the key railroaders, described by a biographer as "the barbed-wire, shaggy-headed, one-eyed son of a bitch of western railroading." In binding the nation together by iron and steel, the federal government had encouraged progress by awarding huge land grants of the public domain along the rights of way. These could be sold for financing capital and in the Pacific Northwest the great timber areas were considered a far lusher plum than the rolling grasslands of the Central Plains. These timberlands were what Big Ben Holladay, the region's first railroad builder, had his sharp eyes upon, ahead of his time, when he laid track hell-for-leather along the floor of the Willamette Valley. Henry Villard calculated the same way, but Jim Hill outclassed them all when it came to backing Uncle Sam into a corner where he would come out second best.

In the Midwest, Hill's Great Northern had acquired land titles of a defunct Dakota railroad. Homesteaders settled upon the tracts, believing this to be public domain and up for grabs. Now Hill, the old partner and friend of Major Griggs' father, threatened to kick them out and there was a bitter uproar in the hallowed hallways of Congress. Farm politicians demanded that the railroad lands be forfeited and of course, the problem farmers were having with railroad freight rates strengthened their case. But Hill turned the screws, putting the government in a position where it agreed to swap him 65,000 acres of federal land *of his own choosing* if he allowed the Dakota farmers to remain. Hill was nobody's fool;

he picked up the rich timberlands of the Pacific Northwest which he had carefully cruised. Later, Hill made another profitable swap when Congress in 1891 set up forest reserves, to become the National Forests, and the Forest Lieu Act of 1897 allowed that acres within the reserves could be exchanged for government land outside. Hill traded gladly rocks, ridges, rills and bare canyons for land which was heavily timbered.

Then the hard-bitten old railroader turned his trump card by selling 900,000 acres of these accumulated timberlands to the Weyerhaeuser Timber Company of St. Paul at six dollars an acre, causing Frederick Weyerhaeuser to comment that this is "not for us, nor for our children, but for our grandchildren." Weyerhaeuser had long cast a sensitive eye at the Pacific Northwest and had even considered buying a huge land grant of 850,000 acres of the Oregon Central Military Road Company, for the region was developing swiftly, spurred not only by the railroads but by the Klondike gold rush which brought frenzied thousands to Seattle. Hill himself was encouraging eastern sales of Northwest lumber with a low forty cent shipping rate to St. Paul.

The deal between Weyerhaeuser and Hill staggered the West, being of a scope beyond imagination and one of the largest single land transactions in the nation's history. It wasn't a matter of simple paper signing either. Like so many railroaders, Hill was hard-pressed for cash to redeem a bond issue. The timber sale included a down payment of $3,000,000, more than half the purchase price of $5,400,000. The remainder was to be in eight semi-annual payments at five percent interest. It required some ready scratching for the Weyerhaeuser outfit to raise the cash, quite a strain indeed on their pocketbooks. In the memory of one lumberman, "it took practically all the lumbermen on the upper Mississippi to raise the money." Finally through three large investors and nine smaller ones, the payment was made to Hill, closing the deal. It proved to be virgin timber at bargain basement prices. Within twelve years the Bureau of Corporations estimated that in terms of the probable cut, the price was about ten cents per thousand board feet.[6] The sale established the Weyerhaeuser empire in the Pacific Northwest which grew over the years to 2,750,000 acres in this western region, with some sixty billion board feet in Oregon and Washington, considered the wealthiest privately owned forest domain in the nation.

To administer this vast old growth area of Chehalis County, Washington, until then rated as a "green desert," came George S. Long, a tall and lanky boss lumberjack of the old school who nevertheless had an eye to the future so that he became one of the most respected lumbermen-foresters of his time. Long could outwalk a giraffe in the woods and when he left one rugged lumberman far behind on a cruising survey, the hard-breathing companion swore, "Hell, you might as well expect to get sweat out of a soupbone."

Long always signed his name "Geo. S. Long" and insisted that he be so referred to in print. He was a sawmill man by blood and honor, first working in his father's small mill near Indianapolis, later hiring out with a hardwood manufacturer, spending time in the South searching for stands of hardwood timber, and finally returning to the North to a job with the Eau Claire mill of the Northwestern Lumber Company, advancing to yard foreman and then sales manager. He was considered an expert with lumber, leading a movement to establish grade standards for pine mills of the Lake States. When Weyerhaeuser wanted him to administer their huge Pacific Northwest tract, they had to make him an attractive offer—$5,000 a year plus $100,000 in stock which Long could purchase on time. But he proved his worth, for although Long admitted that he knew little about the Pacific Northwest, he learned rapidly and wisely the policies, traditions and the way of lumbering, with its fluctuating instability and problems of overproduction, feast and famine, from roaring good times to panic and back to high ball again.

One of the worst tragedies ever to strike Puget Sound occurred on November 18, 1906, when the steamer *Dix* with seventy-seven passengers aboard sank on the way from Seattle to Port Blakely, taking the lives of over half the residents of that tiny place, all sawmill employees. Captain Percy Lermond, who had plied the route for thirteen years, had gone below to take tickets, leaving his mate, Charles Dennison, at the wheel. The freighter *Jeanie* loomed suddenly on the starboard side, Dennison became confused and spun the wheel the wrong way, and the *Jeanie* rammed the *Dix* in the side with such force it nearly cut the passenger steamer in two. The vessel heeled over slowly and sank swiftly, stern-first. There was no time to lower a boat or issue lifejackets. Half the passengers went down with the ship.

Thirty-nine died in the mishap, or maybe forty-five. Authorities weren't sure because there were a number of Chinese coolies hired as mill hands by the Blakely Mill Company aboard and seemingly no sound record of them by name. But nearly every family at Blakely lost a loved one. The sawmill was shut down and flags flew at half-staff during this time of great sadness.

"No mill company on the coast or perhaps the world lost so many employees in one tragedy as did the Port Blakely Mill Company," observed the *West Coast Lumberman*.. "In this one . . . twenty-three mill employees out of a total of forty-four residents in Blakely were lost."

It was a passing sorrow, felt by all the industry, but things had to go on. The lumbermen continued to be at a disadvantage

when negotiating rates with the railroads to allow them an outside chance of competing with the southern yellow pine and
northern white pine in sections of Nebraska, Kansas, Colorado and
Missouri. Furthermore, they were bucking strong trade associations of the southern region, which had a forceful inside track
with the railroads. Puget Sound and Grays Harbor manufacturers
were also pinched by competition from southern Washington and
Oregon, where changes in shipping rates had made things more
favorable.

The direct result was formation of the Pacific Coast Lumber
Manufacturers Association in 1901 with James E. Bell of the huge
Bell-Nelson Lumber Company at Everett its first president, followed the next year by Everett G. Griggs. Victor Beckman who
advocated many of the association's patterns and policies became
its permanent secretary. Beckman was a strong believer in unified
action. He had come to the Pacific Northwest in 1889 from the
Mississippi Valley and edited the *Puget Sound Timberman* at Tacoma. In 1895 he started the *Pacific Lumber Trade Journal.* It is
an interesting point that over the years the lumber industry drew
heavily upon members of the journalistic profession through either
hiring them or retaining their services. Beckman was long considered
"the best informed person in the Northwest on the problems of
the lumber and shingle trade," and advocated such things as controlled and planned production, the establishment of uniform grades
and prices, and a united front against the railroads. He pioneered
also the gathering and compiling of statistical information on the
industry to help establish trends and keep from overproduction,
one of the industry's biggest headaches.[7]

At first the Pacific Coast association had little trouble openly
carrying on matters of fixing prices and curtailing production by
its members. There were overtures to bring more harmony into the
industry, region-wide, through cooperative agreements with associations of southwestern Washington and in Oregon. But at times things
were near to chaos as maverick lumbermen engaged in practices
that nearly ruined the industry.

Still there was hope of some form of permanent harmony from
time to time when the Southwest Washington group fell into
line with the price lists of the Puget Sound mills or joined with
the Oregon association. In 1905 lumber interests seemed to have
reached their greatest accord when the two Washington associations negotiated the "Centralia Agreement" which would be void
unless signed by eighty per cent of the manufacturers and wholesalers. Later in the year a joint agreement was made with the
Oregon lumbermen, involving in all an estimated ninety percent of
the nation's fir production, an annual cut of 2,574,000,000 board
feet for rail shipment from the entire region. But such agreements
were hard to enforce, since they required association members to

squeal on each other, there would be publicity by open criticism of offenders at the meetings, and mills were urged not to sell to wholesalers who were out of line. The Centralia Agreement lasted only a short time, then everything blew up again like a forest fire, only this time it was caused by an earthquake.

Before dawn on April 18, 1906, the City of San Francisco suddenly got the shakes. Buildings began coming down, brick walls toppled into the streets, and people fled their beds to the safety of the parks as the big town built on gold and silver literally fell apart. Fires raged out of control for more than three days, gutting the heart of the metropolis and causing widespread misery and death. Some 300,000 were homeless and panic stricken, crowding the hilltops while Jack London penned for *Collier's* one of his most noteworthy and vivid reports. San Franciscans, with only the clothing on their backs, looked from the high places on their beloved city laid waste, causing Lawrence W. Harris to write the oft-quoted lines about "the damndest finest ruins, nothing more and nothing less."

When the fires were checked at last, using dynamite hauled by the son of Big Ben Holladay in his taxicabs, the city took stock of over $300,000,000 in ruin. Lumber yards on the fringes were for the most part saved, a fortunate thing in the present need. Among them were the Tacoma Lumber Company, Pope & Talbot, Charles R. McCormick & Company, Grays Harbor Lumber Co., E. K. Wood Lumber Company and Inman-Poulsen Lumber Company.

Right off, Northwest lumbermen rolled up their sleeves to help rebuild the city, for San Francisco was their best customer. The demand was for lumber, all kinds, immediate and urgent. Whenever there is great disaster, the survivors turn first to lumber. It was needed now for temporary shelters, homes and street repair, ramps and bridges, docks, walls, siding, studding, framework, finishing, plastering and to hold up the tottering walls of the gutted and sorry buildings. A national relief agency was set up, receiving great donations in cash, food and clothing. The sawmill men and those of allied fields contributed huge amounts, among them members of the Order of Hoo Hoo, the lumbermen's own fraternity. Sawmill employees donated a day's labor and forty-two cars of lumber, worth $17,500, were given by Oregon mills responding to an appeal for material to erect shelters for the homeless.

"The mills of the Northwest in less than two weeks can cut enough lumber to cover all the burned district with lumber boards an inch thick," boasted the San Francisco correspondent of *The Timberman*. "The consumption of the city has been about 200,000,-000 annually; this year it will be about 300,000,000. The rush for

Old-time sawmills were flimsy-appearing affairs, but they turned out the lumber to build up the country, and helped reconstruct San Francisco many times. Note show-off on the roof.

lumber will be over in sixty days and the trade should not take advantage of the necessities of San Francisco."[8]

The industry was surely moving the stuff, too. Three years earlier in 1903, John Eddy and D. E. Skinner of Seattle bought the Port Blakely Mill Company, becoming owners of what was considered at the time "the world's largest sawmill under one roof." The mill's 1,200 men daily turned out 400,000 board feet of lumber and during this time of emergency, the big plant was really pouring out the lumber, exemplifying the pace the industry had set for itself. Ironically, a few months following the *Dix* tragedy, the big mill itself was destroyed by fire.

In fabulous Grays Harbor, which we will consider later in more detail, millions of feet of logs were above the splash dams awaiting heavy rain, for February had been uncommonly dry and the spring rains were below normal. The rains held off, worse luck, shy an inch in May and a freshet not expected in June. Suddenly it came in a deluge for a solid week. The logs poured down to the tidewater booms and there was supply for every mill, at the best price the struggling loggers had ever known. The saw-mills were putting out the stuff so rapidly that San Francisco couldn't place its orders fast enough.

The sudden demand in this single year created more mills so that by the spring of 1907, there were 1,036 sawmills along the Pacific slope, compared with 557 two years earlier. And they were running at a fantastic capacity, one mill at Everett stating that it was operating "thirty hours a day and producing 82,000,000 board feet in the two years of 1906 and 1907."

Then the roof caved in. The rising prices inevitably caused repercussions in the Bay Area. The Bay's lusty newspapers, which had it in for the lumber industry anyway, charged noisily that there was a "lumber trust." Others took up the cudgel and the chant spread afar. Consumers of the Bay Area knew only that prices had advanced and couldn't understand why. A San Francisco grand jury asked the United States Attorney General to investigate the lumber prices. In other regions district attorneys haled the lum-bermen into court to answer for their deeds under the Sherman Anti-Trust Act. The lumber leaders explained that the law of sup-ply and demand governed the price of lumber—and right now there was a whopping demand. There had been a big increase in the price of logs and wages. Shipping costs by both water and rail had gone up with water rates being boosted $2 per thousand. There was an exasperating shortage of boxcars, an embargo by the railroads, and a critical strike that tied up shipping.

The trust-busting scare had its lasting impact upon the Northwest lumber associations in the issuing of price lists under their own names. Changes had to be instigated to avoid any further accusations of price fixing. The Oregon association dropped its official lists in favor of "unofficial lists" distributed by an inde-pendent Portland printing firm. The Pacific Coast group abolished its committee on values and stopped all price lists that carried the association name. In its place, Victor Beckman worked out lists of "prevailing prices" which he compiled as the secretary-manager and then as editor of the *Pacific Lumber Trade Journal*. He created an information bureau to keep tab on prices, supply and demand, and to summarize competitive conditions which be-came a "barometer" of the trade. Four years later, in 1910, the three main Northwest associations worked out an arrangement for a standard basic price list, drawn up by their representatives and taken as a milestone of joint regional cooperation among the three groups, the most extensive in five years.

But it was not altogether the harmonious time that one might think. For years the industry had hounded the big railroads about the shortage of freight cars, which was so critical at times that it choked the lumber industry and caused serious slumps in production.

The lumbermen, who had become highly proficient in handling the big timber and turning it into fine and varied products, were still faced with the headache of getting lumber to market. The industry had grown so rapidly and tremendously that there was often an overbalance in the flow of east-west rail traffic, bunching up the cars in the East. Then the San Francisco disaster created such congestion that the Southern Pacific, Great Northern and Northern Pacific slapped embargoes on lumber shipments and prepared to increase their freight rates.

The railroads held little love for the Pacific Coast Lumber Manufacturers Association anyway, for the PCLMA legislative committee had crammed some distasteful legislation down their throats in Washington State concerning the weighing and equipping of freight cars and was hoping to force the railroads to a forty cent shipping rate. With things critical in San Francisco and the over-all market the best in years, the railroads couldn't deliver the cars or maybe didn't care to do so without hiking the freight charges. Millions of board feet of needed lumber rested at the docks and there were loaded cars standing on the sidings. The Washington and Oregon lumbermen were frantic over an estimated 20,000 cars of lumber "that the railroads could not or would not move. . ." creating the gol-derndest lumber-jam the timber country had ever seen.

Northwest lumbermen carried their grievances before the Interstate Commerce Commission and rammed through laws in legislatures creating railroad commissions and providing for reciprocal demurrage or penalties on the railroads for failure to supply cars. In the Willamette Valley a new group, the Western Oregon Lumber Manufacturers Association, was organized to fight the Southern Pacific. Mills closed down, orders were canceled, and many a desperate sawmill owner lost sleep over whether to "take a chance of winning out" by keeping the saws running or "close down and be eaten up by insurance and other items of expense."

Only the Union Pacific which operated into Portland and was considered by those particular lumbermen as their own private railroad continued to handle lumber shipments with hardly a hitch. Washington lumbermen were blocked from using the line because of the Northern Pacific's stubborn refusal to allow an exchange system of railroad cars, which meant that shipments had to be reloaded at an additional cost in Portland. There were also high local and exchange rates. But the Puget Sound timbermen were desperate, standing idle while Portland sawmills continued to ship lumber. Their only hope was somehow to secure the services of the Union Pacific. So in March 1907 they filed suit with the Interstate Commerce Commission demanding an interchange of equipment and a freight rate from western Washington via Portland equal to that of the Rose City to the Rocky Mountains and Midwest region.

That blew the lid off. Portland millmen beat their chests, for not only were the Washington operators likely to tap their exclusive railroad, but they would be faced with competition for cars and markets. In what Washington lumbermen viewed as a bold double cross, the Oregon manufacturers sided with the railroads. The Portland Gateway Case came mighty close to a shooting war, for tempers flared hotly on both sides of the Columbia River and there was howling through the tall timber, especially after President Philip Buehner of the Oregon association had the audacity in his testimony to declare on behalf of the railroad that they were competent men "who must look after the railroad interest, as we do the lumber interest." Buehner's statement just about severed all relations between the two timber regions. Washington lumbermen would just as soon put Buehner through a gang saw.

The railroads, with a decided advantage, now made the fatal mistake of announcing a ten cent per hundred pounds increase in its rate in June 1907. This low blow called for united action by the lumbermen and Buehner, eating crow, wrote Griggs pledging full cooperation of his association to fight this new freight rate. There were second thoughts now as the Gateway matter cooled and the two associations got back onto speaking terms, although some of the lumbermen would hold a lasting grudge.

Victor Beckman was chosen to coordinate the new rate battle and all stops were pulled for a high ball resistance, since the lumbermen were publicly described as "mad—fighting mad." The associations levied special assessments against their members, the Pacific Coast association alone providing a $100,000 fund for the general war chest. A joint rates committee and a central press bureau, with Beckman in charge, were set up in Seattle, where a huge force of clerks and stenographers was put to work compiling data for the lumbermen's case, since it was believed that not only were the profits of the lumber products involved, but that the value of timberlands was also at stake.

The lumbermen gained an injunction against the Southern Pacific, submitting vast quantities of statistical evidence that the freight increase would indeed cripple the industry. A series of hearings was held and during this time the industry was virtually paralyzed. Lumber dealers denounced the railroad practices as contrary to the Sherman Anti-Trust Law and the Washington lumbermen even openly advocated public ownership of the roads. Their attorney tried calming them down, pointing out that public ownership was a last resort and that other kinds of regulations were more desirable. Above all, the lumber associations wanted a rate review act adopted for interstate commerce laws so that the commission would review any rate changes before they became effective. Half a million pieces of literature advocating this amendment were sent out across the nation and representatives of the Pacific Coast Association testified before a House of Representatives committee on interstate commerce. The ICC commissioner, Franklin K. Lane, said he favored the amendment "on the order of that proposed by the lumbermen of Oregon and Washington."

The joint association action had its effect. The rate-review provision became part of the Mann-Elkins Act of 1910. The ICC decisions went entirely in favor of the lumbermen, the rates being restored to their former level and all rates collected in advance had to be returned. The Portland Gateway matter was also solved, the Oregon lumbermen being granted a slight differential, but a through rate was available to the Washington industry and the Southern Pacific was ordered to restore its former charges from the Willamette Valley to California. The Southern Pacific tried an appeal, but the original decision was upheld. It was a sound and full victory for the lumbermen.

It was no wonder that Griggs, Beckman and others who believed in associated effort were jubilant, for this had demonstrated better than anything so far how unified action could win a war This victory might change the minds of a lot of the region's lumbermen, despite the fact that they were an independent breed by nature.[9]

Then the bottom collapsed in another panic, curbing shipments in 1908 to the Bay by 81,000,000 feet. Hard-pressed timber rivals were once more at each other's throats and the industry was again faced with the problems of overproduction. There was little that could be done without bringing down the wrath of the federal government upon them. The lumber associations had to be careful how far they went in urging price cutting and production curtailment, and guarded language was often used in letters which were submitted prior to mailing to the attorneys. Officials stressed continually that they weren't attempting to coerce the mills into shutdowns. But there was much quarreling and bickering among competing mills, whose owners were hungry, and threats of legal prosecution. Financially it was the worst of times, making Everett Griggs sick at heart and causing him to remark sadly:

"Everybody seems to be fighting everybody else and yet, if we try to get together and secure better prices, we may go to jail. I don't know but what I would rather go to jail than continue in the lumber business under the present conditions."

The one bright beacon in all this gloom was the forthcoming opening of the Panama Canal, which would likely change the shipping picture completely and might bring the railroads to their knees. Northwest lumbermen had a special interest in the Big Ditch, for their own massive timbers were helping to build it. That required tremendous stuff, too, some of it logged along Rapid Creek in Washington by the Simpson people, logs that squared up to thirty-six inches in timbers and were one hundred twenty feet long. In Portland a deal was being negotiated between the Robison Lumber & Raft Company and the Panama Canal Commission for 40,000 sticks of piling, 32,000,000 feet, to be rafted to the Isthmus for work on the canal and construction of barges, houses, wharves and other facilities needed to dig the ditch. But the region's industry had to battle for this business, even with the size of timber it could provide, and at one meeting the Oregon association voted a resolution urging the canal commission to open purchasing headquarters in Portland and submitted a list of facilities available for loading lumber which might well run to several million board feet.

The action was necessary, for Northwest sawmill operators were being by-passed, either through politics or oversight. Editorialized *The Oregonian* angrily:

"That the first effort of the new Canal Commission to secure lumber at the lowest possible obtainable price should be a failure—even a fiasco—is to be much regretted. Whether the fault be due to the ignorance of Major Gallagher, the purchasing agent of the commission, as to the centers of production on the Pacific Coast, or the omission of Portland as a probable source of supply be due to similar ignorance in still higher quarters, there is no means of determining. This first quantity of 26,000,000 feet is only a circumstance of what will be required by the commission . . . To advertise twenty three days ago in a San Francisco paper, ignoring Portland, would be about as sensible as advertising for lemons in the Portland paper and ignoring Los Angeles . . .Neither direct nor indirect notice of the chance to bid has reached any of our lumber companies. The commission refused to extend the time for bids as 'inexpedient.'"

Even with such setbacks, the West Coast lumbermen acquired considerable stake in the Big Ditch, not only its construction but because it promised them cheap accesses to the big eastern market and also the Midwest by shipping by barge along the Mississippi. But some lumbermen, among them J. H. Bloedel of Bellingham who was a powerful, outspoken leader among Puget Sound mills, sounded a note of warning that the canal would create new problems for the industry.

But the transcontinental railroads were worried, for coming of the canal—it was finally opened April 15, 1914—would put lumber and other producers in a far better bargaining position for shipping east, where in the past railroads on the West Coast had had everything pretty much their own way. Bloedel observed:

"If a rate can be found by rail or water low enough to enable the manufacturer to save an increased portion of the tree he is now cutting, and if the Panama Canal is the means of producing such a low rate, it will by the same token have accomplished more in the cause of conservation than anything else. Conservation and low freight rates are twin brothers traveling the same road."

Only time would tell. . .

NOTES TO CHAPTER IV

1. From *Forests and Men* by Colonel William B. Greeley.
2. From the early record book of the Pacific Coast Lumber Manufacturers' Association. Griggs was referring to the Panama Canal.
3. Speech before the Pacific Coast association, August 1905.
4. From *American Lumber Industry,* proceedings of the National Lumber Manufacturers' Association, May 1912, Cincinnati, Ohio.
5. *The Timberman,* February 1909.
6. *Timber and Men,* the Weyerhaeuser Story.
7. *Pacific Northwest Quarterly,* October 1950.
8. *The Timberman,* June 1906.
9. *Pacific Northwest Quarterly,* October 1950.

Chapter V
Some Little Bags of Cedar

One night at a banquet of loggers in Seattle's New Washington Hotel, Major Griggs was giving the main after-dinner address. Secretary Thorpe Babcock and Dwight Merrill slipped from the room and went down the street where they collared a policeman, offering him a stipend to come to the hotel and pretend to arrest one of the loggers.

The officer burst into the room and marched among the tables to the man the pranksters had indicated, seated with three other lumberjacks. There was a sudden uproar, for the logger hadn't been clued in. He was a burly fellow up from the ranks and now the owner of his own logging operation. He gave orders; didn't take them. He exploded with a series of expletives and logger thoughts on the matter that nearly took the plaster from the ceiling. Then he let the poor officer have it left and right to the jaw. Others leaped into the fray and the policeman beat a hasty retreat to confront Babcock and Merrill who pleaded innocence to the affair. The lawman was cooled off with an additional piece of change, order was restored, and the Major finished his speech.

Gatherings and conventions of the lumber world were often loaded with pranks and horseplay, for the lumbermen were fun-loving in a unique way when removed from their hard daily tasks. The long tradition of rough horseplay was there in force, even to the pinnacle that once in the staid Multnomah Hotel, Clyde A. Corman and Robert Conklin placed a fiesty wildcat in Roaring Ed Baker's bathroom. Ed really roared when he went looking for a tumbler. All of which caused George S. Long, who was forever bursting out with the unexpected, to bellow fondly when he viewed a milling timber gathering of loud talk and laughter:

"Loggers, when you are sober I admire you. When you are drunk, goddamn you, I love you!"

Major Everett G. Griggs, the first president of the West Coast Lumbermen's Association, set the pattern for his long line of successors who evolved from overalls to business suits. Griggs was a man of stature both physically and in the industry, yet despite his inherent good nature you couldn't shove him around or drag him through a knothole, for he'd cut his teeth on sawlogs and had been in the business most of his life. It was no wonder he was both willing and able to tackle successfully the job of guiding a united organization of free wheeling and dealing lumbermen through stormy times.

Griggs was a round-faced, jovial and carefree man who was liked and respected throughout the industry. As an avid horseman, he had difficulty making the transfer to the gasoline age. When he bought a large Packard car able to go over seventy miles an hour, the sudden change from horse to gasoline power was so radical that Griggs, driving about Tacoma, sometimes shouted "whoa" to the automobile. He came from robust stock, solid as a Douglas fir. His family were lumbering pioneers both in the Lake States and the Pacific Northwest. Griggs was one of four sons of Colonel Chauncey W. Griggs who had numerous enterprises as a coal and wood dealer, and in the wholesale grocery and contracting business at Chaska, Minnesota, where Everett was born two days after Christmas in 1868. His father, a native of Connecticut, was a Minnesota state senator for a time and served as a colonel with the Third Minnesota Volunteer Regiment during the Civil War. Later he turned to contract railroad building in the Midwest.

Young Everett took his early schooling in St. Paul and later entered Sheffield Scientific School at Yale University where many of his forebears had gone, the first in 1823. Then he spent a year in Europe.

It was during this time that Colonel Griggs made his deal for purchase of that huge timber area in the Pacific Northwest which led to the start of the great St. Paul & Tacoma Lumber Company, one of the region's big ones which helped develop Tacoma into the touted "Lumber Capital of the World." Young Griggs came west after his year in Europe and starting as a time-keeper in his father's mill, worked his way up to superintendent and into the company's executive offices. As vice president, he succeeded his father as president in 1908, two years before the elder Griggs died.[1] He married Grace Isabel Wallace of Portland in 1895. There were no children, although he had a nephew named for him, Everett G. "Spike" Griggs, who was quite active in WCLA in later years and succeeded his uncle as head of the St. Paul & Tacoma Lumber Company.

Griggs was a man of positive action and one of the most progressive in the Pacific Northwest, not only for his strong opinions on associated effort but on the many fronts within his own company. The St. Paul & Tacoma mill was among the first to change from the old-type circular saws to the band saw. Griggs became a leader in creating many safeguards for his men, for

sawmill work was plenty dangerous. Often other lumbermen said
Griggs kept his plant going at a heavy loss when a shutdown
would have laid off many loyal workers. The great plant on the
Tacoma tideflats, with logging operations in the hills beyond Or-
ting, became a regional landmark visited by hordes of eastern
tourists. Throughout his life Griggs remained active in affairs of
his community, was president of the Tacoma Chamber of Commerce, served on the board of the United States Chamber, and
contributed time, energy and money to many Tacoma projects,
among them construction of the Hotel Winthrop. His town looked
to him as one of its stalwart leaders and upon his death in 1938,
the *Tacoma News-Tribune* declared that Tacoma had lost "a loyal
and energetic citizen who did much for the growth and upbuilding
of the city."

Yet it was to the industry he loved so well and where he
spent his life and energies that Major Griggs made his greatest
and most lasting contributions. For a decade he had been the bulwark of the Pacific Coast Lumber Manufacturers Association which
had grown to be one of the largest and most powerful trade
associations in the West. Much of its success could be credited
directly to Major Griggs. Where other associations came and went,
the PCLMA continued to wield its influence over the industry,
the railroads, state and federal governments, and the public. Even
the most rebellious mill operators needed to consider the PCLMA.
Griggs could be hard and bull-headed when the situation called
for it, but he looked at life matter-of-factly and could employ both
patience and tolerance when the need was there. The Major
and many of the other leaders of this new generation were college-
educated so that much of the outer roughness of this lumber world
had been planed off. Griggs understood nevertheless what made
lumbermen tick and why they reacted as they did, and it was
this basic perception of his own breed that brought him into high
regard throughout the industry. If it hadn't been true, his association would have been short-lived and ineffective.
  There was plenty to be done now that the new West Coast
Lumber Manufacturers Association was formally under way, with
offices opening in Centralia and branches at Portland and Eugene. (The central offices were later shifted to Tacoma and then
Seattle where they remained for many years.) The Northwest Douglas fir region was apportioned into eleven districts, extending into
British Columbia, with Griggs heading it all as the association's
chief executive officer. Dues were set at a minimum of $20 per
annum and two cents per thousand on each member's annual
cut. The association, with a broad program in mind, had expenses right off the bat, including the hiring of the manager, a
secretary and retaining an attorney.

W. C. Miles was employed as manager at $416.66 for two thirds of a month's services and Thorpe Babcock as secretary at $200. Attorney Joseph N. Teal of Portland was retained for $400 a month. The first department committees were appointed, their chairmen as follows:

Freight and claims, A. C. Dixon, Eugene; inspection and cargo branch, E. G. Ames, Seattle; grading, J. H. Bloedel, Bellingham; insurance, R. H. Burnside, Raymond; statistical, W. H. Boner, Everett; publicity and market extension, W. C. Yeomans, Pe Ell, Washington; and taxation and conservation, George B. McLeod, Astoria.[2]

Babcock who would have a key role in early WCLA affairs was born in Massachusetts and educated in private schools there, later working as a naval architect before entering Yale. Following graduation from Yale Law School in 1907, he headed for Ketchikan, Alaska, on the tailings of the great Klondike gold stampede, but his ambitions fell short "on what turned out to be a mining swindle." He made it back to Seattle and about broke, got a job stacking lumber and loading cars at Startup, near Everett. It was his introduction to the industry and it took hold of him. Babcock worked for Bolcom, Canal and Seattle lumber com-

—Oregon Historical Society
Steam power invaded the Northwest woods in many forms. This quaint little logging locomotive was used on an Oregon show shortly after the turn of the century.

panies, then having passed his Washington bar examination—although he intended to stay in lumbering—he was hired as secretary of the new Lumbermen's Information Bureau, an experiment in keeping tabs on sales and prices as reported by its members.

Thorpe Babcock succeeded Victor Beckman, the well-known secretary of the Pacific Coast association, under rather sudden and strained circumstances. Beckman had been snuggling too close to John Barleycorn of late and Major Griggs, perhaps sadly, decided he had to go. One day on the streets of Seattle, Babcock met C. C. Bronson who belonged to the information bureau.

"I suggest you go to Tacoma and see Major Griggs and apply for the job of secretary of the Pacific Coast association," Bronson said.

Babcock was surprised, thinking of Beckman and his long standing, but he took the tip anyway. Next day found him nervously in Griggs' huge mill office. The Major, characteristically, didn't bother urging Babcock to sit down. Babcock made his brief speech and left, feeling that it was all a waste of time. But Griggs was a sharp judge of men and quickly made up his mind. Two days later he appeared at Babcock's office in Seattle and asked bluntly:

"Can you take Victor Beckman's job tomorrow morning?"

Babcock must have choked at the suddenness of all this, but said he could if proper arrangements were made with the bureau. He might have hesitated had he known the full story, for it seems Griggs, despite his ruggedness, hadn't the courage to inform Beckman.

"The next morning I had the very delicate and I must add heartbreaking job of relieving Victor Beckman of his position. . . a position which he had held for many years," Babcock recalled half a century later. "He handed me the keys and walked out. And there I was, knowing nothing about the whole business. It was not my first experience at being thrown overboard and told to swim or else . . ."[3]

Babcock was able to swim; Griggs wouldn't have kept him otherwise, for the play was rough in these years and the stakes were high. Babcock must have learned well, for the Major took him into the new West Coast association where he stayed until 1917, contributing much in ideas, aggressive energy and know-how to the growth of this lumber organization. Many of the patterns and policies of the old Pacific Coast association quite naturally became the foundation of the West Coast Lumber Manufacturers Association, for they had been tested under fire and were universal matters affecting all mills which needed to be dealt with by the board of trustees and the various committees. These were familiar things—workmen's compensation, freight rates and car shortages, legislation, tolls of the Panama Canal, tariffs, taxation, building codes, dissemination of statistical information, promoting and advertising the use of wood products, and good relations with both the general public and the press.

By the second meeting in the autumn of 1911, the WCLMA was truly rolling up its sleeves. The word had gotten around and there were three new applications for membership — the Carlton Consolidated Lumber Company of Carlton, Oregon; Nelson Neal Lumber Company of Montborne, Washington; and Silverton Lumber Company of Silverton, Oregon. By the third board meeting there were nineteen more applicants of mills ranging from British Columbia, where Richard Alexander had been appointed resident agent, to Medford in southern Oregon. But there were some resignations, too, by disgruntled members who didn't like the manner in which things were being handled and growled over their beers that the association's "expenses were too high and needed reducing."

The shuttling in and out of the association became something to be expected, for many of these leathery mill owners remained unconvinced that Griggs and his crowd knew what they were doing and that it just might be better to go it alone as they'd done for years. There was no holding them; if they didn't like a piece of legislation that the association was backing, the grades and codes, or the color of a man's hair, they cut and got out, although later they'd eat crow and drift back, snorting and blowing that things sure weren't as they were "in the good old days" when a fellow could cut and peddle timber without all these snags and barber poles.

Not all the single-footers were small independents or fly-by-nighters either. Once Thorpe Babcock tried selling the huge Grays Harbor Commercial Company at Cosmopolis on joining the association, but stubborn Neil Cooney thought it was a haywire show. Babcock tried overriding him by appealing to William Talbot of Pope & Talbot, owners of the Grays Harbor concern. He was rebuked soundly for breeching protocol and Talbot informed him firmly that Cooney was the manager and that he, Talbot, didn't tell Cooney how to run the business.

Problems of getting the lumber to market, fairly and cheaply, were constantly arising and the association's traffic department was on the run keeping track of freight charges, shipments and scalings. Some members felt that because the states of Oregon and Washington had testing cars to see that scales for weighing shipments were kept in good condition, the weight problem soon would be largely eliminated, but Attorney Teal told the West Coast board that "poor scales were only partially responsible for bad weighing." There were many, many instances of malpractice. Teal blamed many weight overcharges to sloppiness and errors. Such careless ways were more often reasons for overcharges than scales that were haywire. The problem seemed especially bad in Oregon where marked tares taxed shippers heavily and only one scaling was made between Portland and New Mexico, "and the railroads refuse to consider any weight but that one scaling." Teal said he knew of cases where part of the locomotive was weighed with a carload, and others "where the scaling was done by the light of a dim lantern and 10,000 pounds or more read into the gross weight in error, where marked tares were as much as 5,000 pounds less than the actual."

"What chance," asked Teal, "has a shipper got with one single scale weight when any one of a dozen things may happen to cause a heavy overcharge in weight? I do not believe that the railroads will ever give us these things voluntarily, and when the lumber business again assumes such proportions as to be considered a burden on the carriers, we may look to see scaling conditions drop back to where they were two or three years ago."[4]

The Interstate Commerce Commission was investigating the weighing problems at this time in Chicago and the West Coast board hurriedly authorized Teal to testify to give a sound picture of the problem as seen by the Pacific Coast industry. There was an initial effort, too, by the association's directors to bring about some uniform system of lumber grades and at the second meeting, the board adopted an "honor roll" plan of qualifying a man at each mill to issue certificates of inspection on car shipments over the seal of the Association Bureau of Grades. But the WCLMA inspection bureau, by the following spring, was essentially eliminated in favor of paying the independent Pacific Lumber Inspection Bureau $400 monthly to handle the work of the various mills.

Griggs and Babcock set up a Lumbermen's Information Bureau to provide a central place where manufacturers could post their prices and perhaps, through increasing their efficiency, be able to improve their lot. All members were urged to join this bureau which became a separate entity since "the officers of the association have not deemed it wise to bring into association work this dealing too much with prices of lumber."

Among the many activities were the selling agencies stimulated by the association, enabling small mills to compete for large rail orders and limiting the activities of "scalpers" or independent wholesalers. It also safeguarded the larger mills from price cutting. One of these selling agencies was the Douglas Fir Export Company which had as its executive committee some familiar names and faces—Everett Griggs, Thorpe Babcock, J. H. Bloedel and Myron Woodard. Through an idea of D. E. Skinner, president of the Port Blakely Mill Company, the Douglas Fir Exploitation and Export Company was launched in 1916 to extend shipments even further abroad. William H. Talbot of San Francisco was its president, with the vice presidents J. H. Bloedel, C. A. Thayer and E. G. Ames.

"North Pacific lumber exporters finally united in a strong agency to develop new demands for Douglas fir in foreign markets," announced the *West Coast Lumberman*. "It is the successful culmination of work covering nearly three years, a very large majority of Northwest manufacturing exporters. It is the first big selling combination of industry manufacturers to legitimately pursue foreign trade in a new era of world-wide trade expansion. . .

Early in the game there was a strong indication of interest among association members in developing promotional and advertising schemes to bring Northwest woods to the attention of eastern lumber dealers, retailers and the general public. On motion of Edgar Ames, the board approved publication of a booklet—the first of what would eventually be a flood of brochures and literature on the industry—touting the wonders of Pacific Coast woods and listing the WCLMA manufacturers. Before 1911 lumbermen of the West were decidedly floundering on the best way to promote their products. "Advertising" meant generally buying space in a lumber trade magazine sporting the name of the company in bold black letters and a sketchy outline of what was manufactured. It was largely vanity advertising, read only by those in the trade and perhaps a few people thumbing through a copy in the local barbershop. Lumbermen often said about the only good such space did was to assure them a fine obituary.[5]

In Chicago there existed a pair of high-bound advertising men, J. B. Crosby and J. J. Rockwell of the Crosby-Chicago agency, who found that they could make chips fly in the lumber industry. Casting about for fields to conquer, Crosby and Rockwell took a good look at the nation's lumber manufacturers and concluded that these people were making no apparent effort to reach their consumers and to tell their story. These advertising men were hardheaded and practical, and out for new accounts. Making a careful study of the situation all over the country, they decided first to tackle the cypress people of the South. Descending upon the cypress association with a sales pitch that would be the envy of Madison Avenue, they managed to line up members with their dollars to sponsor a national advertising campaign, targeted at the consumers. It took some doing, but they were able to swing an association assessment of five cents per thousand board feet.

Now what was needed was something known today as a "gimmick," a slogan or catch phrase that would take the reader's eye and fire his imagination. Crosby and Rockwell came up with a key phrase, "Cypress—the Wood Eternal." From coast to coast it was emblazoned in huge advertisements in leading popular magazines. The pitch was that the reader might be planning something that he hoped would last, like a home or office building, and that for such a purpose, cypress was the right product. Crosby and Rockwell didn't concern themselves with the retail dealer and the wholesaler. What they wanted was to create a consumer demand for cypress, knowing full well that if customers were turned away from a yard empty-handed, it wouldn't happen a second time.

The pair put their feet on their desks and waited; so did a great many doubtful lumbermen. If those advertisements about cypress went against the grain with lumbermen of the Lake and Northwest areas, the southern millmen had a field day. The demand exceeded their supply, mills were turning out more cypress than ever, and the price shot up as much as a dollar a thousand, which was plenty good in those times. The joyful manufacturers dug into their overalls, stepped up the advertising, and forecast the dawn of a new age for the lumber industry.

The campaign was so effective it even sold some Northwest lumbermen, surrounded though they were by the best timber in the world, on the long-lasting qualities of the cypress. When Thorpe Babcock tried to convince Paul E. Page, a rugged individualist from the Page Lumber Company at Eagle Gorge, Washington, that the Northwest industry should sponsor a similar campaign, Page remained stubbornly doubtful.

"But look at the great success of cypress," Babcock remarked.

"Yes," replied Page coolly, "but they have something to talk about. It's the 'wood eternal.' What can you say about Douglas fir?"

Crosby and Rockwell hoped to point the way. They realized it would be a hard sell to convince these cynical and somewhat embittered Northwest lumbermen. Thorpe Babcock, who knew the story of the cypress, met several times with the advertising men in Chicago. Then they came west, telling their story again and again to gatherings of WCLA members. At Aberdeen the lumbermen voted to sponsor a program similar to that of the cypress promotion, Major Griggs was picked as chairman of the advertising committee, and $20,000 was pledged to finance the experiment.

As Paul Page had put it, what can you say about Douglas fir? Easterners thought it was some kind of animal pelt, and it would soon be discovered that all advertising copy needed to carry the full phrase "Douglas fir wood." The struggle became long and hard to convince the lumbermen, but finally there was enough financing on the line so that Crosby and Rockwell could sit down with Babcock and question him in detail, seeking the right gimmick to start the ball rolling. Babcock rambled on and on, finally raving about wonderful cedar as ideal for shakes and siding.

"Besides," he laughed, "it has a peculiar, delightful aroma that dispels moths, thus protecting clothing."

Rockwell bolted upright and Crosby slapped his thigh in glee. They pumped Babcock excitedly for more details. He boasted of cedar's potent qualities, giving them the idea that moths fled at a single whiff. Well, it was good enough and already the advertising men were envisioning copy targeted at Mrs. Housewife. All she must do is clip the coupon, giving the name of her local lumber dealer besides her own and on this request, a small free bag of moth-eradicating cedar shavings would be sent to her, to be placed in her closet or bureau drawer. Presto! No more moths . . . simple as that . . .

The industry certainly needed some push, for competition was proving tougher all the time and things were generally bad. Somehow the sinking of the *Titanic* in April 1912 seemed symbolic; she was considered a "floating wood exhibit" of ornate interiors and furnishings, her doors, paneling, beams, posts, floors and other millwork of the best and costliest woods that the forests and mills of the world could supply. Her lifeboats of which there had been all too few were of Western red cedar; and when she struck that iceberg and went down, she carried with her a way of life of nabobs and American top-hat society of the 19th century that would never rise again.[6]

The lumber industry was feeling the stiffening competition from other building materials, among them steel, concrete, brick and fiber. Half the wood output went into building construction, a tenth into boxes, a twentieth into railroad car construction. Now the railroads were turning more and more to steel for their box-cars.[7] It seemed incongruous that the lumbermen, whose product had built thousands of railroad cars, were now being forced to ship in carriers of steel, but this was the way of the times.

Promoter J. J. Rockwell, explaining the importance of the proposed campaign, pointed out:

"There may be some of your members who do not appreciate the extent to which the people of this country, especially in the East, have been educated by advertising to the idea that wood in commercial quantities is almost gone, that the use it entails is an exorbitant expense, and that good lumber, particularly for structural purposes, cannot be secured at any price."[8]

Some WCLA members objected to part of the advertising budget going into the lumber publications. It seemed that they were back in the same old rut. Crosby and Rockwell were patient men; they explained that 40,000 lumber dealers who were the "delivery wagons" for the product had to be educated, too. Now they were preparing pamphlets describing the various Northwest woods and their uses, suggesting such things as fir for porch flooring and silo construction for farmers, cedar for lining closets, a com-

bination of fir and cedar for buildings and warehouses, the use of
spruce for winding shafts in the nation's textile mills—uses that
were widespread and so varied that the average consumer wouldn't
normally think of them. A special booklet was written telling
about the four leading Northwest woods, aimed at the casual consumer who would be asking for the cedar shavings. Upon learning
of his or her local lumberyard, such follow-up literature could be
sent there.

The initial advertisement about cedar and moths was scheduled
for the *Literary Digest,* one of the nation's largest circulation magazines of general popularity. Crosby and Rockwell warned Babcock
to get set for a deluge by having the little bags of cedar shavings ready. Babcock was skeptical, so he ordered only a modest
supply of small cloth bags, similar to tobacco pouches, with address tags attached. Why, any office girl could take care of the
requests as they came in, filling the bags from a gunny sack
of shavings in the corner.

Shortly after the advertisement appeared, Babcock arrived early
one morning at his office, well ahead of the others. Slipping his key
into the lock, he couldn't budge the door. Pushing hard, he squeezed
his way inside. The floor was piled high with letters "that must
have taken the postman half an hour to drop through the slot."
Over the next few days, the volume mounted and Babcock was
wholly unprepared to follow through either with bags or shavings.
Scouting frantically around, he and his aides found that the "fall-
out" from the shingle mill saws gave them what was needed.
A special room was rented, several girls hired, and a truck operated between a shingle mill at Ballard and the association office
to bring material for thousands of bags.

Rockwell and Babcock circulated through the timber region,
soliciting more support for the campaign even among independent
loggers and timber investors.

"It may surprise you to learn that quite a large portion of
people in the eastern states never heard of Douglas fir and do
not know what it is," Rockwell said. "Some replies show that readers believe Douglas fir is some sort of animal skin; others believe
red cedar shavings are a potent medicine preparation."

It was good fun while it lasted, but the major trouble came
from the lumbermen themselves. Removed as they were from the
consumer, they had no tangible evidence of how much lumber
they were selling as a direct result of this expensive promotion.
Sure, the association office was receiving thousands of requests and
there was opportunity to distribute pamphlets about their products,
but were the orders coming as a direct result of the advertising?
The old doubts returned and interest waned as the novelty wore
off.

But something caught fire and the WCLA leaders, who saw

the broader picture, approved plans to participate in a national forest products exposition first at the Chicago Coliseum, then going to Madison Square Garden in New York. The exhibit would be a four room home, full scale but without the outer walls to display the many interior uses of Northwest woods. Built at Tacoma, it had to be knocked down for rail shipment, then reassembled in two days at the exposition. Babcock was placed in charge. Arriving in Chicago, he found the coliseum in turmoil from a circus moving out as they moved in. Time was of the essence. Wanting to hurry things along, Babcock grabbed a screwdriver. A whistle blew and all work stopped throughout the great hall as carpenters and plumbers walked off the job.

A union steward angrily dressed down Babcock who pleaded ignorance and innocence, that he was merely a boy from the wilderness of the Pacific Northwest. The steward shook his head sadly, but signaled for work to resume, issuing another stern warning for the secretary to keep his hands off.

Then the West Coast group hit another snag when the city inspector condemned the entire exhibit for failing to conform to the town's building regulations. A second man, tagging the inspector, mumbled on the side something about getting the ban lifted for $50 cash to each of them. Babcock dug into his wallet and the exhibit was allowed to open on schedule. But the West Coast men were happy to leave the Windy City, for they'd had enough labor difficulties in their own region with the Wobblies—the Industrial Workers of the World.[9]

Life was never dull around association headquarters and Babcock, like secretaries who came later, sometimes allowed his enthusiasm to run away with him. Once he told members to wire their representatives in the legislature at Olympia to defeat a bill detrimental to the industry. Then metal spikes struck the head rig for Paul Page, chairman of the association's legislative committee, had made a horse trade to defeat another bill considered far more dangerous. It appeared Page was pulling a fast one with his fellow legislators and Page was understandably wild when the wires poured into the state capital. He heaped his wrath upon Babcock, but in time Page cooled down and was even able to laugh about it, putting it down to Babcock's youth and inexperience.

Despite the fact that the association appeared to be off to a good start, within two years following the Raymond meeting it was in trouble, due largely to a depression which curtailed the members' incomes. In the beginning, the board had voted to become affiliated with the National Lumber Manufacturers Association. Now Major Griggs was done as West Coast president and although he remained active, he moved up to take the national presidency, which assuredly didn't hurt the prestige and position of the Northwest industry. Walter B. Mackay, popular manager of the North

Pacific Lumber Company, moved into the president's chair. The selection for the still floundering young association was considered a good one, since Mackay was young (forty-one at the time), vigorous, energetic and possessing strong feelings about the ultimate success of this association. He was to the Columbia River area what Griggs was to Puget Sound, having been a lumber leader with the Oregon-Washington association since its inception in 1905 and in the lumber business since 1895 when he quit college to join his father, Donald Mackay, in operating one of Oregon's largest mills, with annual production of 100,000,000 board feet.

Young Walt Mackay realized full well that the association was on shaky ground late in 1913. By the following spring there wasn't even a quorum at one board meeting. The payroll couldn't be met and W. C. Miles resigned as manager, Babcock taking over a combined job of secretary-manager. The association owed Attorney Teal about $2,000, but Teal didn't press the board. He agreed instead to serve the association on a piecemeal basis rather than the monthly retainer. The Portland branch office budget was reduced to $200 and Babcock was instructed to see what money he could raise so that the services of the information bureau might be continued. Association dues were further reduced to one cent per thousand.

Business continued to drag. The August 1914 cut was down eighteen per cent from the previous year. Shipments had dropped ten per cent and were twenty-one per cent below August 1912. Fifty-seven mills that month cut 137,790,772 feet compared with 167,372,872 feet the year before.

When the association was only fourteen months old, Ralph D. Brown joined the organization, then headquartered in Tacoma; and during the next forty years as comptroller and assistant secretary-manager, Brown became one of the steady hands of WCLA and one of the region's most prominent lumbermen. He came to West Coast from the historic Tacoma Mill Company which was liquidating after half a century. During this time the plant had grown to tremendous size so that Brown recalled the monthly payroll in 1909 "was about $13,000, paid in gold and silver across the counter in about two hours; it took two men to carry it from the bank in downtown Tacoma."

Brown grew to be a national figure and recognized authority of the lumber world and was said to know more Northwest lumbermen at close range, even to being their confidant, than most any other individual in the industry. He ranged the West Coast region of Oregon and Washington, calling on hundreds of mills to keep owners and managers personally informed on association activities, and probably did as much as any single individual in times of crisis to hold the organization together when members threatened to quit and when collecting dues was more difficult

Logging trains unloaded the big stuff with spectacular splashes along rivers and bays, to be boomed up for the mills.

than yanking molars. Other WCLA executives came and went, but Brown continued on. Round-faced and spectacled, he knew his way around and understood what made things tick. He had a high regard for hard-nosed facts and figures. He helped develop an orderly method for lumber grading standards, set up the first reinspection service, compiled the early statistical reports on shipments, orders and production, and developed the association's weekly "barometer," used throughout its history, for reporting the fluctuating position of the industry. During both world wars, he served both government and the industry as an advisory official at government lumber auctions and helped develop some of the basic rules for lumber for the Office of Price Administration, working on numerous committees. He had the reputation of being a walking dictionary of complicated facts and figures, carried in his head.

Although the association broadened its responsibilities in these first years, it remained essentially a two-man organization in its central office which moved to the White-Henry-Stuart Building in Seattle in 1915 and absorbed the Lumber Information Bureau. P. D. "Pete" Ryan who worked for the Pacific Lumber Inspection Bureau was the first WCLA man sent east for lumber reinspection work, because of Brown's continued efforts. Prior to the time, reinspection was accomplished by other regional associations on a mutual exchange basis, but the WCLA tyees found this highly unsatisfactory. The association also arranged for meetings to dis-

cuss current market conditions and the future outlook. These were
mostly attended by mill owners and managers, since not many outfits had yet employed sales managers.

Something of a milestone came, however, following opening
of the Panama Canal in 1914 when the first Northwest lumber
went east by this route. It became apparent that with freight
figured on a net measure, it would be desirable to work out
some method of quoting delivered prices on lumber on a net
freight basis for any combination of delivery costs that might become involved. The Atlantic Coast List, prepared under WCLA
committee direction, was one of the most complicated lists the
association would issue, consisting of thousands of computations reducing the per thousand gross feet measure rates to a net basis
so that they could be quickly added to the f.a.s. or shipside value
for delivered price quotations.[10] The terms of sale and shipping
practices, followed by the industry for many years, were also distributed through the association.

The least change in shipping rates, a slight shift in any regulation, a forest fire, a change in attitude by the public. . . wages. . .
labor conditions. . .talk of an eight-hour day. . .the wild activities
of the Wobblies . . . shutting off of the new Panama Canal because
of the war in Europe. . .rising costs. . .price fluctuations, a sneeze,
a cough, the clearing of the wrong throat seemed vitally to affect
this sensitive industry. The association watchdogs had to ride herd
on it all, to learn the reasons why, and try to drive home its own
program of correction.

The rough and tumble trials of the lumber business, however,
didn't claim the headlines that John Turnow was making on the
lower Olympic Peninsula in the Simpson Logging country north of
Satsop. Turnow, a strange and burly misfit, was disrupting lumber production in his own way, living like a wild man in the
deep forest and scaring the vinegar out of loggers and ranchers
of the remote areas.

But Turnow killed, not once but many times, and became the
object of a massive man hunt by loggers, lumbermen, ranchers
and sportsmen. He was thought to be seen many places and the
newspapers called him the Wild Man, Mad Daniel Boone, the Cougar Man, a Thoreau Without Brains, who traveled through the
treetops, was a crack shot between the eyes with his old rifle,
and could survive even the severest winters, living in caves like an
animal. Finally in 1813 he was killed and his burly body brought to
Montesano for exhibition.

Certainly Turnow's "press" was not much worse than that experienced by the lumber industry itself. Lumbermen were eternally
among the damned, ever since the first comers and even in Washington State which had taken the lead in lumber production to

hold it for a long while. No matter where a lumberman set up shop, even in pioneer times, he was cursed by the people. Cutting timber in a watershed brought down the wrath of ranchers and villagers and sometimes their six guns. Miners could ruin the land with their placer equipment and farmers could plow under the rich prairie grass so that winds swept away the topsoil, but when you cut down a tree, it was a personal thing.

When I was newspapering years ago at Forest Grove, Oregon, the landmarks of that area, as they still are, were some clusters of beautiful, century-old sequoia giants brought as cones from the California gold fields by John Porter, a pioneer nurseryman and farmer of that area. Two of these wonderful trees stood before a pioneer frame home in town. They were continuing to grow, as they would for centuries, pushing upward and outward to break up the sidewalks and crowd the house. The home had been moved once and the lady owner refused to do it again.

Felling those giants proved quite a logging operation. The Portland newspapers and wire services made a lot of it. For almost a week my stories and photographs occupied a huge amount of *front page space,* no less, and there were even editorials bemoaning the death of these great trees. My editor, Harold Shirley, shook his head sadly when I brought one story to his desk, and I still recall his words:

"It's a shame. Why is she doing it?"

Personally, although I felt that it was too bad, I couldn't entirely blame the lady. What was she to do, abandon her property to those giants? Yet all the while that they were coming down and for months thereafter she suffered great public abuse in telephone calls and mail rebuking her for ordering the axe to those sequoias. Cruel things were said and in reflection, she confessed to me that had she known what she did now, she doubted that she would have had the courage to destroy the trees.

Lumbermen, loggers and their associates are faced with such stormy criticism most every day. It seems to be an occupational hazard of the business. Few people, myself included, ever give much thought to the world of wood that surrounds us and where it came from—the floors we walk upon, the chairs we sit in, the desks we work on, the frames and walls of our shelters, the fine wood alleys where we bowl, the smooth places where we dance, the huge beams that support gymnasiums and coliseums. . .cartons that contain goods . . . paper that we scratch notes on . . . the books to read and educate our youngsters . . . everything from telephone poles to jewelry boxes . . . thousands of items, for we live with wood every day. America's first and oldest industry has even permeated our language with richness and color: chip off the old block, rough and ready, going against the grain, two axehandles across, broad as a beam, pulled through a knothole . . . Even in American politics, the programs of candidates and parties are "planks in the platform."

Yet no major industry has been more cursed than that of lumber and certainly in the old days the lumberman did little to improve this condition. The free-wheeling years left permanent scars on the public as the lumbermen harvested the trees and were blamed for the roaring fires, the clogged streams, the obliteration of places of beauty for future generations. No sportsman or camper was ever blamed for a forest fire with the heated passion heaped upon the lumberman. Even in 1964-65, when great floods ravaged the Far West and logging operations and sawmills suffered heavy losses along with everyone else, the lumberman was criticized by anglers and boaters for not quickly clearing the rivers and streams.

Visionary lumbermen of WCLA realized there was a vast educational program to be done, and that better relations must somehow be established with the nation's press and the general public. Newspapers and magazines of 1915 viciously attacked the industry with charges of trusts and double-dealings and would print few things favorable about lumbering, not considering as to how they would publish at all if someone hadn't felled a tree somewhere. Forest fires were always played big, for conservation was coming of age in American thought, and the blame was invariably fixed on the "damnable logger." Unfortunately, it was too often true and timber leaders knew there was much to be accomplished to clean their own house, too.

The present animosity of the press was blamed by lumbermen on two things: the industry had vigorously opposed a Canadian reciprocity bill promoted by the newspapers to gain tariff-free wood pulp and paper; and second, the industry because of its peculiar circumstances spent little for advertising in the nation's dailies.

The national lumber association was ahead of WCLA in thought and actions, but in 1915 the West Coast hired its first press and public relations director, Robert B. Allen, personable editor of the *Pacific Coast Lumber Trade Journal.* His initial efforts produced little results, largely because the lumbermen themselves took a negative attitude toward publishing the truth and were generally uncooperative with even their local newspapers. But Allen stayed on with WCLA and when Babcock resigned in 1917 to take a position with the Northwestern Lumber Company at Hoquiam, Allen stepped into his job. Brown might have been moved to Babcock's chair, but the board wanted a glad-hander, a back-slapper and a friendly outgoing individual and Allen was the type. Brown's personality was against him. The suave Allen came off a sports editor's desk back in Pennsylvania to turn to lumber trade journal work. He acquired a good working knowledge of the industry and could talk shop with the best men in the business, on a golf course or in the club rooms. He also created through his polished personality something of an image that the industry direly needed for too many lumbermen were rough-shod and hell-for-leather outspoken in their own colorful language to be appreciated away from the head saws and green chains. That Bob Allen would one day "do them in" seemed as improbable as taking lumber to the moon.

The association, like a sawmill, needed overhauling and changes in its bylaws to admit other lumber manufacturing groups such as the shingle men who were increasing in number with one hundred fifteen mills counted around Bellingham alone, and Grays Harbor blossoming with numerous specialty plants to utilize different kinds of wood, including spruce for airplanes and hemlock for paper. In recent years the general industry, once so single-footedly independent, had become organization-happy. Even the burly transient loggers had come together, not only in the radical Wobblies but in the founding of the logging congress, conceived during Seattle's 1909 Alaska-Yukon-Pacific Exposition by George Cornwall, when he was striding down First Avenue with Uncle Ed English of Mount Vernon, Washington, who was the first to use wire rope instead of manila in the woods. At the moment Cornwall was thinking about having a bath. Suddenly he said:

"Ed, wouldn't it be wonderful if we could provide baths for the loggers? They get so hot and dirty in the woods."

"George, I think you've got a swell idea," replied Uncle Ed. "Let's form a loggers' association or congress where we can bring this and other such matters up for discussion."[11]

Cornwall had been approached by Henry Reed, the famed Portland newspaperman, for a logging exhibit in the exposition's tremendous Forestry Building. This was apparently the first rendezvous of the logging congress. When word got around, some of the industry's biggest names stepped forward to help—George S. Long, A. W. "Skookum" Clark, Charles Spaulding, Robert and Alex Polson, Tom Bordeaux, Cutler Lewis, E. P. Blake and Frank H. Lamb. Blake was picked as the first president, Lamb as vice president and Cornwall for secretary; and when Cornwall was asked by a Seattle reporter how they were selected, he replied, "Why I did it!" That about floored the reporter, for the congress had been promoted nationally as one of the highlights of the exposition.

But Cornwall served fifteen years in the office as the Pacific Logging Congress grew to sprawling size as principally a forum of the industry for exchange of ideas on basic problems. In 1963 when Robert Conklin was president, the biggest congress of all in Portland attracted 2,000 loggers from across the country. Cornwall became a major figure of the industry as founder and editor of the *Columbia River and Oregon Timberman* which evolved into *The Timberman,* a leading journal of the industry. As editor, he ranged

Dobbin was moving lumber in the yards and to market when WCLA first brought North-west sawmills under a single banner.

all along the West Coast and thus in a dual capacity was able to create a strong logging congress. While the congress was never an affiliate of the West Coast Lumbermen's Association, there was a camaraderie between the two groups and in the mutual exchange were many members of both organizations.

Plywood, pulp and paper were coming in stronger and the changing fortunes of the industry were dominant in the minds of men like Julius Bloedel, often an outspoken and rebellious critic of WCLA programs. Bloedel had a lifetime of lumbering behind him. His family were French Huguenots settling in Wisconsin in the 1840's where he was born. Bloedel studied engineering and then went to railroading, but felt the pull of the forests and turned to harvesting timber. He migrated to Seattle in 1889, arriving just a few days after the Great Fire, found nothing to keep him there and went to Bellingham to settle at Fairhaven which appeared to be booming. Along the way he met another young engineer, J. J. Donovan, and the pair staked a timber claim and organized the Samish Lake Logging Company with Peter Larson, a railroad contractor. The firm evolved into the Larson Lumber Company, one of the largest shippers of Pacific Coast lumber products. Bloedel became secretary-manager and in 1913, when it became the Bloedel Donovan Lumber Mills, he moved to the presidency and chairman of the board. Larson was famous for its huge shipments of lumber. Once Mill B at Larson, Washington, shipped by single order 1,800 carloads of bridge timbers to Edmonton, Alberta, Canada.

President Bloedel pushed hard for reorganization and the WCLA trustees voted nineteen to two to move the offices to Seattle for a less expensive operation, with branches and departments scattered from there to breakfast through the tall timber. In Seattle things would be consolidated under the watchful eye of the secretary-manager and Bloedel was happy to report that "the efficiency and spirit of the organization has been very tangibly increased by this move to the tenth floor of the White-Henry-Stuart Building, a fourteen-story structure on Fourth Avenue where WCLA would have its stronghold for the next thirty-one years.

It was official now; the name was *West Coast Lumberman's Association,* the word "Manufacturers" being dropped. In the trade it would be known as WCLA and The West Coast.

The association seemed to be hitting full stride in its duties and responsibilities, and getting the desired results. Unfortunately, Thorpe Babcock was leaving. But there was growing prosperity and rising prices from the war in Europe, in which the United States would likely soon be involved. WCLA would need all its organizational strength to meet the challenges of this national emergency.

NOTES TO CHAPTER V

1. From the Griggs' family scrapbook.
2. From first WCLMA record book.
3. Thorpe Babcock's own reminiscences to Arthur W. Priaulx.
4. From WCLMA records.
5. Reminiscences of Thorpe Babcock.
6. James F. Stevens, *Out of the Woods,* No. 711.
7. Manager's report, W. C. Miles, Aberdeen meeting, 1913.
8. Minutes, Portland meeting, 1913.
9. Thorpe Babcock's writings.
10. Reminiscences of Ralph D. Brown to Arthur W. Priaulx.
11. From writings of Arthur W. Priaulx.

Chapter VI

The Great Spruce Harvest

LUMBER is a prime material in time of war. Once a U.S. Department of Commerce employee compiled a "partial list" of uses of wood by the military and enumerated one hundred and thirty-seven needs ranging from barracks and cantonments to tent frames, warehouses and latrines. The lumber business has been called by authorities "the most important war industry in the country."

Weeks before the United States declared war officially in April 1917, preliminary efforts were being made to organize the nation's great lumber industry. Lumbermen everywhere had pledged their support to the nation and the president of the National Lumber Manufacturers Association offered full assistance and volunteered his own services.

There was anxiety on all sides and in such an atmosphere, knowing war would come, some lumbermen were anxious to see it made official to clear the air. As it was things were badly stymied by conditions at home and abroad for, while lumbermen of the West Coast were ready to give their all to the war effort, the region's industry was faced with two critical matters that might well block its wartime participation. One involved boxcars; the other, labor.

The boxcar shortage had periodically plagued the industry for several years like an incurable disease, but for two months before Congress declared war, mills could not find transportation for even fifty per cent of their production. When the government slapped on embargoes, conditions were worsened and at times traffic was so congested at the ports from the mounting volume that all shipments east of the Mississippi were halted until things could get untangled. And despite yeoman's efforts by members of the West Coast Lumbermen's Association the shortage continued throughout the conflict, injuring the Northwest's contribution to the war effort since at best, Western sawmills could obtain only about forty per cent of the boxcars they required.[1]

At a Seattle meeting in February 1917, WCLA issued a strongly worded resolution hoping to jar the railroads and governmental authorities to the seriousness of the intolerable situation.

"The forest products industries of the two states (Washington and Oregon) have been seriously hindered since last October by the failure of the western roads to supply cars required for the transportation of products of said industries," the association statement declared. "The excessive accumulation of stocks sold and awaiting shipment is now seriously interfering with the operation of a majority of the mills which, if no relief is obtained in the near future, will be compelled to further reduce operations. Be it resolved, the West Coast Lumbermen's Association, viewing with alarm the unprecedented congestion at the mills, the unparalleled shortage in cars, and the great need of eastern, middle west and western buyers for stocks purchased in anticipation of spring trade, urge upon the railroads the necessity of getting a supply of cars to western loading points; at the same time respectfully representing that a substantial proportion of such car supply be set aside for the loading of forest products."[2]

George S. Long was already in Washington as a member of the Lumber Committee Council for National Defense, organized by the War Department which drafted William Buckhout Greeley of the U. S. Forest Service as secretary. Object of the committee was to assist federal officials on lumber purchases and in this capacity, Greeley worked closely with Long and other West Coast lumbermen, J. F. Gregory of the Fir Tree Lumber Company at Tacoma; E. T. Allen of Portland, manager of the Western Forestry and Conservation Association; and E. A. Selfridge of San Francisco. The committee, numbering fourteen in all, designated that government contracts be allocated through nine regional committees. The West Coast Lumbermen's Association organized a fir emergency committee, headed by Long and Gregory, which evolved after several reorganizations into the Fir Production Board, a regional group under the War Industries Board headed by Bernard Baruch. J. H. Bloedel took charge for a dollar a year, with authority over all fir production for government agencies. Serving with him were H. B. Van Duzer, Colonel Brice P. Disque, C. W. Stimson and William G. McAdoo, representing the federal government in handling the railroads.

The WCLA board voted to send Secretary Robert Allen to Washington, D. C., as anchor man there for the duration of hostilities. Allen would spend most of his time working with the production boards and civilian agencies in the problems of lumbering in wartime, while WCLA assistant Ralph D. Brown would coordinate things on the Pacific Coast. Later, the association set up a system whereby its members, two at a time, would rotate to Washington to help Allen in dealing with federal officials under the countless problems, the stresses and strains of the war program.

One of the first calls was for over a billion board feet to build cantonments. However, since most of the Army camps were located in or near the South, it became quickly apparent that the southern yellow pine belt would grab off the bulk of the orders. The Northwest was able, in any case, to supply lumber for cantonments at American Lake, Washington; Des Moines, Iowa; and later an arsenal at Rock Island, Illinois.

Freighting was assuredly the problem, but whatever lack there was in the cantonment program, Northwest sawmills and logging camps made up for by supplying quantity material, including some big heavy stuff, for construction of a great fleet of five hundred wooden ships on the Pacific and Atlantic coasts and in the Gulf ports. The great shipbuilding program got under way in May 1917 and the WCLA mills really moved the boards to make Major George W. Goethals, skeptical head of the Emergency Fleet Corporation, eat his words that "birds are still nesting in trees of which the wooden ships are to be built." As the trees came down in fury, many a winged family had to move quickly.

The Douglas fir steamships were built to specifications and the cuts made accordingly for the rubber stamp vessels with a dead weight of 3,500 tons and a speed of ten knots. Each ship contained 1,684,233 feet of Douglas fir, almost all that was required, with only 8,501 feet in other woods. Under strict specifications, mills could pre-cut lumber to fit so that upon reaching the shipyards, it could be speedily put together to make each vessel. The long clear cants were often so green that the vessels spilled their calking on the first trip out.

By the fall of 1918, when the war was about over, shipyards of Seattle, Tacoma, Portland and other ports had launched two hundred eight ships and the government was contemplating orders for two hunderd forty-four more. In all, the Emergency Fleet used 790,000,000 feet of lumber, while the Navy consumed 122,000,000 feet. By the end of the first half year, there were purchases of over one billion board feet of lumber for the war effort and at the close of hostilities, this had reached nearly six billion feet.

The wartime need further spread the acceptance of Douglas fir around the nation as an important and leading wood variety, for large quantities were freighted to Atlantic and Gulf ports for shipbuilding, once WCLA got things organized. It was only after a lengthy battle with authorities of the Emergency Fleet Corporation that the *West Coast Lumberman* was able to point out that Douglas fir, once used in such huge quantities for windjammers, was "finally recognized" and that there had been a transfer of orders totaling 40,000,000 board feet of shipping lumber for eastern yards.

Much of the change in attitude came because Bloedel's committee

—Oregon Historical Society
Diamond stack woodburners hauled out the heavy logs being turned into lumber for ships and planes of World War I. Logging and lumber companies owned much railroad equipment.

was able to get the transportation problem licked in an amazing way. Certainly it was a huge feather in the industry's cap in supplying Douglas fir for the cantonment at Des Moines.

"The best bit of advertising of Douglas fir was the prompt and speedy delivery for cantonment construction at Des Moines from Oregon and Washington mills," Robert Allen wrote *The Timberman* from Washington. "One hundred and one cars of fir arrived before any southern yellow pine arrived that could be used. The first cars of fir were on hand four days before any came from the South. There has been much publicity on the remarkable showing made by the Pacific Coast mills. With the exception of only 16,000 feet, the entire consignment of Douglas fir was well up to grade. Officials in charge of construction were enthusiastic over the fir material, and Douglas fir is even going into building of ships on the Gulf."[3]

Hundreds of orders were being placed with Northwest mills and the woods resounded to the logger's axe and saw, but there was a good deal of confusion. Bloedel's board discovered that many war orders were being sent to mills not equipped to handle the specifications. Then there was that damnable matter of shipment, which caused countless delays and turned both lumbermen and shipbuilders frantic. Lumber for the shipyards was being sent helter-skelter in single carlots which would take forty to sixty days to reach its destination. The Fir Production Board found many single cars sidetracked indefinitely at intermediate points, often from breakdowns of the rail equipment.[4] There was little regard for timing and the needs of the shipyards. The yards often received decking first, the keels last, and sheathing and framing somewhere in between. And the Northwest supply was vastly important, for its mills were sending enormous timbers squaring at two feet and one hundred twenty feet long; framing timbers and ribs twenty to thirty feet in length; enormous quantities of ship's planking six inches thick, eighteen inches wide, and sixty feet long; and filling an urgent demand for clear ship's decking two and one half inches by five and one quarter inches, vertical grain on edges. As in the days of the windjammers, Northwest timber was proving itself ideal for building vessels.

But things were chaotic in this mad rush and the first step by the Bloedel committee was to coordinate the allocating of orders to the mills best prepared to handle them. Some mills refused, but pressure was applied by threatening to deny them rail equipment which caused a lot of cursing yet had its immediate results.

Then Bloedel turned to the freighting problem. It was suggested that rail shipments be made into entire trains of thirty-five to forty cars, containing virually all the material needed for construction of a complete vessel. So far as was feasible, each car would be loaded with a single type and cut of lumber, and the trains would be moved through division points intact, so as to arrive as a single unit at the designated shipyard. If there were material for more than one yard, the train could be broken at certain division points and rerouted accordingly.

In the Pacific Northwest, three shipping places were designated—Auburn, Washington, for the Northern Pacific and Milwaukee lines; Everett for the Great Northern; and Portland for the Union Pacific. Railroad traffic managers didn't like the idea, feeling it simply wouldn't work and that it might "upset our regular schedules."

"That's too bad, gentlemen," Bloedel replied firmly, "but you've got to help us meet a national emergency."

"But what happens when we get a bad-order car in one of your trainloads? We can't hold up a train for one defective car."

"Drop it out for repair, just as you do on other train movements," Bloedel snapped. "We'll put a soldier with railroad experience on every train to attend to that and pick up any cars that have been repaired and are ready to move."

Gradually order emerged from the chaos and lumber cars were reaching the eastern break-up points in eight to ten days. A. D. Lasker, chairman of the Shipping Board, was jubilant as shipyard production soared and sought out Bloedel personally to shake his hand. He won the full respect, too, of John Henry Kirby, described as the grand old man of the southern pine industry.

"I don't see how you did it, Bloedel," Kirby commented in Washington. "There's actually more lumber in the shipyards now than they can use."

When the war was over, Bloedel cherished the one dollar check he received in Lasker's handwriting and the accompanying note lauding him "for the real service you performed."

There was trouble in the woods, too, for the boys going to war created a critical labor shortage; then, to heap insult onto all the other problems, bright officials of Uncle Sam's wartime Food Administration set up logging menus that demonstrated how little the government agents understood about lumberjacking. The menus called for "meatless meals" and eggs for breakfast. The loggers were furious, for they required meat . . . meat . . . meat to stick to their ribs and give them strength during the long, energy-sapping days. The West Coast association went to bat for the loggers in this beef about beef and the point was reluctantly won, so that the timbermen got their full supply of meat.

All of West Coast's tall men were involved in the war effort, one way and another, and the various committees were working long hours to keep the industry running high ball. Major Griggs was serving on the Spruce Production Board and Arthur L. Paine, of the big National Lumber & Manufacturing Company at Hoquiam and one of the association's original stockholders, was master-minding things as president. Paine was not a lifetimer to the industry as were most of his colleagues, having been a stove salesman in Spokane. He was attracted to National Lumber's million dollar plant at the mouth of the Hoquiam River, built by Coeur d'Alene mining money of the Wicks and Campbell families at Spokane. The owners were having operating difficulties and urged Paine to see if he could straighten the mill out. He got it on its feet and continued as manager for two decades, becoming a leader among Grays Harbor and West Coast lumbermen.

The industry had been harassed by labor troubles for a decade, many of them instigated and projected by the Industrial Workers of the World, founded in 1905 by a group of socialists and evolving into an organization of radicals with a Marxist philosophy. The Wobblies grew in number and became a movement of bold irritants in the mines and the woods, capitalizing on any rifts between management and labor to stir up trouble and cause confusion of the issues. Wherever possible they seized control, yet they had an appeal for the Northwest loggers, for conditions in the camps at the time were primitive. Some of IWW goals were commendable, however, including the termination of the ten-hour day and a three dollar per day minimum wage, but they preached revolution and hate, and fomented strikes and rioting in most all the lumber centers, often wresting control from the less resourceful American Federation of Labor. The Wobblies played rough, too, with sluggings and beatings, and driving bolts and railroad spikes into logs to sabotage the saws at the mills.

In the summer of 1916, the IWW's attempted to move in on

a Shingle-Weavers' strike at Everett, but were driven off by the sheriff and a group of local citizens. Promoting a freedom of speech cause, they were back in November aboard the *Verona* and the *Callista* from Seattle, bent on invading the stricken lumber town. The sheriff and a large group of armed deputies, millmen among them, were determined that the crowded *Verona* wouldn't dock. The *Callista* hovered safely in the background to see what would happen.

The Wobblies, leaning over the rail, shouted their defiance as the steamer drifted toward the pier. As it brushed the dock, a deckhand threw a mooring line around a bollard. Then the shooting started, from which side first no one knew for sure. Men fell both on the ship and on the pier. The crowd rushed to the opposite side of the *Verona* to escape the swelling gun fire. The ship listed, straining at the mooring line. Part of the railing broke away and men toppled into the water. Then someone cut the line and the *Verona* backed off. When casualties were counted, seven were dead, two among the shore party and five aboard the ship. Fifty others were wounded. Others may have drowned, for in the excitement no one knew for certain what happened to them. On the return to Seattle, seventy-four men suspected to be Wobblies were held on a murder charge, although later they were released from lack of evidence.

There were other incidents of bloodshed, but the Battle of Everett was significant in that it was the first instance where the IWW's were met with armed resistance. There was no love lost among the A. F. of L., the Shingle-Weavers and the IWW, nor any united front against the companies, but all agreed on certain main objectives, including the adoption of an eight-hour day and improvements of working and living conditions in the woods. Now with the Great War in full sway, the Shingle-Weavers and Timber Workers coordinated plans, taking advantage of the labor shortage, to press their demands, unpatriotic as it might appear. They called for a strike by mid-July. Then the Wobblies pushed into the picture and because their loud and angry name-calling could rally support among the unhappy and ignorant lumberjacks, they got some camps to walk off the job ahead of the July 16 deadline.

The lumber employers ignored the strike threat until July 9 when they met in Seattle and formed a Lumbermen's Protective Association which strongly condemned the eight-hour day as "impossible in wartime" and to keep to the ten-hour schedule "for the purpose of maintaining the maximum production in the lumber industry."

But public sentiment, despite the critical war effort, was running against the employers and following the deadline from 40,000 to 50,000 workers walked off the job. By August 1 not over fifteen per cent of the logging camps and mills were running. It was truly an impressive demonstration of union power.

President Paine had plenty on his mind before the West Coast Lumbermen's Association:

"This is no time to talk hours. It is no time to figure profits. Every man in this country should be willing to go to the limit of strength, brains and capital which God has given him to assist in lightening the burdens of this war. . .I almost regret that I have lived to see the day that my country would permit men to go unhanged who would go about spreading sedition at a time like this, as they are doing in this state and in many places throughout the land."[5]

The employers had already begun improving living conditions in the camps and mills—clean bedding, spring beds, electric lights, new bunkhouses, better sanitation, social halls and places for entertainment, libraries of books and magazines, and special housing for married men, all comforts that would make the old-time snoose-chewers turn over in their graves. But the owners stood firmly against lessening the working day which would bring a substantial increase in lumber costs, even if Uncle Sam was paying for it, because the day would come when the war would be over and they would be turning to private consumption again.

The boxcar shortage and a healthy inventory strengthened the employers' position. There were also prospects that the Army would move in to help get out the lumber, especially in the sudden rush for vast amounts of Northwest spruce for airplanes. An Army take-over would discourage strikes. With better working conditions and because they were hungry for pay checks, thousands of men began drifting back in September. The lumbermen held to their ten-hour day and also required that returning workers sign statements declaring they weren't members of the trouble-making Wobblies, and at last the big strike was over.

All at once the cry was for the lordly Sitka spruce of the Pacific Coast which Major R. Perfetti, head of the Italian Military Commission for Aeronautics in the United States, described as "a wood . . . which is consecrated by the Creator to insure liberty of the world and is the harbinger of peace and good will among mankind." Material from the fat spruce trees, eight to fifteen feet in diameter and three hundred feet high, was needed not only by Uncle Sam but by the Allies who were ahead of the United States in the production of aircraft as weapons of war.

Through the West Coast Lumbermen's Association, manufacturers formed a Spruce Production Board as a clearinghouse for the mills involved in spruce manufacture. John P. Keating of Hoquiam was appointed manager with offices in Portland to work with E. T. Allen who represented the federal government in the purchase of quality spruce for airplanes. Bloedel who was doing such an excellent job handling the rail traffic situation was named to this board a short time later, although apparently Bloedel had his hands very full for he was soon replaced by Major Griggs.

The critical importance of spruce to the war effort was never better stressed than at a meeting in an Aberdeen hotel in an atmosphere of cloaked secrecy, attended by Thorpe Babcock, now manager of the Northwestern Lumber Company which was one of two Grays Harbor mills assigned to handle the government spruce cut in that locality. Behind closed doors, Babcock and the other mill manager were confronted by three men in strange uniforms. They turned out to be Italian, English and French pilots, brought to the Northwest to emphasize the need for great quantities of blemish-free spruce for airplane frames. The entire war effort hinged on this product. Unless production was speeded to high ball, the war could well be lost, for German air power was far greater than that of the Allies. The Germans were putting many planes unchallenged into the air for observation rather than combat and were thus able to check on Allied preparations and troop movements. The Allies needed a huge air armada to knock the Germans out of the air.[6]

The war effort would demand an estimated 100,000,000 to 117,000,000 board feet of spruce in the next year, representing about one billion board feet of logs, since only about one hundred sixty-seven board feet out of every thousand met G-list specifications for aircraft production. It was like mining for gold and *The Timberman* reminded its readers that "Pacific Coast spruce is the only satisfactory wood for airplane construction in the world available in sufficient quantity to make possible the successful aerial offensive against Germany."

But this loud clamor for aircraft came in the midst of all that labor strife and the great strike, so that now there was an even greater need to expedite things to serve the war effort. Major Charles R. Sligh, a former furniture manufacturer from Grand Rapids, Michigan, was serving in the Signal Corps and undertook to push the program by sending E.T. Allen to the West Coast along with George S. Long of the Emergency Spruce Committee. A month later Sligh followed them and by September, the government had commandeered all available spruce lumber inventories and cold decks. The situation was in turmoil from the summer strike and the yet ugly mood of the men returning to the camps and mills and Sligh, growing impatient with Allen's slow-bell progress, demanded his resignation. That got Long's back up, too, and Sligh charged that Long was out "to get my scalp." Long denied any such intention although other public officials were also sniping at him, including Oregon Governor Oswald West.

Out of the quarreling and continued harassment by the Wobblies, Colonel Brice P. Disque, a West Pointer who had served as a

—James F. Stevens Collection
This sawmill crew found a unique way to demonstrate the strength of Douglas fir for aircraft and carrier decking, in great demand during two world wars.

Michigan prison warden and then re-entered the service, secured the necessary authority in Washington and hurried to the Northwest to view the spruce matter. He took charge and Sligh resigned, later attacking his successor as an incompetent and blowhard which boiled the tempers of Disque's fellow officers and the many lumbermen who were working with him for the good of the cause.

Disque had his faults, but he took a firm hold on the situation and began bringing soldiers into the Northwest to help get out the spruce lumber, thus starting his famed Spruce Production Division. They had to be trained, but it was possible; by February 1918, he had 5,500 men in the industry and this grew to 30,000 men at the peak wearing combat hats in the woods. Disque arranged things so that the soldiers were assigned to mills and camps that were shorthanded. Employers made up the difference in pay between the Army wage and the equivalent total given a civilian employee doing the same work. Disque began work on a thirty-eight mile railroad to tap some rich but isolated spruce stands, built a remanufacturing plant at Vancouver, and contracted with both loggers and sawmill men not only for spruce but for fir, encouraging the cutting of Douglas fir to supplement the vitally needed stock of available spruce. Soon fir for planes was being shipped in increasing quantities.

"Fir is now entering upon its own," Major Everett Griggs told a gathering of West Coast lumbermen. "It is equal to spruce for aircraft material and in some respects superior to it and is being so recognized."

By the fall of 1918 the ratio of spruce and Douglas fir was about three-to-two; for every 30,000,000 board feet of spruce cut for aircraft, 20,000,000 was cut in fir.

Disque was quick to realize something must be done to handle the labor difficulties which were slowing and halting production on all sides. The Spruce Division helped, but wasn't the full solution, for spruce shipments were at only half the desired 10,000,000 feet per month. Disque launched a new organization of employees and employers called the Loyal Legion of Loggers and Lumbermen, commonly known as the "4L," something of an industrial council. The idea may not have originated with Disque, but may have come directly from President Woodrow Wilson and Samuel Gompers of the A. F. of L or through a group of lumbermen anxious to better labor conditions and reduce the power of the Wobblies. In any case, Disque was quick to put the plan into action. Gompers and Secretary of War Newton D. Baker approved of it, for this would merge the best efforts of both groups for the national cause and at the same time help keep the labor peace by jointly considering such knotty problems as wages, hours and working conditions.

Disque and his assistant, Lieutenant Colonel Cuthbert P. Stearns, selected personable young officers as ambassadors of good will to the camps and mills to talk with employers and workers. They found the two groups largely receptive. Workers had had their fill of strikes, the lack of pay checks, and the Wobblies; and from the founding of the first 4L local on the last day of November, the plan which was described as a "fifty-fifty" organization and was born under the cloak of patriotism "took like wildfire in the woods." By the end of the year there were over three hundred locals and 10,000 members, and by the following April the 4L had 70,000 members. The organization spread across the mountains into the pine country, also essential to the war, and soon boasted 100,000 members. Through the 4L and its mounting power, even though it was to be merely a wartime organization, Disque made progress in production, improved camp and working conditions, and laid the groundwork for changing the pay schedules.

The board of the West Coast Lumbermen's Association took action to work closely with Disque in filling the government contracts and in organizing the 4L; and at its meeting a few days before Christmas 1917 voted to place "two active heads of lumber producing plants in the districts covered by the association" in Washington, D. C., for the period of the war and as long as necessary thereafter to facilitate and coordinate matters of this industry and the war effort. The board voted also to have President Paine and Colonel Disque work out in conference an arrangement for appointment of one or more men from each association district to work with Disque to step up production. A central agency was set up as a clearing house for all government orders and contracts, so that they could be assigned to mills able to handle them; and the WCLA pledged the industry to a minimum of six hundred carloads of airplane material per month and urged each mill owner to devote a complete day to studying his operation to step up production for aircraft.[7]

Now Disque pushed for the eight-hour day, which the timber companies so vigorously opposed, as Ralph Burnside of the Willapa Harbor Lumber Company—often described as the "peace-maker" of the industry—took over the WCLA presidency in this second year of war, and H. B. Van Duzer of Inman Poulsen, in Portland, became chairman of the Fir Production Board. Lumbermen were heatedly critical of Disque, accusing him of trying to cram the eight-hour day down their throats and hating it especially since the IWW had promoted it. But the schedule was highly popular with the general public and a coming thing in American industry, despite the bad timing due to the war.

With public opinion running hard against them, the lumber-men grudgingly accepted the eight-hour day on February 27, 1918, and Disque issued an immediate order for adopting this schedule throughout the region's lumber industry, with a forty-eight hour week and time-and-a-half for overtime. The workers were jubilant, to say the least, but there was mounting bitterness among the employers over Disque and his power. The lumbermen could only express the hope that the workers would now settle down to business and make "a more honest effort," as Long put it, to winning the war.

NOTES TO CHAPTER VI

1. *Timber and Men*, the Weyerhaeuser Story.
2. West Coast Lumbermen's Association record book.
3. *The Timberman*, August 1917.
4. *18 Men and a Horse*, by Donald H. Clark.
5. From WCLA record book.
6. Reminiscences of Thorpe Babcock.
7. From WCLA record book.

Part II
SONG
OF THE
SAWMILL

Chapter VII

Landmark of Industry

A visit to a sawmill, large or small, is a memorable thing. You never forget trodding across the soft wet earth heavily carpeted with sawdust, chips and shavings; of watching the great logs splash down into the millpond; of climbing the steep stairs and clapping your hands over the ears at the scream of the whirring saw biting through the thick logs; of thrilling to the flashing hand signals of the skillful sawyer as the huge logs are turned and slammed against the dogs; of watching the freshly cut lumber running along the green chain where the pieces are quickly sorted and graded in a language you would never understand. The sawmill is a wonderful and mysterious world all its own. The massive cold decks . . . the tall stacks of bright lumber . . . the marvelous sweet fragrance of the cut wood, as sweet as orchards in springtime . . . these are the lasting impressions you carry away and remember from a first introduction to a West Coast sawmill.

Yet, to the casual observer, the average sawmill of the old and traditional type is outwardly an unpretentious thing. Today there are many big and sleek sawmill plants along the Pacific Slope — clean, efficient, light, airy, safe, and utilizing most everything of what was once waste material so that the great wigwam burners, long the distinctive feature of any sawmill, are bowing out, being replaced by huge chip bins. But even the most modern mills adhere to the basic problem of slicing up the log, albeit scientifically, in a system that started with the first grunt and groan handsaws. The old-time mill, and there are numbers of them yet spread over the hinterland, remains a rustic affair, looking as though it might fall apart at any moment or that its roof might cave in. Actually, it is stoutly constructed to withstand the pounding and vibrations of the work being done there, so that long after these sawmills are abandoned they remain landmarks of the lumber region as are the shafts, tunnels, rockers, cradles, tailings and stamp mills of the mining country.

The ideal site for a simple sawmill has a land topography with a gentle slope, so that the logs may be easily rolled onto the saw carriage. There should be a level or downhill haul on the opposite side for running out the lumber. In this age of machines, these requirements are not as necessary as once they were. There should also be easy access to transportation — a major matter which haunts the industry from beginning to end — for bringing in the raw logs and taking away the finished lumber to market; and there should be adequate space for stacking and drying the new lumber. In days of the steam mills, the plants had to be near a good water supply. Mills powered by diesel, gasoline or electricity don't need this.

The logs roll out of the hills on powerful trucks to be dumped into the pond adjacent to the mill. Many mills today also use "cold deck" stock piling. Boom men sort and float the huge logs to the incline or ramp below the log deck where they are pulled up by a heavy chain conveyor. Sawmills are built on stilts above the ground to allow for a certain amount of sawdust and chips falling beneath. In small mills logs are often rolled to the deck from above, then shifted onto the carriage as needed. In the large modern mills, the bark is peeled from the logs by a high-pressure water or rotating burr system as they are hauled to the deck.

Some logs will supply lumber of fine appearance; other logs will supply lumber that is not good looking but is rugged and strong. Each piece of lumber, whether it is of best appearance or not, has a use for which it is especially adaptable.

Inside an operating sawmill there is an endless hurricane of noise, the booming thunder of rolling logs, the whir and whine of many saws, the low chortle of moving carrier chains.

Each man in the mill has a definite part to play in the manufacture of a piece of lumber. From the first cut to the last grading, the processes of manufacture are the processes of selection.

At the head rig, where the big saw takes its first cut, stands a master craftsman, the head sawyer. He swiftly sizes up the log, deciding whether or not various cuts will supply fine finish lumber, structural material, or boards and framing items. The final product will depend on the number of knots and other characteristics the log contains.

The head sawyer turns the log to proper position for the cut, then decides what size of cut to make, and signals the operator of the log carriage to adjust the log accordingly. Then the sawyer pulls the lever that moves the log into the saw; the whine takes on a deeper note as the saw teeth bite into the wood, sings again as the cut is finished and the cant moves onto the carrier chains. The making of lumber begins.

Endless chains and rolls carry the lumber to each succeeding saw. The men at the controls interpret the decisions of the head sawyer, and move their blades to cut each piece to its best advantage.

Mill machinery is powerful, ingenious and intricate. At the head rig, lifting bars and iron claws turn huge logs lightly as pancakes. The gang saw makes a dozen slices through a square of timber like a cheese-cutter going through a chunk of cheddar. The trim saws drop like triphammers, cutting off the ends to improve grade and appearance.

Beyond these machines, still on the moving chains, the lumber travels the long sorting table. Trained graders examine and mark each piece for grade. And as it moves along the line, each piece is taken from the table by a sweating puller and stacked with others of the same grade, size and length.

The work of the sawmill is finished. Logs have been converted into rough green lumber. Nearly all of this lumber is surfaced later in a planing mill and even now more than half goes to the planer and is shipped without seasoning. Today lumbermen are installing more and more dry kilns, so that in a few more years more than half of production will be shipped dry. Lumber may be stacked in towering piles in the mill yards for partial drying before going into the kilns, where huge ovens finish off the drying process.

In the planing mill the tempo is picked up. The whir of saws changes to the scream of razor sharp planing knives; the chains and rolls move faster as they feed the smaller strips of lumber to the machines.

Here the lumber is "finished"; cut to exact measurements and patterns, surfaced satin smooth. And again and again it is examined and separated by the graders according to the purpose it may best serve.

This is lumber manufacture: sawing . . . planing . . . grading . . .

Nowadays there is a true art in cutting up the log, for each one has its individual grain patterns, knots and other characteristics, as distinctive as fingerprints. Cutting for sheer beauty in this day of unique grains for homes and office buildings calls for great skill on the part of the sawyer. A sawyer must know his log and his woods.

Lumber can be cut from a log in two distinct ways: Tangent to the annual rings, producing "plainsawn" lumber in hardwoods and "flat-grained" or "slash-grained" lumber in softwoods; and radially to the rings or parallel to the rays, producing "quartersawn" lumber in hardwoods and "edge-grained" or "vertical-grained" lumber in softwoods. Usually so-called quartersawn or edge-grained lumber is not strictly parallel with the rays, and often in plainsawn boards the surfaces next to the edges are far from being

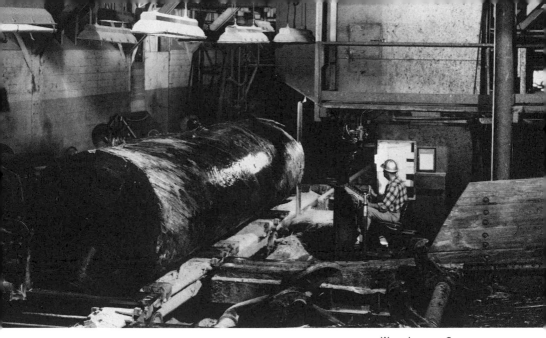

—Weyerhaeuser Co.
Head rig saws logs into long thick slices called cants. These cants are later cut to lumber sizes. Modern sawmill workers are required to wear metal hats for safety.

tangent to the rings. In commercial practice, lumber with rings at angles of 45 to 90 degrees with the surface is called quartersawn, and lumber with rings at angles zero to 45 degrees with the surface is called plainsawn. It is plainsawn that produces the flat grains and the more richly swirling patterns.[1]

Principal drawback to the circular saw which remains in widespread use is its kerf, as thick as five-sixteenths of an inch and causing much waste in the cutting which buried the early mills beneath huge mountains of sawdust. One early-day wit described the mills as "sawdust factories with a by-product of lumber," an exaggeration that made its point. Getting rid of that surplus brought about the great burners which were considered a mighty step forward in their day, for the heavy leftover was a major headache to every sawmill man. Sawdust furnaces became a popular home heating means in the Pacific Northwest as one outlet for the surplus. But today the mills sell their chips and sawdust to other woodprocessing plants; and huge bins to save the leftovers have replaced the knobby burners on the sawmill skyline, so that the burners themselves — long the symbol of wood waste — are now a subject which the lumbermen would just as soon forget.

The large and progressive modern mills now use great band saws, sixty feet in circumference, sixteen inches wide, and running at terrific speeds of over one hundred miles an hour. The band saws have a thinner kerf, but require a sizable investment. The endless steel band operates in circular fashion on two large wheels, above and below. Single band saws have only one cutting edge, while the double heads are toothed on both edges and can make a slice each way, with the log carriage operating and adjusting the log in each direction. The band sawmill must be housed in a very sturdy structure, able to withstand the stresses and strains and keep the saws in proper alignment. Several sets of head rigs or complete mills may be housed under the single roof of a big lumber manufacturing plant to increase volume of production. The modern push-button sawmill is something to behold and attracts throngs of tourists to such semi-automatic plants where there are guided tours.

Leftovers find their way out of a sawmill in another direction. Slabs, edgings and miscellaneous pieces move by conveyors to the chippers, for they are suitable for pulp. Bark, sawdust and planer shavings make cheap fuel, too, for the company's powerhouse. The chips go to pulp mills for remanufacture into paper, container board, hardboard, insulating board, cellophane film and a wide variety of other uses. Yellow wood chips are now said to be the "blue chips" of the timber industry, with a dozen paper mills able to eat up three thousand tons of wood fiber every twenty-four hours. Chipping plants consist of heavy steel wheels of six to eighteen sharp blades turning at a high rate of speed and cutting the wood into even-size pieces about five-eighths of an inch long. The chips fall into screen hoppers which sort out the sizes and eliminate the splinters and coarse pieces. Then off to the pulp mill they go, by ship, barge, truck or railroad car, part of the ever-changing scene of modern lumbering.

Two old-timers sat side by side on stools of a greasy spoon cafe. One had a deformed hand, four of the fingers gone.

"You a shingle weaver?" the other man asked, glancing at the hand.

The other man nodded, for he wore the brand.

The old-time sawmill was a dangerous place to work, on a par with the high balling logging operations. An old-time labor leader described safety in the early sawmills as "nil." Most of the mills were free-wheeling and little thought was given to safety. The millowner wasn't much concerned and didn't know how to cope with the situation; and the men who worked for him were reckless and "damned if I care," adopting a philosophy of life that what will be will be . . .

Fingers were the most vulnerable and many a sawmill man lost his digits to the spinning steel teeth, sometimes not even realizing it for several seconds, so quickly and painlessly did it happen. Bad lighting which cast false shadows was sometimes to blame, although more often human failure was the reason. One sawmill man ran his fingers through a saw. He glanced down and then passed out.

"How in hell did he do that?" asked the bossman, rushing up.

"Just this way," answered a young buck and, demonstrating, did the same thing to his own hand.

But accidents were sometimes spectacular. Circular saws, running at high speed, broke loose and sailed through a wall or the mill roof. If a saw struck an imbedded iron bar or spike, all hell broke loose. The circular saws, without adequate guards, threw wood chunks and splinters with great force. Edgers and resaws had terrific kickbacks. A piece of board flying at the speed of a missile could crush a man's skull; a smaller piece could cost him an eye. A javelin-like splinter once broke from a board, sailed through the air and right through a man's abdomen, killing him outright.

A log carriage, moving fast, broke loose from the cable and went spinning off the end-of-track and through the wall, taking the rider to his death. Boilers exploded and slipping logs fell on men, crushing legs, arms and chests. Huge belts operating the

—Forest Industries
Great double-edge band saws travel at high speed, must be removed for sharpening. This is typical sawmill filing room.

machinery off the central power plant snapped and whipped through the air, clobbering any man in the line of the great lash.

When the mighty band saws broke loose from metal fatigue or at the welding line, the mill was suddenly alive with a monster of whipping steel, going in every direction like a giant clockspring on the loose. Harry Jenkins, manager of the Jones Lumber Company, remembers a snapped band saw dancing all around him like a serpent, while other men dove for cover. Jenkins was trapped and forced to stand his ground, afraid to move yet knowing he might be cut in two at any second as the great blade shaved his whiskers and then danced off in another direction without scratching him.

Sometimes the rampaging band saw went right through the side of the building. Then again, the saw might roll into a corner where it crouched like a quivering rattlesnake, poised for a strike. The big band had all its energy still coiled up there and the men were afraid to touch it. In one case, they blocked it in and cemented it up, leaving it there, for there were no demolition experts in the sawmill industry.

Occasionally there were more terrible accidents that grabbed deep at a tough man's insides. Harry Jenkins once saw a man fall into the gang saw which cut him to ribbons and years later, shuddered when he told about it.

But gradually sawmill owners and the men developed an awareness for safety. Precautionary devices were installed, better equipment required, and safety codes adopted. Modern mills, with their push-buttons and remote controls, sounder equipment, better lighting, and a stress on programs of preventative maintenance have reduced the accident tolls considerably, to where plants boast of millions of man-hours without a mishap. Both management and labor have become safety conscious and the continuous accident-free hours are given places of prominence on outside billboards for the public to see, since human error remains a primary cause of accidents today. It is through constant reminders, with the mill crews in regulation metal hats patrolling each other plus company meetings and schooling sessions, that the toll has been so greatly reduced. Like many other industries, modern sawmilling has grown up . . .

Even so, the darned sawmills were always catching fire; and a sawmill fire, while spectacular, was a terrible and frightening thing. Among the worst was the million dollar holocaust of the Ballard mill, Seattle Cedar Lumber Manufacturing Company in May 1958. The causes of mill fires were many—sparks from a burner or locomotive in low-humidity weather, friction, combustion, sabotage and smoker's carelessness started many a fateful sawmill fire. The mill of wood, built as it was on stilts that created good up-drafts, was a marvelous place for fire. On a high wind, the flames would travel with the speed of a forest crown fire through the main plant, the resaws and planers, the machine shop, the docks, ware-houses, into the fine lumber of the yard, onto the waiting boxcars and to the logs of the cold deck and the pond. Little could stop the flames once they were on the rampage.

Next day, only the damnable burner which may well have started it all stood amid the charred ruins, with thin wisps of smoke rising from the graveyard of the dead mill. Somewhere near-by, the lonely figure of the millowner poked about, muttering to himself, wondering what he could salvage and whether he would ever build again or get out of the business. Chances were that he would rebuild, somewhere, sometime, for sawmilling was in his blood and would be so long as he stayed on his feet in this wonderful timber country.

NOTES TO CHAPTER VII

1. From *Wood Handbook,* prepared by the Forest Products Laboratory, Forest Service, U.S. Department of Agriculture. Agriculture Handbook No. 72.

Chapter VIII

Cut 'Em and Brand 'Em

In frontier sawmilling, grading was a simple matter. Each sawmill man rated boards to suit himself and by and large, there were only two grades: No. 1 Clear for lumber of no serious defects and knots no more than a foot from the end; and No. 2 Clear—everything else. Many mills classified lumber as "good" and "refuse." Another way of putting it was "suitable for the use intended."

Lumbermen sliced up the logs according to need and mood to suit their fancy, or upon specified orders. From mill to mill there was no uniformity in size and shape. Wagonloads of lumber were hauled to the yards in all widths, thicknesses and lengths, and the customer went through the helter-skelter piles like a bargain basement table till he found what might fit into his particular building project. A board was a board, and that was that. One mill tried piling its output like jackstraws in the yard to save the trouble of sorting and stacking. The plan didn't work at all well, since what was needed was usually at the bottom of the heap.

The very idea of bringing some sort of order out of all this chaos seemed like the logger's "pie in the sky." By Nature's own way, no two trees were ever exactly alike. Each had its own personality and design. Yet lumber leaders felt that some kind of uniformity was not beyond reach, even for such a far-flung timber region as the Pacific Northwest. It became one of the primary objectives of the West Coast Lumbermen's Association. But grading lumber was a touchy subject which almost tore WCLA apart.

Other lumber regions had managed to develop some rules of standardization, handed down from Swan Alverdson who in 1754 wrote the first grading rules for Scandinavian pine at Stockholm, Sweden. Alverdson's classifications were best, good, common and culls. Yankee ingenuity, over the years, was bound to make things vastly more complicated. The State of Maine adopted simple grading rules for lumber in 1833. The Popes and Talbots in the West knew about them and their families may have influenced the writing.

In the early 1870's in Michigan and Canada, there was the Saginaw Inspection, with six grades or classifications — uppers, good, fine common, common, shipping culls and culls. On the West Coast, the first meager effort to sort lumber into categories was attempted in 1850 at A. M. Simpson's mill at Gardiner, Oregon, with the grades being "flooring," "select," and "refuse," the latter applying to dunnage lumber for the Pacific trade cargo ships of that era.[1]

During the gold rush, San Francisco was rebuilt may times by cheap and quick construction. Among the many disastrous fires were five major conflagrations. Any kind of lumber, as we saw earlier, was a hot item, going for fabulous prices. The clippers, barks and schooners dumped great quantities on the San Francisco wharves, much of it roughly cut by primitive muley saws powered by waterwheels or hand cut by back-breaking misery whips. Tapering boards and scantlings, planks with waves that would put the width at three inches in the middle and a half inch at each end, and many ripples between bulges and tapers, left Bay carpenters fit to be tied. There was loud and prolonged shouting among San Franciscans for standards, even general ones, in lumber manufacture.

The Popes and Talbots, who had their own large distributing yard in San Francisco and understood the Maine grading system, found themselves "under the gun" to do something, so they tried to bring order to the region's manufacturing and selling. But their efforts were not widely accepted, for among many pioneer lumbermen, cutting in small and crude mills, a log was a log and a board a board.

Other regions were making progress, however. Before the turn of the century, Mississippi Valley and Wisconsin lumbermen had sets of grading rules. In 1894 the rules were revised and adopted by the white and Norway pine region of the Lake States. And as this occurred, the lumbermen were migrating to the Pacific Northwest.

When the first West Coast trade associations were formed and the industry grew to importance internationally, the talk turned to uniformity in grading. Rules were adopted by the pioneering Pacific Coast Lumber Manufacturers Association in 1901 and the following year an eight-page booklet was printed by the Seattle Lumber Manufacturers Exchange, the region's first published rules.

Standardization of grades became a leading matter of concern with every early lumber trade association and was indeed an essential part of price determination of the time. The constitution of one early Northwest association stated flatly that the purpose of the organization was to adopt uniform grades for lumber inspection "as the only legitimate basis for more nearly uniform prices." The Oregon Lumber Manufacturers Association insisted on something of this nature in 1905 before signing an inter-association price agreement; and by 1908 the three Northwest associations were jointly maintaining a Bureau of Grades with inspectors of full authority to see that standard patterns and grades were maintained by member mills. The cargo mills, except from January 1902 to 1904 when there was a successful export pool, had no joint agreement on grading until 1911. However, separate Washington and Oregon cargo inspection bureaus operated from 1907 until July 1911 when they combined to clear the way for the merger of the three regional lumber associations a month later at Raymond.[2]

The effectiveness of drawing up these sound standards and then maintaining them contributed substantially to the long-term survival of the West Coast Lumbermen's Association. As much as from the internal pressure among the lumbermen themselves, there was growing public demand for standards so that the consumer could feel that he was getting what he paid for when purchasing lumber at any yard. Other industries had their standards — why not lumber? The *West Coast Lumberman* at one point observed that there were so many names and grades that "they rival the tongues spoken in building the Tower of Babel, with the same resulting confusion."

"Lack of standardization of lumber and timber products increases litigation, buying expenses, the mis-use and waste of lumber, loss of good will and common honesty, and stimulates cut-throat competition, and the blending and substitution of grades," the trade magazine editorialized.

It was a hard thing, since no two sticks were alike; there were many wood varieties, classifications must cover all conditions, and then you must ride herd on every mill owner. The Pacific Lumber Inspection Bureau, which engaged primarily in cargo lumber, was incorporated in January 1903, with E. G. Ames of Seattle as president; and it was through the efforts of Ames and R. H. Alexander of Vancouver, B. C. that well-founded adjustments were made of values on the export lists, but not without "a great deal of diplomacy being exercised from time to time," as the *West Coast Lumberman* described it. In the decades before World War II, grading was a department of WCLA and was mainly involved with rail inspections. It became a separate organization after the Department of Justice contended in 1940, at the time of an antitrust campaign by Uncle Sam, that non-members of associations didn't have equal opportunity in competition with member mills and thus forced either separation or changes which would assure impartial treatment in inspection matters. The West Coast Bureau with its two hundred or more inspectors became the police force of the industry and was sometimes called the Scotland Yard of the timber world, with the inspectors developing into conscientious experts in the complicated matter of judging lumber.

Members of the industry often stood upon their heels and yelled "foul" at the manner in which their products were being rated. Grading was, and is, dollars either in or out of pocket. The difference of a shade of an inch, spread over thousands of board feet, could mean the loss of many dollars and influence the way that a log was cut. If you operated close to the line, it could send you into the red columns. As a result, there was a goodly amount of cheating.

There are countless things to consider — the kind of lumber, its appearance, size and dimension, quality, intended use, blemishes or individual characteristics, slope of grain and the end growth rings to determine the stress a piece of lumber can stand, size and frequency of knots, pitch streaks, moisture content, pin holes, heavy torn grain, shakes, splits, pith, stain, wane and warp, and a great many other factors. Shakes are long splitting cracks. Skips are changes in the planed surface. Outsized knots may weaken a beam, making it unable to withstand full pressure.[3] All things are relative and that is why lumber must be graded according to its intended use, be it beams, joists, industrial flooring or lath. Over the years, the matter of grading has become more and more intricate. In 1913 the West Coast Lumbermen's Association published a sixty-three page booklet of standard grading rules, with twenty-six pages devoted to the rules, the remainder to diagrams of sizes. By comparison, the last edition of grading rules published in 1962 by WCLIB contained 357 pages of fine print.

A key matter in the judging of lumber is knots and knot holes. One lumberman, a whopping big fellow, judged his knot holes as to the size of his palm. That was fine, except that his hand was several times larger than the average man's. The common knot has given lumbermen and builders many headaches, and the grading book breakdown is enlightening. Knots are classified as to form, size, quality and occurrence or frequency, with the size of each determined by averaging its maximum and minimum dimensions. There are a great many kinds of knots. A red knot results from a live branch growth in the tree and the knot intergrown with the surrounding wood. A black knot comes from a dead branch which the wood growth has surrounded. A round knot is cut at right angles to the limb. An oval knot is cut at slightly more than right angles, while a spike knot is cut either length-wise to the knot or diagonally across it. A pin knot is less than half an inch, a small knot is limited to three-quarters of an inch, a medium knot less than 1½ inches, and a large knot is no more than three-fourths of the width of the piece containing it.

A sound knot contains no decay, while a firm knot is solid across its surface but contains "incipient decay." A fixed knot will retain its place in dry lumber under ordinary conditions, but can be moved under pressure although it cannot easily be pushed out. There are tight knots, ingrown knots, water-tight knots, star-checked knots and knot clusters. This is just one segment of the grading picture. The grader must keep these things and all the patterns and other qualifications in mind as he goes over the lumber quickly and accurately. He operates generally on the law of averages and with personal but impartial judgment.

The West Coast Lumbermen's Association pressed for hard-headed development of standardization regulations. It became a predominant feature of most every meeting, for in dealing with the railroads, the cargo vessels, the retailer and the consumer there was need for more than a rule of thumb. Lumber rules needed to be national in scope. Following World War I, the entire industry expressed a desire for simplification and standardization of softwood grades and sizes, but nothing specific was done until 1922 when Herbert Hoover, as Secretary of Commerce, offered the services of his department.

"Lumbermen should take it upon themselves," said Hoover, "to protect the grades of forest products rather than have regulations forced upon the industry."[4]

"Lumber manufacturers . . . must commence to give serious consideration to the question of grade marking their products," agreed the *West Coast Lumberman*. "Secretary Hoover pointed out there is growing agitation for protecting the lumber buyer so that he may have some means of knowing that he obtains the grade of lumber that he purchases. . . The question of standardization is one of the biggest issues facing the lumber industry."

"Ninety-five per cent of the complaints registered by purchasers of our lumber is justified," declared President R. Webb Vinnedge of the North Bend (Washington) Lumber Company in 1921 before the annual meeting of WCLA. "We are shipping our customers something they do not want, and which they cannot and will not use. I do not believe this is done with design. I think it is largely the result of either improper grading, loose inspection at loading, indifferent labor, or a misapprehension of what the market needs and must have."

There was a great amount of chest beating in WCLA gatherings over this constant hassle on grades and classifications. At times things got pretty heated for there seemed no common meeting ground, especially involving other lumber regions. The Pacific Northwest had special problems regarding shrinkage and the matter of shipping green lumber, since it was difficult if not impossible to open air dry a sawmill's output during the long, dreary and wet Northwest winters.

The U.S.-wide standardization movement was initiated formally in 1920 by the National Lumber Manufacturers Association. Hoover stated that he would rather see the industry act than have the government adopt a "pure food law" for building materials. The need was to develop standards among mills manufacturing the same

—Weyerhaeuser Co.

Lumber grading is a specialized and highly important function of the manufacturing process. Grading became a hot national issue during the 1920's.

or similar woods so that a given grade would be of the same value and could be used for the same purpose regardless of the mill from which it came. The several softwood groups tried to firm up some national standards. A Central Committee on Lumber Standards was created by the American Lumber Congress. There was much haggling back and forth, and a goodly amount of regional politicking by vested interests over matters which to the layman seem unimportant but were terribly necessary to segments of the timber industry. Standards had to be set for odd lengths, bundling, rough dry sizes, flooring pattern, tally cards, edge and flat grain. Provisions needed to be made for measurement and for inspection and reinspection. But the big stickler proved to be a mere thirty-second of an inch!

The Battle of the Thirty-Second, as it became known, raised a good many tempers all around the country. There were nearly as many opinions as there were groups, or lumbermen for that matter. The officiating committee of lumbermen recommended that the thickness of a dressed board of inch stock be 25/32 of an inch, although the Forest Products Laboratory, drawn into the fray as a sort of peacemaker, supported a 1/32 additional thickness. Many lumber groups, including those within the West Coast Association, weren't about to accept 25/32 as standard, due to the unique shrinkage and log cutting problems along the Pacific Slope. The harangue went on and on, with no sign of any final settlement until at last it was referred to Secretary Hoover himself. He handed down the decision which still exists: 25/32 is standard thickness for a dressed inch board, while 26/32 was recognized as "extra standard size" and later was officially designated as "standard industrial lumber."

This cleared the way for publication of the first edition of the "American Lumber Standards" manual which defined the basic grades for softwood lumber, gave a sound foundation for continuing efforts to equalize the many grades, and established a system of standard sizes which reduced by nearly sixty per cent the number of actual finished yard-lumber items. Furthermore, the ALS approved of a system of grade marking to show that lumber met the rules under which it was graded. The American Lumber Standards became the basis for all softwood grading rules, while a central committee rode herd over regional and species rules to make them conform with national regulations.

But Hoover's decision didn't settle the matter for WCLA members, many of whom were bluntly outspoken and rebellious, even though leaders like Victor Beckman, Frank B. Cole,[5] Thorpe Babcock, Ralph Brown and Robert Allen had worked long and hard over the years to put together a sensible grading system. In this agreement on a national scale — and the national and international picture was now vastly important to these far corner mills — there were threats of a breakdown within the association which might ruin all that had been accomplished during the past two decades.

The situation was serious. President Ernest Dolge of Ernest Dolge, Inc., a lumber company of Tacoma, feared for the association's very existence when he found himself in the middle of a civil war at the Tacoma meeting of stockholders in November 1924. WCLA had met crucially at Grays Harbor some months earlier and accepted the American Lumber Standards system; now the membership was threatening to go back on its word, primarily because of the shrinkage problem when dressing green lumber. Dolge wasn't about to let it happen.

"The West Coast has repeatedly, after long and earnest consideration, pledged its unstinting support to this standardization movement," Dolge reminded the membership. "The eyes of the country, including government officials who promoted the program, are upon us and failure now to fulfill our pledges would greatly discredit us and might defeat the entire American Lumber Standards program. In our judgment a large number of distributors and consumers desire to see it fail. If this occurs, we may look for a flood of both state and city legislation regarding building material standards that would make our worries with the present program seem insignificant."

Some lumbermen were threatening to cut out, but Dolge stood his ground and told them that he held no truck for the tactics of quitters. He had made up his mind to use all his power as president to hold the association to its commitment.

"You are the association," Dolge declared. "It is for you here to state your point and it remains for some of you to be sufficiently persuasive to convince the rest, or the majority of the rest. I am glad to submit your motion, except to this extent: I feel that we have pledged ourselves to do certain things. As your spokesman I refuse to be the one who will take the message back that our membership is guilty of repudiation. That is a thing I cannot do."

Dolge reminded the lumbermen that WCLA representatives had constantly tried to tell Washington officials that many Northwest mills could not — and would not — dress their lumber dry because they hadn't the room to stack and store, or didn't have the money backlog to hold up their shipments. To meet the new standards, they must "dress green" and allow a slightly larger thickness for the shrinkage.

"We must dress green," Dolge stressed. "Now let's be consistent and stay with that. Those who can and want to dry, let them do so; but the majority who cannot, what will they do? Will they dress green to standard size and expect the buyer to take whatever he gets? Is that the interpretation of standards? I don't take that to be . . . I think the interpretation is that it shall be dry when dressed, or the equivalent. The great difficulty that confronts us, as I see it, is on the part of the rail mills that want to dress green and ship immediately. They say that the extra thickness is too much; it will affect the weights too much; it will work too much against them." The membership must decide what course to take: whether to allow standards to be based on green dress, an interpretation Dolge didn't accept, or whether to "follow in the lines that seem to the best interests of the nation at large, or ourselves at large, and of keeping our promise on standardization."[6]

The green mills continued pressing for their position and urged that WCLA publish two sets of standards.

"If you print both standards," said Dolge, "how are you going to know which standard the buyer wants when he sends you an order?"

Trouble was, the new standards hadn't been published by either the central committee or the National Lumber Manufacturers Association, adding to the confusion and distress of Pacific Coast lumbermen. Major Griggs expressed much concern for mills that had leftover stock which didn't conform to the new national rules. He was reminded by George M. Duncan, of the Luedinghaus Lumber Company of Portland and a member of the Grading Improvement Committee, that the millowners had had ample time since the adoption of the national rules at Grays Harbor. The problem involved the manner in which various mills handled their product.

"If we are dressing green right from the sizer and piling that stock in the yard, we take the responsibility of a complaint if it reaches the customer under size," declared Myron C. Woodard of the Silver Falls Timber Company at Silverton, Oregon. "At the

Aberdeen meeting, we voted this proposition down of this extra thirty-second of an inch of oversize green, owing to the fact that our lumber did not stain or deteriorate in shipping. It is apparently a proposition for the association to decide whether they want to adopt universally the method of kiln drying their common, their dimension, or whether they want to continue to ship it as we are at the present time and see that our cutomers get the sizes that we sell them."

Woodard was strongly opposed to the association dictating what individual mills should do in this regard. His company would alone be responsible for shipping their lumber to customers so that it reached them in standard sizes. Woodard had a lot of supporters in the room.

The big meeting continued to cuss and discuss the lumber sizes through one hundred fifty-six pages of typewritten testimony. Thorpe Babcock finally observed that if they didn't soon settle things, it would be up to their children and grandchildren. There was an attempt to adopt a flexible rule, whereby individual mills would have the responsibility of cutting an additional thickness of their own judgment, but it was defeated. In the end, after all the talk and threats, the lumbermen voted to reaffirm the position taken at Grays Harbor so that the new WCLA rules could be published in line with the American Lumber Standards.

"We have started on a line that is a big step," commented Major Griggs. "Some of us don't agree and some don't quite understand the importance of it . . . what a big thing it is."

That didn't end matters, however. More than half the association's sawmill members asked to be released from the WCLA pledge to the American Lumber Standards, placing the association on shaky ground. But by January 1926, after much calm diplomacy and yeomen's work by the leaders, WCLA President E. D. Kingsley of the West Oregon Lumber Company at Linnton announced proudly that sixty-five per cent of the mills had now agreed to go with the national standards and that none of the original fifty-seven per cent who rebelled refused to come back. The way was clear for adopting an official rubber stamp grade mark design, like a cattle brand, to be used with ink of a glycerin base, since a castor oil base would quickly destroy the rubber; and now things were pointing toward the conclusive national standardization conference in April in Washington, D. C., where WCLA representatives would try to swing some necessary changes in the rules for the Northwest industry and make a last attempt for legalizing the additional thicknesses.

A. H. Landram, sales manager of the St. Paul & Tacoma Lumber Company who headed up the West Coast delegation, had a rough time protecting the WCLA interests. He had gone east accompanied by Webb Vinnedge, L. A. Nelson who was in charge of the WCLA department of grades, and Chester J. Hogue, WCLA engineer who was also an authority on grading. They were under the impression that it would be smooth sailing, that adoption of the West Coast rule changes by the Woods Utilization Committee would be a routine matter. However, upon reaching Chicago a few days early, Landram attended a meeting of the National Lumber Manufacturers standardization committee. He was shocked to find that producers from other areas were strongly opposed to granting any modifications to the West Coast. The matter of the thirty-second of an inch leeway made them see red.

Dashing to the nearest Western Union office, Landram wired WCLA· headquarters to rally support among the membership to meet the onslaught which the Southern yellow pine people were spearheading. For five hours, Landram and his aides pleaded before the committee for relief from some of the rigid standards which didn't suit West Coast problems of manufacture. They were voted down on every point. When the meeting broke up, Landram and the others attempted to huddle with some of the other representatives. Landram found quickly that "they were not in any mood to give us consideration on anything.[7] He therefore took the position that "we were literally kicked out of the standardization movement because they had sizes in there that made it impossible to perform." He told the opposition as a parting shot that he saw little use in going to Washington, the way matters stood.

This was bluff, for Landram had no intention of giving up. On the way, Hogue and Nelson worked up some charts to show graphically the sizes under discussion and the peculiar harvesting and cutting problems of the Northwest. Landram had difficulty convincing other lumbermen who were cutting short logs that the conditions were far different; they couldn't believe that the West Coast industry was cutting logs thirty feet and longer, which demanded consideration under the grading standards. He also considered, in planning his maneuver, Herbert Hoover's ardent interest in conservation, having seen many articles inspired by Hoover's office about the strides made by the lumber industry in eliminating waste.

Using the charts in a last-ditch stand, Landram asserted that if the West Coast were forced to adhere to the present standards, it would result in *a great amount of waste*. Those were dirty words! Figuring on percentages of the industry's impressive annual cut of some ten billion board feet, the loss from a slight difference in cut might run to half a billion board feet a year. Conservation was the watchword of the times. Put that way, Landram's case had a hard-hitting impact on the standardization committee and most of the desired WCLA changes were approved.

Landram returned to the Northwest to urge that WCLA swallow its pride and adopt the long-fought 25/32 size which would therefore make the region's rules one hundred per cent American Lumber Standards.

"I think it would be a wonderful thing if we do this, because we are reaching out into other markets more than ever before, competing more than ever with other woods, particularly yellow pine," Landram said. "It would reduce our sales resistance if we give those people in that territory sizes and grades as nearly comparable as possible to the sizes and grades that they have been accustomed to using all these years."

Landram had done a terrific job in Washington, the WLCA lumbermen realized, and they awarded him a thundering ovation. His suggestion was adopted without a negative vote. Grade standardization was now secure. . .

Yet the complexities of grading still go on and changes are made to suit the times. Today lumber is graded in two general categories: appearance grade—paneling stock, cabinet work, moulding, siding, flooring, etc.; and strength grades—all framing, studs, rafters, joists, posts, beams and stringers.

Complicated — yes! — for the average person. The best way for the layman or student to acquire an understanding of lumber grading and its benefits is to get acquainted with his local lumberman and have him demonstrate first hand . . .

NOTES TO CHAPTER VIII

1. According to James F. Stevens, *Seattle Times*, April 22, 1956.
2. From *Pacific Northwest Quarterly*, October 1950.
3. From 1962 Standard Grading Rules No. 15, West Coast Lumber Inspection Bureau.
4. *West Coast Lumberman*, April 15, 1922.
5. Frank D. Cole was early editor of the *West Coast and Puget Sound Lumberman*, and was once described by the *Columbia River and Oregon Timberman* as the "dean of lumber trade journalism and an authority on lumber lore."
6. WCLA stockholders' meeting, Tacoma, November 7, 1924.
7. A. H. Landram report, WCLA stockholders' meeting, Portland, Oregon, June 4, 1926.

Chapter IX

Getting the Wood to Market

A t dusk on a Friday afternoon, a long freight train heavily laden with logs, lumber and produce rattled down out of the great Tillamook Burn and snaked beside the Salmonberry River toward the Oregon Coast.

The train was running late and the crew was unhappy at the overtime, since they were looking forward to the weekend with salmon thick in the coastal bays. Suddenly there was the sharp scream of steel, the smash of breaking wood, the thunder of tumbling logs as the locomotive and several freight cars flip-flopped from the rails and into a slight ravine, strewing their loads in the tangle. The men "joined the birds," hit the dirt, and then shouted to each other, checking that all were safe and sound, without a scratch. They gazed at the sorry sight, swore, and started walking the ties to town. There would be no train anyway till Monday.

"To hell with it," growled the engineer. "We'll pick up the mess next week."

The old and rugged P.R.&N. (The Pacific Railway and Navigation Company) which crawled and lunged its way through the jagged Coast Range was a lumberman's railroad of the first order. No mere logging company line, the "Punk, Rotten & Nasty" was a main line branch which served a dozen back country logging operations and fifteen sawmills of what was until 1933 a great timber region — and from the way the trees are growing, will again be so one day. It was one of the most rough and tumble branches in the Far West, sixty-seven strenuous twisting miles of roller coaster track from the tiny railroad center of Timber through the 1,835 foot summit logging village of Cochran with its millpond and remains of an old sawmill, and down through the logging camps to the coastal communities of Wheeler, Nehalem and Tillamook. The grades were two and three per cent, with one place an unbelievable five per cent. The line which cost millions to build climbing a grueling 833 feet between Timber and Cochran, a distance of seven miles. Then it wheeled and cut back on itself through thirteen tunnels, the longest 1,437 feet, and across black ravines and into the deep slot of the Salmonberry canyon. There were many spectacular trestles — thirty-five over one hundred feet in length and among them a bridge that was reputedly the tallest single pile span in the world. This was a memorable freight and passenger line, matching any of the high Sierras or the Rockies.

In its heyday the P.R. & N. was a hustling, bustling system serving many logging operations, camps and mill towns of a region so sparsely settled that there were almost no roads and all the people depended on the railroad as their link with the outside world. During the summers inland residents climbed aboard the "Suntan Specials" to ride to the coast; hunters, fishermen, loggers and settlers rode the mixed trains into the deep forest where deer ran for cover from the snorting locomotives and black bear ambled across the right-of-way.

Whipping coastal gales roared up the canyons, knocking down fat firs across the tracks. Huge crosscut saws stood in the corners of the cars beside the potbellied stoves and when the route was blocked by a fallen tree, railroad men and passengers leaned their backs to the task of clearing the track. In some trips following a bad storm, there would be many such encounters.

From five to seven huge steam locomotives pushed and pulled the heavy pole trains of seventy cars up the long grade from Timber to Cochran, two or three steamers on the head and the others cut into the train toward the rear. It was a spectacular sight to see the great engines huffing and blowing up the hill, while between Cochran and Mayo, the other side of the summit, you could sit in the caboose or rear hog and wave at the head engineer far below yet directly opposite on a sweeping horseshoe curve, with the center of the train buried in a long tunnel. It was one of the toughest, orneriest railroads in all the West.

When the Tillamook Forest blew up on a hot August afternoon of 1933, the P.R. & N. was nearly destroyed. Trestles and tunnels were gutted, along with much of the roadbed ties. The fire was so hot it melted the rails. The logging camps at Cochran, Ripple, Mayo and Enright were wiped out and the Enright depot leveled. It was many weeks before the railroad could be put back into service, and some of the collapsed tunnels were completely bypassed, never to be restored. The line might have died, for its mainstay was logging and lumbering but within a few years began an amazing job of logging for World War II when the P.R. & N. hauled billions of board feet of this salvage to the mills and the subsequent lumber to market.[1]

Transportation — traffic they call it in the industry — has always been, and probably will always be, a major headache for the West Coast timber region. Getting the logs to the mills from out of the rugged hills was a challenge of no small dimensions.

The lumbermen tried everything and devised ingenious methods to move stuff that weighed fantastic tons — skid roads, flumes, log booms, oxen teams, the Benson rafts, wooden cars, railroads, steam donkeys, flooding streams which sent them hurtling down to splash, and lastly the heavy logging trucks. Millions of dollars were invested just to get out the logs.

But the matter wasn't made simpler after the logs were sliced into lumber. In the beginning the sawmill men had little choice than to haul the cuts to local markets by wagons over the muddy roads, to load them on the river sternwheelers or, for the more distant markets of California and the Pacific Rim, aboard the windjammers and hope to blue blazes that someday they would get back their money.

The lumbermen looked forward to the coming of the railroads and the railroads in turn foresaw a leading source of business in the Northwest timber country. But the honeymoon was quickly over for the two interests became disillusioned and began fighting each other like turkey cocks. Northwest lumbermen, who envisioned new markets opening up with the completion of the Northern Pacific to the Midwest and East, found the freight rates too high to meet the retail price competition from the Lake States and the South. The railroaders saw the West Coast lumbermen constantly pressing for lower shipping rates, which if granted would cut heavily into railroad profits. Yet the Northwest industry was under a terrific handicap of being far removed from the major American markets and geographically isolated, with over sixty per cent of the national lumber consumption east of the Mississippi River. The tremendous burden of transportation costs to reach those markets proved to be the main limiting factor in development of the West Coast industry.[2]

When the railroads attempted to raise their rates, the lumbermen roared in pain and took the matter into the courts. The railroads brashly tried to put the squeeze on the lumbermen by refusing or delaying shipments, or slapping embargoes on lumber as in the Portland Gateway case. In retaliation, the lumbermen rammed bills through their state legislatures to force the railroads to meet their terms. Lumbermen were always cursing the railroaders and the early associations were formed primarily to battle the railroads on the matter of shipments and rates. One Oregon group was organized for the express purpose of battling the Southern Pacific, and made no bones about its aims. And, when the West Coast Lumbermen's Association was founded, dealings with the railroads and water cargo owners were major activities.

The opening of the Panama Canal gave the lumbermen another prime outlet to the Atlantic Coast and also to barge shipments up the Mississippi River, thus placing them in a better bargaining position with the railroads. Yet keeping the freight rates competitive continued to be a major concern of WCLA traffic managers and staff which acted as watchdogs over the freight problems and time and again went into battle armed with volumes of detailed statistics to prove that unless consideration was given to the Pacific Northwest, the lumber industry there would die of strangulation.

The problem was graphically summarized in the early 1930's by Colonel William B. Greeley, the powerful secretary-manager of WCLA, in testimony supporting Congressional legislation for fairness in rail and water transportation. Colonel Greeley pointed out that freight rates had a direct effect on conservation. The average western Washington mill value of lumber at that time was about $19 per thousand board feet. Rail shipment cost about $18 per thousand to Chicago, $21.25 to Cleveland, $22.50 to Pittsburgh and points east. Seventy-eight per cent of total production was in timbers, plank, framing lumber and common boards. On much of this low-grade production, rail rates doubled the dollar value of the material. The costs were prohibitive, Greeley stressed, and as a result West Coast operators left in the woods about twenty per cent of this low-grade timber which was normally untilized in lumber producing regions nearer the markets.

Lumbermen tried to overcome this problem by shipping in great quantities, up to ninety per cent, by water via the Panama Canal and then back-hauling by truck or rail into Michigan, Ohio and Indiana. The lumber flow by water became so voluminous that the railroads grew quite concerned and tried to win back the business by obtaining better and more equitable rates through government legislation. The West Coast lumber industry moved for a more active competition between rail and water carriers, since there were advantages to shipping dry mixed orders needed by retail yards via the railroads instead of diverting everything to green cargo shipments.

In later years with the advent of better highways throughout the West, trucks came into the picture, primarily for short hauls of a few hundred miles, since their costs proved prohibitive for transcontinental shipping. Trucks in large numbers are used, however, for hauling lumber to California, which remains a prime market for Northwest wood products.

A shortage of boxcars also plagued the industry decade after decade, and any serious shortage over a long period could vitally affect production, causing mills to curtail their shifts and even shut down until they could move the lumber from their docks and warehouses. Lumber sitting on a dock brought no income and could quickly make a sawmill "lumber-poor." Part of the car shortage problem has always come from the fact that the Pacific Northwest is principally a producing region rather than one of a consumer of goods. The heavy flow of cars has been outbound and the railroads hate to return empty cars to the timber country.

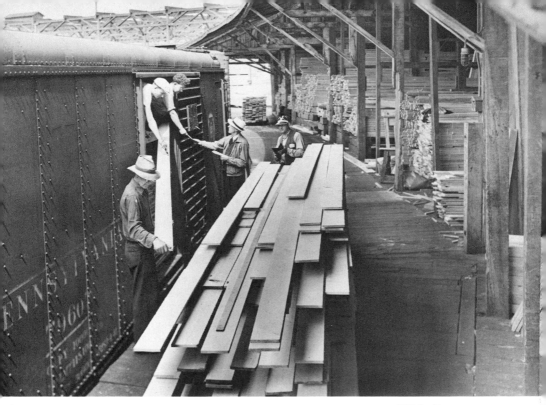

—WCLA files
Great quantities of lumber have long been shipped by rail from Pacific Northwest mills. Many plants have own spurs and special loading docks and warehouses.

The cars bunch up in heavy consumer areas back East or in southern California. In the past decade, from 1955 to 1965, railroads have also lost about 107,000 cars to deterioration.

At first WCLA dealt with its shipping matters through committees of lumbermen in rail and cargo divisions, but it soon became apparent that the job was too intricate and complex, and the demands too heavy for a part-time committee to function effectively. The association attorney, Joseph Teal, handled some of the problems. About 1914 WCLA signed on F. G. Donaldson as its traffic manager, headquartered in Portland. Donaldson stayed with the association for only two years, then resigned to become traffic manager and secretary of the Willamette Valley Lumbermen's Association. He was replaced by L. S. McIntyre who came from the Chicago, Milwaukee & St. Paul railroad and who worked with Julius Bloedel in the gigantic and often frustrating task of organizing trains of lumber for ship construction during World War I.

McIntyre was a hard worker who established many patterns for the traffic department during his forty-two months of service and won victories for WCLA in several critical cases. On the shingle reparation case which he personally argued before the Interstate Commerce Commission, his preparation was so effective that he won a reduction of two cents per hundred in the shingle rates to Chicago, St. Louis and the intermediate territory and provided the reparation of more than $60,000 to the shingle manufacturers of Oregon and Washington. He stopped cold an attempt to increase rates to the Central Freight Association territory and was again successful when carriers tried for a fifteen per cent increase in rates, finally denied by the ICC. He was also instrumental in organizing all lumber producing regions in an attack against a cubical minima loading rule which was again decided in favor of the industry. By the time McIntyre quit, the WCLA traffic department was recognized nationally as a power to be considered in any rate changes.

In 1920 Herbert N. Proebstel became traffic manager, a position he maintained for the next fifteen years, steering WCLA through many a stormy time to secure better water and rail rates and protective regulations through the ICC. Proebstel was well grounded in traffic matters with fourteen years' experience behind him, working from the Portland area for the Southern Pacific, Union Pacific, and North Bank lines. He also served for a year as traffic manager of the Wittenberg-King Company, dried fruit packers, and then as examiner for the Portland district freight traffic committee of the U. S. Railroad Administration, because of his special knowledge in rates and rate-making.

Proebstel built a solid department for WCLA which furnished many services to the members and saved them thousands of dollars in auditing their freight bills, acting on their behalf in claims with the railroads, protecting and improving the freight rate structure with other lumber regions, and serving as an envoy for the industry with the railroads, cargo companies, other lumber associations and government agencies. The department also compiled and published a detailed rate book, summarizing the rates to various shipping and marketing points, and interpreting the rail and cargo rates, calculated by the railroads in hundred pounds, in terms of board feet of lumber. The books which Emil Hanson, veteran assistant traffic manager, helped develop, included details of regulations for loading lumber on cars which needed to be clearly understood by every lumberman, large and small. This compilation of information, brought continually up to date, proved not only of value to the lumbermen but a source of strength for the association.

At the end of 1935 Proebstel resigned to become assistant general freight agent of the Northern Pacific at Seattle. The WCLA position was passed to Kenneth C. Batchelder, well known to John D. Tennant of Long-Bell Lumber Company at Longview. Batchelder had become assistant traffic chief of Long-Bell at Longview in 1923 where he gained not only considerable experience in rail shipments to eastern roads but in the cargo field. In 1930 he resigned to become secretary-manager of the Longview Chamber of Commerce. He was selected for certain obvious reasons. "Batch," as he was known, had been with both railroads and shippers; among his credits were the Northern Pacific, Spokane International, Spokane and Inland Empire, Pacific Coast Shippers Association, and the Portland & Northern railroad. Some of his work with the Longview chamber concerned traffic. He handled several cases before the ICC on behalf of the "planned city" of the Columbia River to obtain a rate structure parity with other Pacific Coast ports. Such work must have impressed Colonel Greeley who was building his own solid team at this time, so he brought Batchelder to the WCLA camp.

In twenty-eight years of service with WCLA, Batchelder set many permanent policies and achieved many victories in the traffic field which were cheered not only by the association membership but the industry as a whole. He saved the industry millions of dollars annually so that he became looked upon as "one of the true heavyweights in the traffic field."[3]

Batchelder hadn't been with WCLA but three months when he boldly challenged an increase of fifty cents a thousand for water shipments east. The opposition caught the shipping companies off guard, since the lumbermen normally concentrated on rail rates. And the shippers had been exercising discrimination by picking on lumber and leaving steel and iron alone. But the lumber industry was shipping over a billion feet of water cargo at the time so that the rate boost would have cost the industry half a million dollars annually. Batchelder won a suspension from the Maritime Commission which ended discriminatory rate increases that hurt Northwest lumber and in doing so gained new recognition and respect for WCLA in the freight rate field.

Following World War II, rail freight costs were climbing ever higher, a step at a time, and the lumber rates were in a category which always took the full brunt of every increase. Each boost caused deterioration in the competitive relationship between West Coast and southern lumber. Batchelder set out to prove that a hold-down in Western lumber was needed to keep the region's wood products on an equal basis with southern species in the national market. The point was won and the hold-down formula became an important segment of WCLA traffic policy, still in use in 1965, and estimated by one association official to have resulted in a yearly saving of $30,000,000 to the industry. The aim of the hold-down is to maintain the market relationship by taking the percentage increase in rates from the South and applying it as a *maximum* to the West.

Batchelder was now a powerful voice in the industrial councils. But he and his four departmental aides credited George T. Gerlinger of the Willamette Valley Lumber Company who served as chairman of the WCLA traffic committee from 1936 to 1945 with contributing many important things to the association's traffic policies and welfare. Gerlinger's principle was that WCLA should never fight reductions obtained by competitors and thus be at war with them, but instead should make its own efforts to get related reductions. He was a wise and knowing man, this Gerlinger, like a well seasoned timber, who had been logging and lumbering most of his born days, having begun in horse logging in 1897 in Clark County, Washington. He was also a builder of logging railroads. In 1896 he helped lay the Vancouver, Yacolt and Yakima railroad. Then in 1903 after the Yacolt fire, he moved to Dallas, Oregon, where he raised a large sawmill and three years later, not satisfied to be a sawmill man only, Gerlinger built the Salem, Falls City & Western railroad which he operated for years as a common carrier. Later he managed the Oregon, Pacific & Eastern which ran some twenty miles from Cottage Grove. He thus understood the problems of traffic from two points of view, the lumberman and the carrier.

Lumbering remained a primary concern throughout Gerlinger's productive life. He built a major sawmill plant at Dallas which was modern and progressive, and he helped to raise the standards of lumber manufacturing. During World War II, this plant did such an outstanding job that it was among the first to receive an Army-Navy "E" award for excellence in war production and for making a major contribution to the war effort. Later, Gerlinger built another modern plant at Foster, the Willamette National Lumber Company, and added the Corvallis Lumber Company mill at Corvallis to his chain.

George Gerlinger was a lumberman's lumberman, a visionary of the Major Griggs kind in Oregon who helped pioneer the tree farm movement of the 1940's and early brought his timber properties into the conservation program. This stemmed from his sincere and active interest for over half a century in forest conservation. From 1913 until his death in 1948 he was a member of the Oregon State Board of Forestry and became its senior member. During his first year on the board, he led a fight for a compulsory fire patrol law and later was a major force in campaigns to strengthen conservation statutes. He was credited with being responsible for much of the state's enlightened forestry legislation, including the 1941 passage of the Oregon Forest Conservation Act, first of its kind in the nation.

This lumber and forestry man also helped develop a sound program for handling the Oregon & California lands, and in 1938 was appointed by Secretary of Interior Harold Ickes to the first O & C advisory board where he helped shape its initial forest policies. He served many years on the WCLA board of directors, much of the time as vice president from Oregon, but for reasons of his own he declined several times to become president of WCLA. He did however accept the presidency for two wartime terms in 1944 and 1945 of the National Lumber Manufacturers Association where he had served many years as a director. In this capacity, Gerlinger spearheaded a highly successful drive for forest conservation, tree farming and sustained yield forest management in every timber state.

As with all that he undertook, Gerlinger's work with traffic left permanent marks of progress on the industry. Batchelder clung to the Gerlinger policy suggestion of not fighting competitor reductions and what's more, he put it to good and workable use. In 1961 southern lumber shippers were granted a rate reduction by the railroads of that region as a result of heavy truck competition. Batchelder found it necessary to preserve a competitive relationship. An historic struggle followed involving lowering of rates and an "incentive" rate to encourage lumber companies to load cars heavier to qualify for this rate reduction. WCLA worked closely with the Western Pine Association and the Douglas Fir Plywood Association in guiding this incentive package through the hoops, first with the midwestern railroads and then with the eastern and southern groups. There was a maze of hearings where the program was attacked and changed to some degree, but the lumber traffic men never compromised on their basic position.

The critical measure was fought by the southern pine lumbermen, eastern port authorities, and intercoastal lumber carriers and shippers. Batchelder's years of experience and seventy-five personal appearances before the Interstate Commerce Commission paid off handsomely. The ICC granted the Western industry a reduction of seven cents, which was worth $20,000,000 annually in savings and also put heavy carloading to work.

There were many other matters for the watchdog traffic department. Over the years a region-wide rate structure was developed for the Douglas fir territory whereby a manufacturer in southern Oregon could ship east at the same rate as another in northern Washington. The department undertook a huge job revising the WCLA rate book, reducing its complicated size from 389 to 212 pages which meant digesting some 30,000 pages of tariff material for accurate compilation of the new book. The traffic department was among the most important to the lumbermen in looking after their dollar-by-dollar interest, since a rate increase of ten per cent or three cents per hundred pounds — small as it might sound to the layman — would mean an additional cost to the industry of millions of dollars annually. WCLA traffic men were constantly trying to convince their friends in the rail traffic departments that the best way to increase their earnings from lumber was to build up and encourage the long-haul shipments from the West. A healthy lumber industry on the West Coast meant more business for the

Since days of the windjammers, much lumber is also sent by water carriers. Northwest lumber has gone to world's far corners.

roads, and the lumbermen were the railroads' leading customer in this part of the world.

When Batchelder retired in 1963, James Manning who had been his assistant for ten years stepped in as the fifth and last traffic manager in WCLA history. A year later when WCLA merged into the new Western Wood Products Association, Manning continued in that capacity. Manning was the first college-trained traffic manager. Following World War II when he served as a Flying Fortress pilot of thirty-five bombing missions over Europe, Manning earned a degree in transportation at the University of Washington and joined the WCLA traffic force. In 1950 he took charge of WCLA's universally-used rate book.

In these mid-century years, under both Batchelder and Manning, the relationship of the lumber industry and the railroads has completely changed. The lumbermen by and large no longer view the railroads as a black-hearted enemy to be fought to the death; and likewise, the rail lines recognize that an industry which pays out close to $300,000,000 a year in freight charges is a mighty important customer along the Pacific seaboard. The lumber industry and rail systems today see each other as "partners" in getting the wood products from the far corner to the major marketing areas at a price that is beneficial to both, and yet can meet the market prices of wood products from other regions. In other words, one can't exist in healthy fashion for long without the other.

Even so, there will forever be hassles over shipping charges, for the industry and the market are constantly fluctuating, as are wages and other costs. Whenever the picture alters in other regions, the impact is felt and the West Coast lumber industry must take a good look at its own situation to make adjustments to keep in pace with the competition. For this reason, lumber trade associations like WCLA and its successor, Western Wood Products, will always need strong and hard-hitting traffic departments. They can't very easily walk away from an upset, as the rail crew did that afternoon on the bawdy old P.R. & N.

NOTES TO CHAPTER IX

1. From *Vacationists to Logs, Story of the P.R.&N.*, by Ellis Lucia, *Sunday Oregonian Magazine* section, March 4, 1951. The Southern Pacific still operates freights over the P.R.&N. and occasional summer excursion specials. sometimes make the spectacular run.
2. From the writings of Colonel William B. Greeley.
3. *Crow's Lumber Digest*, October 10, 1963.

Chapter X
Down to Splash

There was no place like Grays Harbor in all the world. It was the epitome of lumbering in North America, the Comstock Lode of the timber world.

Everything was near to perfect around The Harbor for harvesting fat trees — the time, the place, the natural conditions, the supply. Most of all the supply. There were more plump trees here than a man thought existed, running three to four million feet to the forty, over fifty billion board feet in all, timber that stood more than five feet in diameter with one hundred eighty feet of sawlog length and some stands twenty million feet to the quarter section, in deep forests where the sun had not touched the soft land of moss and ferns and needles for centuries. The trees were several hundred years old and just ripe for harvesting when the lumbermen arrived. The land was slotted by many good streams which swelled on the year-round heavy rains so that the logs could be sent speedily down to the mills which sprang up around the inlets and the main rivers dumping into the great bay that itself was of size and depth to welcome the ships of the world.

Life was bigger, bolder, brawnier, rougher and tougher around The Harbor than anywhere else. Some twelve thousand men were employed in nearly half a hundred sawmills and wood-processing plants, strung along the water's edge of the triple cities of Aberdeen, Hoquiam and Cosmopolis. The biggest logging equipment in the world was built here to handle the tremendous logs and finished cants, the logging railroads were greater in number, the lumberjacks were taller and tougher, the skid road area wilder, and the bay was a mad scramble of sailing vessels and steamships which came by the thousands to take the lumber away. In the single year of 1925 a thumping 733 ships, not counting 17,905 freight cars which carried 447,625,000 board feet, hauled out 1,116,110,691 board feet of lumber. The following year topped even that enormous volume when the cut was 1,557,223,000 feet, of which ninety-one per cent — 1,416,295,000 feet — went to market by sea in 880 ships. In half a century, The Harbor shipped thirty billion feet,

Around Grays Harbor tough lumberjacks cut some whopping stuff, hundreds of years old, in thick stands beyond belief. The area became the Comstock Lode of old-time lumbering. Legend has it that the "Mother Township" of the Douglas fir region was in the area.

an enormous volume equal to a year's production of all mills in the United States. During the six climactic years of 1924 to 1929, the annual output averaged 1,352,000,000 feet and the destinations of this production are impressive — Kobe, Shanghai, Taku Bar, Batavia, Sydney, Adelaide, Antwerp, Callao, Antofagasta, South- hampton, Cape Town, Boston, Newark, Philadelphia, San Pedro San Francisco, a hundred more ports . . . There has been nothing like it, either before or since.[1]

There was nothing like that timber and its excellence, either, two million mist-washed acres of it fronting on the two harbors.

"The noblest growth of fir, spruce, cedar and hemlock ever found in the civilized world," one early observer enthused.

J. A. McGillicuddy, father of Jerry, Cornelius and Dan, all cruisers and specialists in timber appraisal, declared that he "never thought there was so much timber in the world" after he had walked and canoe-traveled from Olympia to The Harbor in 1881. Some of the stands were far beyond belief. Up in the Humptulips country north of Hoquiam towered what came to be known affectionately as "old 21-9," which some believed was the premier mother township of the Douglas fir region. The twenty- eight privately owned sections in this township had produced more than two billion board feet of lumber by 1950. Township 16-6 south of Elma, site of today's Clemons Tree Farm, produced over one and a half billion feet of the original crop. On the Willapa, Satsop, Wynooche, Wishkah and other rivers were sections and townships of noble stands of similar excellence.

Sawmills had been humming on Puget Sound, in southern Wash- ington and in Oregon for over two decades when Charles Stevens and William Anderson set up the first mill at Grays Harbor, up the Chehalis River at what would become Cosmopolis. They cut Grays Harbor's first lumber in 1881.

That same year a San Francisco shipping man, Captain A. M. Simpson, sent his associate, George H. Emerson, into Grays Harbor to "search for timber" and the site for a sawmill. Captain Simpson was a lumberman of the first water, having pioneered things in many coastal places of the redwood empire, at Coos Bay, Gardiner and Shoalwater Bay (Willapa Harbor). His original mill of the Washington coastal ports became the South Bend Mill and Timber Company at South Bend. George Emerson didn't have to search far for timber, staking claim to three hundred acres at Hoquiam before returning to San Francisco. Next spring the little brig *Orient* dropped anchor at the mouth of the Hoquiam River and began unloading a sawmill that Simpson and Emerson purchased at Cres- cent City. The mill was set up during the summer, using timbers from the Stevens-Anderson mill, and began cutting in September. Shortly thereafter, its initial cargo was shipped aboard the vessel that brought the mill gear. This was the first real sawmill of notable size on Grays Harbor, evolving into the Northwestern Lumber Company, which ran well into the Twentieth Century before cooling its boilers and bowing out.

Emerson stayed with The Harbor to become one of its industrial leaders, founding a shipyard and a large store, still operating in the mid-1960's as the F. G. Foster Company, while a grandson and great-grandson guide the world-wide enterprise of the Lamb-Grays Harbor Company, manufacturing machinery for forest products industries. The influence of Captain Simpson was also long felt on Willapa Bay where his early sawmill cut logs over the many years. The plant later was purchased and rebuilt by Charles Lewis of Olympia. Simpson's substantial shipping operations became the Sudden & Christenson empire.

Simpson was truly the father of Grays Harbor, but there is no marker or memorial to him today. However, Simpson was memorialized in a unique way. Among his employees was Peter B. Kyne, a bookkeeper who labored long hours over the lumber ledgers in the Northwestern mill office before 1910 and observed Captain Simpson at close and critical range. Kyne had a creative talent; he liked working with words rather than figures, and he saw Captain Simpson as a crusty but lovable shipping tycoon engaged in battles of wits not only with rival shipping interests, but with henchmen within his own firm, among them his own shipmasters. Thus was born one of the most beloved best-selling fiction characters of the Twentieth Century, the doughty Cappy Ricks. Kyne not only patterned the famed Cappy after his boss, but also drew many of the incidents and true-to-life facts of his novels from affairs around The Harbor.

Another local personality who excited Kyne's special interest was a tall, walrus-mustachioed mate of the barkentine *Gardiner City* named Ralph E. Peasley, a Down East sailing man who had shifted his base to Aberdeen. He grew into Kyne's Matt Peasley, hero of several Cappy Ricks novels. As in the books, Peasley became a skipper in real life, but not from marrying the boss's daughter. Peasley was pleased at being immortalized, but he wasn't a braggart. In all the ports o' call, he took his nautical literary eminence in stride with a modest but proud skill. In sixty years as a mariner he handled a number of commands. His final ship was the big schooner *Vigilant,* Harbor-built for the E. K. Wood Lumber Company and one of the last sailing ships to plow the seas in the lumber trade. She was a beauty, too, 241 feet long and 1,600 gross tons, and making many historic voyages with Peasley at her helm. Waterfront reporters from Bellingham to Adelaide broke into lyrical song whenever the colorful skipper hove in with the big windjammer:

"My name is Matt Peasley,
The Mate of Cappy Ricks.
I'm the skipper of the *Vigilant*
With all her five sticks."

The *Vigilant* was equally as famous and beloved around The Harbor as was her legendary skipper, who died in the early 1950's. In 1927 she was sold to the City Mill Company of Honolulu and for years thereafter continued in Pacific service. The last trace of her was that she was being used as a barge on the coast of Chili. Loyal sailing men talked about bringing the historic vessel home to be outfitted as a museum but never did.

Kyne had long since left The Harbor which gave him so much inspiration and background material, moving to San Francisco. But the robust Northwest lumber ports were a source of supply for other yarn-spinners of that generation, among them Norman Reilly Raine who drew another colorful character from a female tugboat skipper on Puget Sound who towed log booms to the mills. Her fiction name was Tugboat Annie.

Everything around The Harbor was done on a gigantic Paul Bunyan scale. By the time of the San Francisco earthquake, there were fifteen or more mills strung out along the waterfronts, able to produce over 100,000,000 board feet annually, the glow from their burners lighting the nights, the hum of industry on all sides, the towns as boisterous and wild as Dodge City. By 1925 there were thirty-seven mills in this Eldorado, nineteen along the Grays Harbor tidewater, eighteen in the territory directly tributary to The Harbor. Their payrolls totaled 5,900 men, while an additional 4,200 men were working getting out the logs for The Harbor's ten large logging companies and a number of smaller outfits. In addition to lumber, a wide variety of other wood products were being manufactured — shingles, doors, (7,250 doors were produced daily), veneer, lath, piano sounding boards, bucket food containers, veneer sides for orange boxes, box shook, moulding, casing and base, garage doors, and other cabinet and factory specialties — employing an additional 2,000 men. The year 1929 was the zenith in old growth lumber harvest of this green commonwealth. From there on came a decline in lumber production, with the rise of pulp, paper and other timber by-products.

Lake States men and machinery supplied much of the go-power for The Harbor's fantastic industry. Michigan's "mitten" and Wisconsin's Green Bay were take-off points for dozens of prominent Harbor lumber families — Weatherwax, West, Fordney, Anderson, Hulbert, Middleton, Miller, Donovan, Bryden, Coats, McClymont, Averill, Corkery, Bishop, Douglas, Wood, O'Connor, MacFarlane, Hart, Hoonan, Morley, Leitch, Johnson, Davenport, Lytle,

More than 12,000 men worked in the sawmills of colorful Aberdeen, Hoquiam and Cosmopolis. Hundreds of little windjammers and schooners took away the lumber to ports of the world.

Stockwell, McLean, Hewitt and Tebb. The Polson brothers, Alex and Robert, came from the eastern shore of Canada to found The Harbor's largest logging and milling operation, employing 1,200 men at its peak. Neil Cooney of Prince Edward Island rose from a modest shipwright status to overlord of the Grays Harbor Commercial Company at Cosmopolis, a famed stop-off place for thousands of workers from Puget Sound and even the Lake States, known as a rough and tumble operation, with Cooney long a hold-out against the labor unions. Ahead of him as manager was C. F. White who was later drafted by Seattle interests to guide the Metropolitan Building Company in handling downtown University of Washington properties and whose name is carried on in the White-Henry-Stuart Building where West Coast Lumbermen's Association long had its offices.

Perhaps most unique of all The Harbor's operations was E.K. Bishop Lumber, engaged in the making of piano sounding boards. E. K. "Ned" Bishop's father came out from the Lake States to obtain coveted Sitka spruce stock for the sounding boards. The operation started at Montesano and shifted in 1920 to Aberdeen. For forty more years Ned Bishop ran this strictly-spruce enterprise which became something of a hallmark for The Harbor when it sailed through the Great Depression without losing a working day. It was believed that, in part, this was made possible by an aircraft factory established at Buffalo, New York, following World War I by Reuben H. Fleet with some Bishop financing, and which later became Consolidated Aircraft of San Diego. In its early years, this was certainly a postwar outlet for Bishop spruce and thus brought about a memorable occasion. In 1927 Charles A. Lindbergh flew into history with the *Spirit of St. Louis* built of Sitka spruce from the Bishop sawmill and the Posey Manufacturing plant at Hoquiam. When Lindbergh made his post-Atlantic tour of the country, he dipped the wing of his famous ship over the place where the structural material had been manufactured. It was an exciting and proud day for Grays Harbor.

Some of the biggest logging and lumbering equipment in the world was being manufactured in the machine shops of Grays Harbor. The famed Lamb Machine Company of Hoquiam, one of the largest foundries in the Northwest, turned out logging blocks not only for the forests of Washington and Oregon, but sent them around the globe. Its sprawling plant at the west end of the town was the last word in modern efficiency, with drafting room, large pattern shop, foundry for casting steel, iron and brass, a forge shop, machine shop, ample rail facilities and space for storing a month's supply of its standard products.[2]

Manufacture of the mighty Lamb blocks was the main item of business, but the foundry also supplied parts and new machinery for many logging camps and sawmills. One of its most noteworthy products was "lamsteel," a specially treated steel which had a strength and hardness that made it ideal for logging tongs and hooks. The Lamb set works for shingle mills — a machine that regulates the thickness of shingles — was another leading product. There were also sprockets, gears, locomotive shafts, bronze and brass parts for locomotives, and small machine parts used extensively in sawmills and logging operations.

In the back country, the loggers in their traditional uniforms — tin pants, suspenders and long underwear — were bringing down the timber. In 1903, the year following the great Northwest fires known as the "Yacolt Burn," Alex and Robert Polson began railroad logging. There was so much salvage that this speedier method was in order and with new mills rising on The Harbor, there was a free market for logs. The Polson Brothers got going in a big way, for the Merrill & Ring people had substantial volumes of fire-kill in the area and commissioned the Polsons to move it to market. The Polsons had set the pattern and before many years, there were twenty railroads hauling logs out to the busy plants.[3]

There were mainline railroad projects a decade earlier. The Northern Pacific reached Montesano in 1890 and was then extended east of Aberdeen to Junction, across the river and down the south shore to Ocosta near present-day Westport. Ocosta-by-the-Sea was to be the Grays Harbor metropolis. Aberdeen was bypassed, which didn't set well with the local citizenry, so they undertook to extend the line themselves from Junction City to the Wishkah River. Lumbermen Charles Wilson, J. M. Weatherwax and A. J. West headed up the ambitious project, with every able-

bodied man donating ten days' work or the cash equivalent
at $2.00 per day. Wilson, Weatherwax and West donated crossties
and rails. The rails came from the British bark *Abercorn*, wrecked
in January 1888 just north of the Grays Harbor entrance. The cargo
was railroad iron and its salvage was a long and costly job, requiring a mile of trestle construction and the services of a diver.
It was six years before the iron was removed. The rails were sorely
pitted from the salt water, and travelers on the Aberdeen branch
knew when they were nearing the town by the rattle of the wheels
on the pits. Before long, the branch became the main line when
the Ocosta boom faded.

There was another spectacular pie in the sky in the rise and
fall of Grays Harbor City, three miles west of Hoquiam, also
boomed as a future metropolis. Lots went on sale for $500 mini-
mum and within three months all the space was gone. Streets
were graded, business buildings and homes erected, a brick factory
established, and a mile-long wharf built to deep water of the bay.
A newspaper was established, too, its editor Edgar B. Piper who
later carved a name in western journalism as editor of *The Oregonian.* That was long after the Grays Harbor City bubble burst,
when the railroad failed to come and the speculation went down
to splash.

Before the railroads, river log drives reached fantastic proportions in the years around the turn of the century. With a drenching
rainfall of seventy to eighty inches annually, it was possible to
drive rivers like the Humptulips, Wishkah and Willapa at intervals
all through the winter and in summer, too. At least thirty-nine
splash or sluice dams of huge timbers were built on the streams
serving The Harbor. The dams contained several gates through which
logs and water were sluiced into the stream below, sending them
hell-bent for tidewater. Some streams had an entire series of dams,
sluicing from one to another. The Humptulips Boom & Driving
Company had eight dams on the Humptulips alone. It was a cooperative firm which, with A. P. Stockwell in charge, drove the
big stuff for several companies, apportioning the cost by volume.
On the Wishkah, Cy McLean had a similar arrangement.

It all depended on the frequency of the freshets.

"We usually had to have a good freshet in June to pay the
Fourth of July wages," an old-timer reminisced. "We usually got it
too." He didn't agree that the climate was changing, that Junes
are drier now. "We still have June freshets," he commented, "but
they don't always come the same month."

When the logs hung up on the river banks, there was no way
of budging them until a bigger freshet came along, since they were
far too massive to be rolled with peavy power. Millions of board
feet lay on the banks for years until tractors made salvage possible.

—James F. Stevens Collection
Loggers in their traditional outfits—tin pants, suspenders and long underwear—brought logs down to splash. The famed Polson Brothers crew paused for this photograph in 1898.

"Splash" was a part of The Harbor's lingo and became synonymous with the annual Fourth of July blowout, when thousands of loggers hit the three towns to let off steam from a six months' stint in the woods. The annual Grays Harbor Splash, held alternately at Hoquiam and Aberdeen, was the West Coast's first big logging show and unrivaled for its sheer magnificence for about thirty years. The splash dams and log drives faded from the scene, as did the old lumberjacking ways, so that by 1930 the big celebration had lost much of its punch.[4]

Timber was cheap, as cheap to these lumber towns as gold was to the mining camps. You could buy a tract for fifty cents a thousand. But prices went up. In 1905 Douglas fir logs delivered to Harbor mills sold for $5.00 a thousand, with two grades — clear and merchantable. Both would be classified largely as peelers now. Wages in the mills were about $1.75 for a ten-hour day, while woods pay ran about $2.00. The City of Aberdeen, called "Plank Island," paid $8.00 per thousand for 4 x 12 and 3 x 12 structural grade planking with which to "pave" its streets. But prices were high in 1906-07 when third grade logs brought $6.00 and better grades $9.00 to $12.00, resulting from the need for lumber following the San Francisco earthquake.

There was a very basic reason for the apparent haste in harvesting The Harbor's virgin timber, which hasn't been given much credence until recent years. It was over-ambitious taxation — the great tree stands were literally taxed right out of the woods.

"Soak the timber companies," cried the assessor when he campaigned for reelection. He did just that and in self-defense, the owners had to liquidate the trees as fast as they could, or perish. Otherwise, the great stands might have lasted for many more decades.

The logs shot down to the mills, the lumber moved out, and the dollars rolled into the saloons and honky-tonks of The Harbor, one of the lustiest ports of them all. The saloonkeepers grew rich as those of the mining towns. Fifty saloons lined the lower streets of Aberdeen and Hoquiam. They grew from eight in 1895 in Aberdeen to thirty-nine in 1914. In 1903 Aberdeen's city income came from three prime sources: taxes, $25,000; water service, $18,000; and saloon licenses, $20,000. A city saloon license cost $1,000 a year.

The nights were plenty wild, with the Palm Dance Hall on Hume Street between G and F epitomizing the roaring era. It had five bartenders, four bouncers and forty girls. On the night it opened, fighting started early and a welter of combatants swirled from the swinging doors. One battler picked up a scantling which had a spike on the end. On the first swing, he caught another on

—Washington State Historical Society
Grays Harbor moved out big logs on freshets and over vast network of some twenty railroads handling heavy stuff.

the head, virtually scalping him, with fatal results. But despite this and a subsequent trial, the Palm had a long run as a favorite play center.

It was rough and tumble, and Aberdeen became known across the land as a wicked city, which caused its good citizens, who had established churches and schools and were law-abiding, much discomfort until the day when they changed the name of famed Hume Street of "The Line" to State Street.

A special Harbor Log Patrol drove pirates from the booms, while hundreds of seagoing vessels thumped against the mill wharves and crammed their bellies with lumber. Many of the pirates were Wobblies, the "I-Won't Work's," reduced to this raiding to get operating cash. Billy Gohl found another way, dumping the bodies of his victims into the rivers and bays; and when they finally caught up with Gohl, his trial was a sensation so that copies of the *Aberdeen World* sold like hot cakes in the early morn.

Even the landlubbers could tell a schooner from a barkentine, a brig from a brigantine, by the rigging. The steam schooner was developed for the Pacific lumber trade and called in large numbers at Grays Harbor. It used both canvas and auxiliary power until sails were finally discontinued. The most popular ships coming to The Harbor were the barkentine, the schooner and the steam schooner.

In the early days, millions of board feet were moved without harbor improvements, indicating the skill of the skippers. In 1884 the steam tug *Hunter,* skippered by Al Stream, began a towing service for both Grays and Willapa harbors. Soon there were other bar tugs — the *Traveler, Printer, Ranger, J. M. Coleman, Daring* and *John Cudahy.* Yet shipmasters often needed convincing and it was long a common sight to see the beautiful windjammers come to port on their own. As late as World War I the three-mast schooner *Lizzie Vance* sailed all the way in to Cosmopolis. The windjammers continued to take lumber from The Harbor well into the 1920's.[5]

The coal-burning "team kooner," as the Scandinavians called them, became increasingly popular as the workhorse of the Pacific shipping lanes. The first to call in Grays Harbor in 1889 was the *Cosmopolis,* operating between the namesake port and San Francisco. Sail began to disappear and along with it, the cargo gaff evolved first into the single long forward boom, then double booms fore and aft. The steam schooner gear was found by other carriers to be just right and was adopted into modern cargo handling.

Until the early 1900's, the steam schooner's capacity was less than 400,000 feet. The first to carry a million feet was the *Nome City,* built for Charles Nelson; and the last wooden steam schooner

Big, rustic mills like this one lined the waterfronts of the bay and rivers around roaring Aberdeen. There were many specialty plants, too.

was the *Esther Johnson* of Portland, built in 1923 by the Matthews yard of Hoquiam, 208 feet long, 611 tons, and with its deckload able to stow 1,275,000 feet. There was a veritable rush in steam schooner construction from 1885 to 1910. Grays Harbor yards built their full share. Among the early ones on the San Francisco run were the *Point Loma, Captain Conway, Newberg, Del Norte, Centralia, Coronado, Chehalis, Norwood, C. C. Lindauer, Fair Oaks,* and *Svea*. They grew larger all the time. The *Lakme* was a big one, 404 tons, carrying 650,000 feet. Before long the builders and skippers learned ways of expanding their capacity without increasing the size of the vessels. Ships the size of the *Lakme* later were rated at 750,000 feet.[6].

The yards at Grays Harbor built many vessels with increased capacities to over one million board feet. The *William Donovan,* named for the tyee of the Donovan Lumber Company of Aberdeen, could carry 1,600,000 feet. At the Aberdeen Shipbuilding Corporation yards the 695-ton *Phyllis* slid down the ways in 1917 with a capacity of 1,275,000 feet. Frazier Matthews of Hoquiam built several noble vessels of over a million feet capacity, among them the *Daisy Putnam,* the *Daisy Matthews,* the *Quinault* and the *San Diego*. And the Grant-Smith yards of Aberdeen in 1919 put together the *Forest King,* 267 feet long with 1,750,000 feet capacity; while the *Cricket,* also of formidable size, could stow almost 2,000,000 feet of 90-foot cargo booms.

Scandinavian seamen mastered and crewed both the windjammers and the steam schooners, big fellows who were skilled descendants of the Vikings. Grays Harbor was haunted by men named Johnson.

—Washington State Historical Museum
Lumber piled along the docks was the barometer of how things were going. A few yards away were the wild skid roads where seamen and loggers intermingled. Vice and crime ran rampant in the tri-cities during the reckless years.

From 1908 to 1915, at least fourteen Johnsons were skippering ships out of The Harbor. There were so many Johnsons around the boats that something had to be done. The result was a distinctive array of colorful nicknames — Single Reef Johnson, Rough Pile Johnson, Glassy Eye, Baby, Drawbucket, Cordwood, Slabwood, Scantling Bill, Swell Head, Doughnut and Scarface. Author Peter B. Kyne picked up the names for his stories, among them a barkentine skipper called "All Hands and Feet."

The old growth timber went out of the land and by 1930 the roaring days of Grays Harbor were a part of history. But with the ebb of the great bonanza and the heedless days came a new philosophy of practical forestry. The old-time logging man has been replaced by the college educated and technically trained forester, professional men schooled in timber management and timber growing with a thorough working knowledge of trees and their harvesting. Lumbermen came around to thinking of timber as a crop and significantly, the first true tree farm was established in 1941 on 129,000 acres at Grays Harbor. Today the Harbor probably has more certified tree farms than any other comparable region in the country, with every major company in the area setting aside managed lands for the future.

Tax laws were revised to be more realistic. Public campaigns lessened the forest fires. The rise in the value of timber brought other changes, to get more use from the wood. The great burners began disappearing from The Harbor, for the trimmings, edgings and other leavings are now converted into everything from fiber boards to broom handles; and chemists labor long hours to discover other uses for the wood, perhaps even the needles and the whisper of the wind through the branches.

On The Harbor, lumber production has leveled off to about a quarter of the output in the glory days. On some of the old mill sites, other types of wood operations have sprung up. The transition is from an old growth raw material economy to one of big hemlock and new growth Douglas fir, and the day promises to arrive when even lumber production will increase as new timber crops reach merchantable maturity. The new age is marked by establishment of two pulp-paper mills, several stud mills and re-manufacturing plants, veneer and plywood, sash and door, furniture and other factories based on wood use. Several lumber mills which weathered the transition, not an easy thing, did so by gearing operations to the available raw material and increasing their efficiency of processing. Following World War II, they were joined by the Weyerhaeuser Company with a pulp mill at Cosmopolis on the historic site of Pope & Talbot's old Grays Harbor Commercial mill and with a sawmill on the site of the old Aberdeen Lumber & Shingle Company. In Hoquiam there is the big Rayonier paper mill, also providing a bulwark of stable economy for The Harbor.

The Harbor is far from becoming a ghost town tourist attraction as is Virginia City on Nevada's Comstock Lode.

NOTES TO CHAPTER X

1. Much of the material on Grays Harbor is drawn from the research reports of Harold B. Olson of Portland, who spent years in that area as a newspaperman with the *Aberdeen Daily World* and knows the subject well.

2. *Aberdeen Daily World,* March 10, 1926.

3. Today there is no railroad logging as such. Only the Polson line, now Rayonier's, Inc., reaching up the Olympic Peninsula northwest of Lake Quinault, remains in log hauling. It is a main-line operation, hauling from a truck reload in the woods. There is, however, considerable log traffic on the common carriers serving The Harbor.

4. The Albany, Oregon, Timber Carnival each Fourth of July is now considered the Northwest's big annual logging show. There are other huge ones, too, including one at Shelton, Wash.

5. Among the windjammers of note visiting The Harbor were the *John Palmer, King Cyrus, Nokomis, Sophie Christenson, Ethel Zane, Alpha, David Evans, Cecelia Sudden, Mary E. Foster, Robert R. Hind, Edward R. West, A. F. Coats, Alumna, Tarus, Holmes, Henry Wilson, Zampa, A. J. West, Polaris* and *Westerner.*

6. Some of the steam schooners were the *Whitesboro, Greenwood, Coos Bay, Pasadena, Alcazar, Westport, South Coast, Signal, Navarro, Noyo, North Fork, National City, Scotia, Homer, Albion, Alliance, San Pedro, Aberdeen, Brunswick, Fulton* and *Charles Nelson.*

Part III
The
GREEN
GLORY

Chapter XI

Lumber on a Seesaw

SAN FRANCISCO was long considered the play town for Pacific Northwest lumbermen. They and their wives loved the place, rating the colorful metropolis by the Golden Gate something special, a far cry from the more rustic cities and towns of their lumber world.

Among the lumbermen who trekked often to San Francisco was Frank Mulkey of Portland, about whom little is known other than that he dealt in lumber and real estate, and over a long period of time made a considerable sum in both fields. Now in his sunset years and lonely, Mulkey enjoyed making periodic trips to The Bay which he found more lively and friendly than his own town.

The old man began hanging out at the Thalia, the largest dance hall on the western shore, located along the Barbary Coast on Pacific Street between Kearney and Montgomery. Night after night he sat at a table beside the dance floor, buying many drinks but never touching them and conversing with the waiters and the pretty girls. When one was particularly friendly to him, the old man would say:

"Thanks so much. I'll remember you in my will. I'm a wealthy man, you know."

Then he would take a small notebook from his pocket and jot down the name of the waiter or girl. No one took him seriously; he was just another of the eccentrics and strange characters frequenting the Barbary Coast joints. But when Mulkey died, he remembered them all in his will with a considerable sum, including the proprietor, Terry Mustain.[1]

The early Twenties were characterized as a time of soft markets, frustration, internal strife within the industry, and many disappointments. The era had begun tragically with the so-called "Centralia Massacre" which long remained one of the blackest events in Northwest lumber history. In Centralia, Washington, a current I.W.W. hot bed, the Wobblies' headquarters hall was wrecked by enemy forces, but they set up in a hotel under protection of the town's police. On the first anniversary of the Armistice, a big parade was planned.[2] Reaching the hotel, the marchers surged forward and the hateful Wobbly emblem came crashing down. Shots rang out: three Legionnaires lay dead in the street. The mob stormed the building and wrecked it. One Wobbly, Wesley Everest, himself an ex-service man, was pursued through the streets and shot another Legionnaire. He was grabbed, beaten, his teeth were knocked out and he was physically mutilated. That night Everest was dragged to the bridge across the Chehalis River and lynched.

The "massacre" and subsequent events made national headlines. It spelled the end of the Wobblies, for despite heated and conflicting opinions, business and patriotic groups held the I.W.W. responsible. Aroused lumbermen saw in the incident undeniable proof of the anti-American and violent character of the organization. It started a steady decline in the Wobbly movement and among those openly denouncing them was the American Federation of Labor which adopted a resolution repudiating "the policy of Bolshevism and I.W.W.-ism as being destructive of American ideals and impractical of application."

Other things kept the lumbermen on a seesaw. The market went into a tailspin, despite efforts to guard against it. This caused much unrest and curtailment of production. When a terrifying earthquake rocked Japan, leveling large sections of Yokohama, Tokyo and other cities, the industry received a sudden and swift upsurge of lumber orders to help rebuild the country, as it had in 1906 when San Francisco was mangled. Secretary of Commerce Herbert Hoover informed the West Coast Lumbermen's Association that the Japanese government wanted assurance that lumber prices wouldn't be suddenly boosted out of sight. WCLA Secretary-Manager Robert Allen promised Hoover that the association would do all within its power to organize the mills and gain their full cooperation.[3]

The Japanese government organized a "metropolitan construction board" of 660 persons divided into six bureaus of city planning, land, adjustment, buildings, materials and supply, and ways and means. The rush orders came across the Pacific for boards, planking and flooring, 18,000,000 board feet; baby squares and flitches, 66,000,000 feet; large squares, 60,000,000 feet; and logs and piling, 120,000,000 feet. Ships were commandeered for this rush job, since it was estimated that 400,000 buildings needed replacing. Douglas fir was to be used "almost exclusively" in the paving program for Tokyo.[4]

The Japanese embassy in Washington, D.C., closed negotiations with the Douglas Fir Exploitation and Export Company, representing one hundred eight West Coast mills, for 96,400,000 feet of Douglas fir and hemlock, about a $3,000,000 deal; and also negotiated a contract with the Bratlie Brothers mill of Ridgefield, Washington, for 750,000 feet of Western red cedar. It was believed that reconstruction and the demand for lumber would extend over seven years.

Major Everett Griggs and Chester Hogue, the great WCLA technical engineer, visited the stricken country for the association early in 1924 to appraise conditions first-hand. Griggs estimated that "it will take two billion feet to rebuild Tokyo." But both Griggs and Hogue were startled by the congestion and bottlenecks at the harbors of Japan which were clogging the steady flow of lumber supplies to Tokyo. Griggs reported that it was virtually impossible to move lumber due to the lack of transportation means, for barges were wrecked and canals blocked. It was costly, too; $17 per thousand feet to move the wood from Yokohama to Tokyo, far above the $10 per thousand charged from Seattle to the quake-torn country. There wasn't much buying either, despite the fact that West Coast mills were breaking their head rigs trying to meet the emergency. The Pacific Lumber Inspection Bureau reported shipments to Japan were 861,774,447 feet in 1923 compared with 590,921,000 feet in 1922.

Now the orders fell off and there seemed no solution to the tie-up in Japan. Over sixty vessels jammed the Yokohama harbor awaiting discharge, but there was no harbor space and both sides of the waterway to Tokyo were "crowded with lumber." The lop-sided balance of trade dislocated the exchange rates and the yen fell in value. Banks refused to issue letters of credit. The *West Coast Lumberman* described the conditions as "distressing" and added grimly:

"Japanese orders suddenly diminished almost to the zero point. Letters of credit were cancelled . . . Shipments were left in the hands of the exporters. Just what happened in Japan will never be completely known."⁵

It was a hard blow for the Northwest lumbermen. The PLIB for 1924 showed a decline in cargo to Japan to 691,919,844 feet or a loss of about nineteen per cent. Many a lumberman found himself holding the sack, unable to collect for the orders. This did nothing to improve his sense of humor or to lift his depression about the market at home, which WCLA President Ernest Dolge of Tacoma described as the "frequent and violent rise and fall in the price of lumber."

The West Coast Lumbermen's Association was itself reflecting this over-all turbulence. The heated hassle over establishing sound grading rules and practices for the Pacific Coast industry and on the national level was tearing the organization apart. Sore-heads resigned and meetings were often given over to time-consuming argument of the grading matter. Several times it appeared that WCLA might disintegrate or lose its effectiveness and most of this trouble stemmed from the grading rift which would go on for years. Strong men were needed to hold the organization together. Secretary Robert Allen wasn't one of them. He tried his best, but while he was a glorious gladhander, it became increasingly apparent to association directors that he was not right for the job in this turbulent time. It reflected in the WCLA books, too, with expenditures outbalancing the receipts, and a few of the leaders began quietly keeping their eyes out for the right replacement for Allen.

Gradually things improved when the grading war was settled, at least for a time, and WCLA took the pioneering step of refusing membership to any mill whose grades fell below ninety-five per cent in a test of grades efficiency, as provided by WCLA's monthly rigid inspection service. Tractor logging, truck hauling, and other marked improvements in technology were coming to the woods and mills, although the forest fires seemed to worsen.

But the mid-Twenties proved the peak production years of all time, despite the difficulties, with the camps and mills cutting over eleven billion board feet, including 7,027,325,000 feet in Washington and more than a billion of it going out from fabulous Grays Harbor. These things caused WCLA to take another pioneering step when a mass open meeting of three hundred to four hundred lumbermen was held early in 1926 at Seattle. The lumbermen voted unanimously to subscribe to a gigantic market extension program over the next three years, involving an expenditure of at least $500,000.

John D. Tennant of Long-Bell, chairman of the WCLA market extension committee, observed that "it really means the definite beginning of an era."

"It has been said," added Tennant, "that this committee has been made up largely out of WCLA, but we want it understood that this is a campaign for the entire industry, for everybody, big and little."

The meeting resulted in formation of the West Coast Lumber Trade Extension Bureau under the management of Henry Schott. Financing came from manufacturers doing their own logging and from independent loggers at five cents per thousand board feet on all lumber manufactured and logs produced. There were substantial appropriations from WCLA. Tennant was elected president of the new bureau, and others to serve as its first directors were: George S. Long, Ralph H. Burnside, C. D. Johnson, Everett G. Griggs, Myron C. Woodard, R. W. Vinnedge and Henry Schott.

The lumber industry played an unwitting role in the solution of one of the decade's most brutal and memorable crimes. A Southern Pacific mail and passenger train was stopped and the mail car blown up, and four trainmen slain in broad daylight, high in the Siskiyou Mountains on October 11, 1923. Loggers, mill hands and lumbermen joined the posses searching the rugged Oregon land.

The killers eluded the posses by hiding under a huge log in the back country where they had earlier stored food and blankets. They robbed a logging camp for more supplies and made their escape.

At first, authorities didn't know who had committed the shocking crime. But the slayers dropped some of their things near the tunnel where they halted the train, including a pair of overalls. Criminology was a comparatively new science in 1923, but one of its pioneers, E. O. Heinrichs of the University of California, was brought into the case. From the overall pockets, he pulled bits of sawdust and wood chips, indicating the owner worked in either a sawmill or logging camp. There was also a postal receipt, and using these threads authorities traced down the identity of the killers as being from Eugene, and one had indeed worked in a lumber camp. They were identified as Ray, Roy and Hugh D'Autremont. The manhunt spread around the world, one of the greatest in the history of the U.S. Post Office Department, and it was three years before the brothers were captured and brought in 1926 to trial in Jacksonville, Oregon.

While the exciting manhunt for the D'Autremonts was the talk of the West Coast, it didn't occupy all the attention. A great deal was being focused on a startling development in the bottom lands of the lower Columbia River, Washington side, between Vancouver and the mouth, where the "biggest sawmill in the world" was being built.[6] In July 1924, WCLA President Dolge joined with the Long-Bell company in sending out a circular invitation to the WCLA membership from the Seattle office, urging the lumbermen to attend grand opening ceremonies for the new mill and the surrounding and very ambitious "company town" which was being developed, "thereby showing the West Coast lumber industry's keen appreciation of the monumental enterprise of Mr. R. A. Long and his associates in establishing the nation's greatest new industrial development in this region."

The town created through the visionary ambitions of Robert Alexander Long of Kentucky and Kansas City was something spectacular. The Pacific Northwest now had two Longs as prominent leaders of its timber world — George S. Long of Weyerhaeuser and this newcomer of the Twenties, R. A. Long of Long-Bell which had only lately invaded the Northwest from the South where its timber reserves were depleted. Physically, the two Longs could pass for brothers, although there wasn't the remotest relationship. Both were tall as bean poles and there it ended. George Long was outspoken, migratory and handy with lusty words and phrases among fellow lumbermen; R. A. Long was conservative and pious, opening his board of directors' meetings with a prayer or two. But the new Long, now in his seventies, wasn't conservative when it came to business and above all, he knew how to move in the lumber world.

When Long-Bell decided it must come to the Pacific Northwest or die, Long came out to have a look at the timber. He found an exciting lush growth in Cowlitz County, Washington, and made a deal with the Weyerhaeuser people to buy 70,000 acres, containing several billion board feet of timber.

Now there had to be a mill. After much harassment from aggressive promoters of various areas, Long and his associates decided on the soggy lowlands where the Cowlitz River dumps into the Columbia, at a place called Monticello where in 1852 a gathering of settlers voted to petition Congress to create the Washington Territory.

In the summer of 1921, advance crews from Long-Bell began clearing out the thick brush and Wesley Vandercook, the company engineer, began directing gangs at diking the lowlands and installing an extensive drainage system. Also nosing around was J. C. Nichols of Kansas City, who set the local tongues wagging since he represented a profession that no Northwest lumber town had even seen before. Nichols was a landscape architect!

It was discovered that there were nine Longviews in the United States and that one, unfortunately, was located on the banks of the Columbia in Benton County. When the backers of Long's city applied for a post office, they were met with a firm denial, since the Post Office Department wouldn't allow two towns of the same name within the same state. Change the name? Impossible . . . Something had to be done to eliminate the other Longview.

Members of the older town's three leading families proved more congenial than expected. Postmaster R. M. Klinefelter signed a petition asking that the name be changed to Barger. Long-Bell envoys sighed with relief. But as they were leaving, a citizen remarked that it would be a welcome thing if the tiny depot had some kind of covered platform to keep the mailbag, thrown from moving trains, from landing on wet and soggy ground. The Long-Bell men were delighted to extend the sum for such a platform which cost the terrible price of $25.

"The only thing cheap about Longview was its name," later wrote the city's historian, John M. McClelland, Jr.

This was true, for other costs took off into the wild blue yonder. The 14,000 acre site cost about $125 more per acre than was thought possible. Long-Bell engineers and officials erred in their estimates. The dike system was estimated at $817,359. It cost $3,250,000. Parks, lakes, sidewalks and other features were far above preliminary calculations. Then there was the sticky matter of rail transportation. The Union Pacific, Northern Pacific, and Great Northern were crusty in their rejection of having Long-Bell cars pulled by Long-Bell locomotives moving over their pooled trackage. That got up the ire of the Long-Bell people who organized a subsidiary company under an ambitious name which was supposed to frighten the big railroads — The Longview, Portland & Northern. The railroad never got to Portland, but operated primarily around the new city and some nine miles up the Cowlitz River to the company logging camps near Ryderwood. It cost a pretty penny, $5,400,000, and a new bond issue was required for this financing and also the construction of two large sawmills.

Now at the end of July, thousands gathered for a four-day Pegeant of Progress to dedicate the "planned city" and see a great sawmill cut its first logs. The bands played, people cheered, and there were endless speeches of praise for the founder, Robert Alexander Long, by the Governor of Washington, a United States Senator, a Congressman, and other dignitaries. On the final day, a sermon was preached by the noted evangelist Billy Sunday who had been secured at a cost of $500 by Long himself; and it was Sunday who now proclaimed in his rousing sermon that he "wouldn't preach outdoors for anybody but God and R. A. Long."[7]

In the building of Longview, the Long-Bell company publicly demonstrated that it was a new force in Northwest lumber affairs and a powerful voice within WCLA. Many of its people were already active in the association. Secretary Robert Allen took a dim view of this, fearing that "outsiders" might be taking over WCLA and would thereby run the industry.

The industry remained largely disorganized and the times were hectic, despite spasmodic prosperity. WCLA was losing influence and members, and much effort was made just to hold things together. President Dolge urged that WCLA adopt a more aggressive program in traffic, market extension and trade promotion, grades, publicity and other services. He tried to sell the industry on what WCLA was doing for them, and cited traffic as an excellent example of good insurance. In one year, with an appropriation of $45,000, the traffic department was able to collect $113,193 in claims for its mills, including $20,000 for a single mill, nearly half the total dues of members during the year. That in itself, Dolge declared, showed how WCLA paid its way.

Yet members remained unconvinced, and WCLA membership reached the lowest ebb in its history. The industry was hard pressed by steel, paperboard, patent roofing and other so-called "substitutes" for lumber. WCLA was spending large sums for trade extension but there was growing dissatisfaction over the lack of concrete results, and the periodic shutdowns of mills from overproduction caused a reduction of the WCLA income which was based on the number of board feet the mills turned out. There was also mounting public pressure to do something in government about the timber lords who were gouging the beautiful woods, and were allegedly the cause behind the many devastating forest fires. Passage of a significant act sponsored by Charles L. McNary, one of Oregon's outstanding U.S. Senators of all time, and co-sponsored in the House by John W. Clarke of New York in 1924 opened the door for new approach to the nation's forestry problems. The chief of the U.S. Forest Service, William B. Greeley, had a lot to do with shaping the bill and the lumbermen were greatly impressed with his attitude. The law's dramatic appeal came from the cooperative action by private owners and state and federal agencies against the enemy of all — forest fires. This made it a hallmark in forest legislation.

In the changing scene, the WCLA leadership felt they needed a new image, a new face, a new leader, someone who was capable of meeting the challenges of the New Age in forestry and lumbering, yet a person of recognized influence who not only knew his way about the timberlands but could command the respect of the more rowdy and rebellious elements within the industry. There was increasing criticism of Robert Allen, who believed that all things could be worked out on the golf course. Allen had made his contribution, but he wasn't wise enough to move on to other things. Someone — the record isn't clear — suggested a daring thing: That the association hire somebody of national prominence in the field of forestry and conservation.

Visionaries like Major Griggs, George Long and John Tennant saw that perhaps the time was right. But did they dare? It would shake the walls of Jericho and send old-time lumber barons rolling in their graves. Great hog! But who? The name of Herbert Hoover, a strong conservationist who was very friendly to the West Coast industry in the grade dispute, was reportedly suggested, but never really considered, for Hoover had many other interests and was well on the way to entering big-time politics. Then the name of Bill Greeley was thrown into the ring. Northwest lumbermen liked Greeley and his ideas. They had worked closely with him in peace and war, and found him fair. He not only had championed the Clarke-McNary Act, but stood staunchly against his former boss, the powerful Gifford Pinchot, who pushed for federal regulation of all private logging. Despite his position as U. S. Forester, Greeley was known to be an outspoken advocate of private enterprise.

Greeley was approached and with him, too, the time was right. He had reached the pinnacle of his career in government forestry. His work was done there, he felt, and he thought that now more might be accomplished as a friend rather than foe of the lumber industry. Greeley believed in the co-existence of lumbering and conservation, that one could complement and support the other in a healthy fashion that could extend the forests forever. The offer from the WCLA people was tempting and challenging, and the more

Greeley thought about it, the more convinced he became. He agreed to come West.

The announcement which was to startle the timber world was made the same day as one concerning the consolidation of WCLA and the West Coast Lumber Trade Extension Bureau into a larger organization of strength and influence. That afternoon, February 17, 1928, George Long gave the word that Colonel Greeley would take charge of the new consolidated organization.

"We feel that the industry needs a big, broad-gauged man, nationally known, a person who can represent the industry properly before the nation," Long said. "We know something of his organization ability. He can handle big things. He made a splendid record during the war. We think he can organize this industry."

Then Long turned to the matter of Allen:

"I dislike to name a successor to Bob Allen, who for many years has been secretary of WCLA. He has done remarkable work. The trouble is that we haven't helped him and he has been criticized for the things we ourselves ought to have done. The time comes when, for no good reason, a man incurs many enmities and under those circumstances, a change became necessary."[8]

There was a rising ovation of appreciation to Allen by the lumbermen, and he was presented with an expensive gold watch as a memento. R. W. Vinnedge, the former WCLA president from North Bend, Washington, expressed the feelings of many for Allen's eleven years of service.

"I cannot praise him too highly," Vinnedge said. "Few realize what he has accomplished for the industry. He was particularly fitted by training and temperament to handle big problems."

Allen stayed several months to help with the change-over on the arrival of Colonel Greeley. Despite additional praiseworthy testimonials, Allen must have felt the association owed him more than a watch. By May, Colonel Greeley was in command. Allen said his farewells and left the Seattle WCLA headquarters. An auditing was begun as part of the change-over. For some reason, Charles H. Paul, the WCLA attorney, had a queer feeling about Allen. He urged Greeley, President John Tennant and others to check over things carefully and especially the association strongbox. It took some prodding on Paul's part, but he finally got them to the bank. The WCLA box had been closed out months before and everything placed in a box under Allen's name. When the box was opened, some $30,000 in Liberty bonds, the WCLA reserve fund, was gone. In their place, Allen left the watch and a note stating that he felt he should return the gift, and expressing his feelings that the association had been taken over by the southern lumber interests, meaning primarily Long-Bell.

WCLA members were shocked upon hearing the news. They found it hard to believe that the personable and friendly Allen appeared to be a thief. He was tracked to San Francisco where his wife was located. He'd given her $6,000 and then disappeared, perhaps fleeing the country. WCLA officials felt sorry for her; to take back all the sum would leave her destitute, so they allowed her to keep between $3,000 and $4,000.

Legal action was taken by Attorney Paul in the Superior Court of King County in the form of a suit which President Tennant explained "the trustees regretted exceedingly . . . but such a course appeared unavoidable in order to protect the interests of the subscribers." The association was able to recover another $7,500 through insurance which added to the amount returned by Mrs. Allen was about one-third of the total sum. Even though current monies weren't placed in jeopardy, the theft seriously reduced the WCLA surplus for lean times and placed the association and the trustees in an embarrassing light with some of the members. It also got the Greeley administration off to a poor start, since this was something he hadn't counted upon.

Bob Allen couldn't be found and if Mrs. Allen knew his whereabouts, she wasn't saying. It was reported that he was "somewhere in South America" and still later he showed up in Florida and was arrested. By then WCLA trustees were sick and tired of the entire affair. It would cost more to extradite Allen catty-corner across the country and bring him to trial than it was worth, and the lumbermen, tough as they could be at times, didn't have the stomach to face this man whom they had always liked. Therefore, they voted to drop the charges.

As for Allen, so far as is known, he never showed up again in the Pacific Northwest. Attorney Paul heard later that he was in the East, working for a trade publication. But that was only a glimpse, for Allen disappeared permanently from the West Coast timber world where his turbulent career would long be a subject of speculation among the lumber interests.

NOTES TO CHAPTER XI

1. From the well researched *The Barbary Coast* by Herbert Asbury.
2. Harvey O'Connor, in his version in *Revolution in Seattle*, says it was no secret the hall was to be attacked.
3. From the WCLA circulars.
4. *West Coast Lumberman*, October, 1923.
5. *West Coast Lumberman*, May 1, 1924.
6. Many West Coast companies and sawmill men, it seems, boasted about having "the largest sawmill in the world."
7. Stewart Holbrook has a lively account of the building of Longview in his *The Columbia*.
8. *West Coast Lumberman*, March 1, 1928.

Chapter XII
'Greeley Speaking'

ONCE when still with the U. S. Forest Service, Colonel Greeley was confronted by a female journalist of the crusading school, seeking a sensational angle for a forestry story she wished to do for national distribution. Lumbermen and industrial foresters of that day were being put on the defensive by a mounting onslaught from writers of the muckraking class who held no interest in forestry, but only in grinding out lurid tales with the lumberman as the villain.

This particular writer urged the Colonel to give her "something graphic."

"It simply must catch the public's imagination," she explained, her pencil poised.

Colonel Greeley was captivated by her abounding ignorance and obligingly gave her the works, his owl-like face sober and wise, while she failed to detect the sly twinkle in his eyes as he tapped his pipe.

"Doubtless," he declared, "the worst example of forest devastation in the world was the clear-cutting of North Dakota by the most notorious of our early day loggers."

"And the name?" asked the girl, her note pad shaking from eager excitement.

"Paul Bunyan," answered Greeley, his face expressionless.

"Spell it," demanded the writer.

Greeley spelled it out slowly, and then expanded on the lurid deeds of this maniac logger of yesteryear. Bunyan not only ran rampant in the Dakota timberlands, but was actually in the secret employ of the King of Sweden who had many subjects in North Dakota. They complained that the timber was so thick they could do no farming. The monarch, through a secret arrangement with the U. S. State Department, allowed Bunyan to move his many reckless loggers to the region. The result was the most classic example of forest destruction of all time.

"Never a tree," said Greeley soberly, "has since been seen in North Dakota."

"Marvelous!" cheered the crusading lady journalist with eyes shining as she closed her notebook, envisioning her scoop.

The Colonel never saw or heard from her again, nor did he ever find her story in print.

"Old Paul did me a good turn," he later recalled to Stewart Holbrook.

The Colonel, as he was most generally called, didn't very often lead people down a garden path. He had other ways of setting them straight, and during his years as secretary-manager of WCLA, as it had been when Chief Forester of the U.S. Forest Service, he was a dynamic personality in the job he had to do. Greeley felt that it was a lifetime crusade and personal mission which drove him on.

In the Colonel's office hung a motto in a large frame:

The business of life is to go forward.

It was his creed and he lived by it with every tick of the clock that measured his days, in accomplishing and doing and trying to better the timber world that he loved. He instilled this forward movement in the people who were part of the pioneering forestry and lumber program that the Colonel cut in a gigantic swath through the American timberlands.

Colonel Greeley didn't cut and get out; he cut and stayed for the follow-through and in doing so committed sheer heresy, for he shocked people of the timber world and the politicians time and again by the unique positions he took on matters of forestry and conservation. Greeley believed that forestry and the lumber industry could be partners, and that the control and perpetuating of the forests for future generations could be accomplished by private enterprise and initiative without rigid governmental controls. It got him into a peck of trouble with a lot of powerful people, including his former boss, Gifford Pinchot, and the Colonel's hide acquired another layer of thickness. When he joined WCLA, it was the final straw; Greeley had sold his soul to the Devil.

Yet to the Colonel, his gigantic step from government forestry to private industry, and a lumber association at that, was a natural move directly in line with his motto. He was merely going ahead with the business of life and working for the betterment of the forest world. Amos Alonzo Stagg, the great football coach, once wanted to be a preacher, but it was generally concluded that he molded more characters of boys as a coach than he would ever have done from the pulpit. It was the same way with Colonel Greeley. He accomplished far more for lumbering and forestry by being a part of the industry than he might ever have done had he stayed with "the enemy" in government work.

By the time he took over for WCLA, Colonel Greeley was as well seasoned as any ripened Douglas fir. He had been through many a human mill, been slabbed, turned, edged, twisted, gang-sawed, planed, graded and dried for shipping. All this made him sounder and hardier than before, a better man so that his inner drive to far-off goals kept him moving without petty vindictiveness or contemplation over old wounds. He was a forester, by the gods, but a practical forester, living to do what he knew was right for America. He understood his work as few men ever do, with a broad view of the future. He was both stubborn and nimble-footed so that he could handle himself well in the political arena and parry the barbs that flew at him from politicians, the press, itinerant lumbermen and the general public.

One of the most biting criticisms of his early career came in 1906 when he was supervisor of California's Sequoia National Forest. Westerners took a very dim view of the Forest Service in its infant days. Greeley found it necessary to crack down on stockmen who were over-grazing. There was a heated debate during a conference with the stockmen, but finally a compromise was reached. Then one cattleman observed that in another area a larger quota of cattle was allowed.

Greeley replied flatly that it made no difference what was done in other National Forests.

"On *my* National Forest, the range is in bad shape and the numbers of stock have got to be cut."

A leathery veteran stockman casually leaned back in his chair, propped his feet on the table, and drew out the makings. Unhurried, he poured the Bull Durham into the paper, then drawled:

"When the young supervisor just now talked about *his* National Forest, it sorta reminded me of the time when the old Devil took Jesus Christ to the top of a high mountain. He offered Christ all the kingdoms of earth if he would fall down and worship Satan; all of 'em, mind you! and the old s.o.b. didn't own a damn acre."[1]

It was a sound rebuke, which the Colonel never forgot, but it helped to mold his character and became a story he told on himself. Such things toughened him for the job ahead. Yet he wasn't far wrong in calling the timber *his* forest. Greeley believed that the nation's natural resources were his responsibility — and the responsibility of every American and every enterprise, private and public, within the United States. He envisioned a reforested America free from the ravages of fire and depredations due to human ignorance. This was no idle dream; he set about turning that dream into reality, although at the time it must have appeared almost an impossible task. But by his efforts and his long career of accomplishments, Colonel Greeley became one of the nation's greatest foresters of all time, although the name of Gifford Pinchot has always overshadowed him.

Forest fires were Greeley's personal enemy. He had good reason to feel this way. He joined the U. S. Forest Service in 1904 fol-

lowing completion of work for his Master's degree in forestry
at Yale University. He rose rapidly as one of "Gifford Pinchot's
Boys" and four years later was placed in charge of the newly
created District One of the Forest Service in Montana, a 25,000,000
acre region considered one of the most primitive and heavily forested sections in the country. Two summers later, the young ranger
was plunged to the depths of despair and helplessness when this
same region "blew up." The woods had become tinder-dry with no
rain for three months. Over three thousand fires were burning.
Then the wind came up and by August 20 was of hurricane velocity,
alarming the population of Montana, Idaho and Washington as the
blow's savagery raced through the narrow mountain gorges, driving
the flames before it and creating massive destruction across a great
expanse of timber.[2]

Scope of the tragedy was shocking, with eighty-five lives lost
and over three million acres destroyed. Bill Greeley had good
reason to think of quitting, of dumping his chosen career for
something easier. Instead, it gave him a new insight into the tremendous job facing the forestry movement. From that time, he
swore to drive fire from the woods. And, if state and private
landowners would not accept federal regulation, in the name of
cold reality the only other course was to cooperate with them.
He abandoned the "Great Crusade" inspired by Theodore Roosevelt
and Gifford Pinchot, and also any last remnants of bitterness and
antagonism toward the lumbermen.

The forest road which the fires of Montana had opened would
not be easy for the son of a New England Congregational minister.
His was one of many successive generations stretching back to
1630 in the New World. In a way, he came by his profession
"honestly," for some of his forebears were sawmill people; it was
bred into him . . . Born at Oswego, New York, September 6,
1879, Bill Greeley came with his family as a boy around Cape
Horn to California, where the Greeleys settled on a ranch in the
Santa Clara Valley. Bill went to school there, then entered the
University of California, earning his Bachelor of Science degree in
1901.

The tall, brawny and somewhat gaunt appearing young forester
— he was often described as "Lincolnesque" — was among the first
to join the ranks of "Pinchot's Boys." He served in the South, New
England and California before taking the fateful Montana post. Yet
despite the discouragement of the Montana holocaust, it was recognized that the disaster was not Greeley's personal fault. The following year, he advanced to Assistant Chief Forester in charge
of forest management, where he stayed until World War I. He
sailed for France as a major with the Tenth Engineers, won a promotion to lieutenant colonel, and became chief of the forestry
section with 21,000 troops serving under him, operating ninety-five

Colonel William B. Greeley, one of nation's leading foresters, became powerful head of WCLA in 1928.

sawmills turning out two million feet of lumber daily. His impressive war record won him the U.S. Distinguished Service Medal, the French Legion of Honor ribbon, and England's Distinguished Service Order. Two years after the Armistice, this same distinguished record of moving ahead brought Greeley to the pinnacle as Chief of the Forest Service, succeeding Henry S. Graves. It was at the time of the turbulent Twenties in the forests and the lumber industry.

Yet ever since Montana, Greeley's approach to forest policy and that of Gifford Pinchot, the man who trained him and whom the Colonel long respected, had been growing apart in their beliefs of how to accomplish the ends which must come. Both were strong-willed men of ability with an active sense of duty and responsibility. They were sincere and loyal to their codes. A contemporary of both men asserted that "either of them would sacrifice himself in the line of duty."

The Colonel and Pinchot were bound to clash heatedly, sooner or later. Pinchot saw lumbering as a "willful industry"; Greeley viewed it as a "sick industry" which could be cured. Pinchot looked upon the lumbermen as selfish and greedy, and bent upon destroying the nation's timber resources for personal benefit. He was bitter over their failure to embrace his principles of forest management. It was an age of trust-busting and muckraking, and journalists turned from oil, sugar, meat packers and other public enemies to leap upon the lumber industry, the devastators of the public domain, the cut-and-get-out-boys, who caused ruination and waste across the land.

Greeley's contacts with the lumbermen over the years convinced him that they were not necessarily at odds with conservation. What was needed was a common meeting ground. He found it in a mutual foe — fire . . .[3] This common enemy couldn't be defeated singlehandedly or through hostility, Greeley believed. On the other hand, cooperation between public and private timber owners would instill understanding and the bonds of partnership, which, Greeley hoped, would eventually take progress another huge step forward to the ultimate goal, *reforestation*. It was upon this premise that he constructed his National Forest Policy, and boldly aired his stand in 1917 through a Department of Agriculture report, *Some Public and Economic Aspects of the Lumber Industry.*

Pinchot read the report, gnashed his teeth, and blew up like a crown fire. He was especially irritated that a forester wrote it, one of his own boys, and branded it as a "whitewash of destructive logging." That Bill Greeley would boldly oppose this policy of hardened dogma was downright unthinkable, beyond the scope of comprehension. Greeley had become a captive of the "wicked industry."

"I found that I had lost caste in the temple of conservation (Pinchot's home) on Rhode Island Avenue in Washington," Greeley declared.

The two great foresters went into verbal battle in the early 1920's when Greeley took the reins of the Forest Service and Pinchot threw his great prestige behind a campaign for direct federal regulation of private forest lands. As Chief Forester, Colonel Greeley also came hard against Albert G. Fall, Secretary of Interior in the corrupt Harding administration. Fall announced plans to take over the National Forests and the Forest Service, and that as a beginning he intended "to fire the impractical forester who is mismanaging the whole show." Greeley stood against his onslaught for more than a year. Then everything became clear as to Fall's intentions in the Teapot Dome Oil Scandal. Fall left the cabinet overnight and later spent time in prison in the affair which touched off other scandals, leaving the Harding administration in shambles.[4]

Through it all, the Forest Service survived without a tinge of scandal. But Pinchot wasn't to be denied and although now out of public service, he still enjoyed a powerful voice in affairs of the woodlands. He pointed out that the lumbermen, the Timber Barons, had shown little tendency to change their cutting habits and as for the matter of planting trees, they argued this was sheer nonsense until trees could financially sustain themselves and be worth the cost of planting and protecting. Pinchot fought openly for use of the Big Stick he had come to enjoy under Theodore Roosevelt; a demand for federal regulation of all private logging in all forest lands everywhere was paramount, in the name of public interest.

Greeley headed up the opposing forces which were needed to fight Pinchot in and out of Congress. Over the next four years, a number of bills were introduced and Greeley reluctantly concluded that some sort of control over destructive logging was inevitable. However, he hoped the forestry and lumber camps might join forces to temper any such legislation. He assigned a number of Forest Service men to rally these forces and work with state foresters and lumbermen to set down specifics as to what they felt the minimum requirements should be in cutting practices. Greeley feared a complete revolt on the part of the lumbermen. Pinchot charged that the lumbermen had pulled the wool over the eyes of the naive Greeley.

"My hardest work," the Colonel recalled, "was to keep the lumbermen in the cooperative tent. They might easily have stampeded off the reservation completely and taken to the warpath. Some of them did."

There was a growing rift within the Forest Service itself, many men staying with the powerful Pinchot, while according to Greeley "some of us could not thrill to the sound of trumpets." Greeley found a sympathetic ear in a newcomer, Senator Charles L. McNary of Oregon. McNary asked Greeley what might be done. Greeley stressed his fear of federal police tactics in the forests, and that sane and practical private or industrial forestry was dependent upon forest fire prevention and the nature of forest taxation. McNary suggested that they write a bill around forest fires. A Select Committee on Reforestation was approved by the Senate, with McNary its chairman. Some twenty hearings were held in the forest regions and Greeley later stated that "I confess to packing the stands at committee hearings with fire witnesses."

The bill, ready early in 1924, was based on fire prevention through cooperative action. When the Clarke-McNary Act became law, Colonel Greeley had won a major victory in his crusade for a better timber world. The act was far more than one against fire, as we have already noted. It provided a stimulus for a concerted drive for reforesting denuded lands and in the Pacific Northwest brought about a cooperative two-state forestry system that paved the way for an industrial forestry program which developed an outstanding record of good cutting practices. Most significant, the annual drain and growth of the timberlands reached a closer balance.

The act opened many other new avenues to the future and cleared the air of much of the heated controversy which had raged for years. And the federal regulation supporters found themselves without a leader, for Pinchot had turned his main attention to politics in Pennsylvania.

The lumbermen were impressed with what was clearly a Greeley victory. This was particularly true in the Pacific Northwest, for his thinking seemed to be closely in line with that of the veteran leaders of WCLA. So the Colonel packed his duffel bag and with his wife and family headed for the Northwest. He had the vision to see into the future and to know where he belonged. It is to the credit of the WCLA leaders that they had the vision to hire him.

The announcement that Greeley was joining the industry brought a storm of criticism from old-guard conservationists who had long suspected that Greeley had "sold out". This was the clincher; Pinchot was right. On the other hand, the more liberal called the charges ridiculous and observed that old-guard conservationists were "just too damn narrow minded." One Congressman asserted that WCLA "ought to be indicted for grand larceny for having taken him away from the government."

Greeley lost no time in going to work at rebuilding WCLA, once the Bob Allen affair was over and done without benefit of scandal in the public press. He was quick to outline some of the problems of the Northwest industry in a letter to President John Tennant.

"It requires building up and holding permanent markets and effective use of raw material standing in the woods," said Greeley. "Commercial timber growing is not possible without well-established industries and sustained markets for their products. Reforestation will be brought into the industrial picture of the Northwest to the extent that lumber and wood-using industries can attain stability and prosperity. It is like the last stone in an arch."

Greeley worked long hours at the task of reorganizing and developing the big new combined association of the West Coast lumbermen and the trade extension bureau. His rumpled, gaunt and lanky form gave little indication of the astounding energy he possessed and the vast knowledge within his head. He would dictate for many hard hours without a break, pacing the floor of his huge rustic office while feeding a steady flow of words into letters, bulletins, communiques, memos, ideas and suggestions, and miscellaneous notices which went to employees, lumbermen, loggers, government officials, editors, private capitalists and those of many other walks of life across the nation and the world. The Colonel fell to working closely with every department of WCLA — grades, traffic, timber engineering, trade promotion, forest conservation, government relations, statistics, accounting, and public relations and publicity. He indoctrinated his staff and the lumbermen with the "Greeley system" for the forests, and stressed that whether you were handling grades, traffic or accounting, all were part of the same team working for the same goal. Most always, he answered the telephone with "Greeley speaking." The phrase was significant, for no matter what the subject where WCLA had voice, it was "Greeley speaking."

"Timber is a crop," the Colonel said many, many times. He pounded it home and the slogan became on a par with his office motto. Yet he knew that any forest conservation movement had to pay its way.

"Men conserve the things they value," Greeley observed. But men are also wasteful under the guise of being practical. Forest fires had to be mastered, but there were other things which the Colonel envisioned for the safe and sound use of the forests of the future. Progress must come through enlightening private enterprise and the efforts of thousands of timber owners and operators. Research must bring about the full utilization of logging and saw-milling left-overs. Constructive programs of forest economics promised ultimate good for forestry. He saw legislation on a broader view, too; it was of concern to conservation not only when dealing directly with forest matters, but when it had to do with lumber tariffs, taxes, traffic, grade standards, industrial wages and hours, social security, federal housing and home financing, and countless other problems. WCLA department representatives, appearing at government hearings on such matters as freight rates and grading rules, stressed the fact that unless such things were adopted, not only would the Northwest lumber industry suffer, but it would be a blow to conservation. The magic word *conservation* had impact beyond all else and no politician or government official in his right mind would speak out against the conservation of natural resources. The points were pounded home to Greeley's staff and they caught the fire of "Greeley-ism," as it became known.

The Colonel's approach in publicity and information wasn't merely backslapping and handshaking, but hard-hitting, wise and practical work, with a real sense of timing. Greeley gained the services of a personable Seattle author who knew his way around the newsrooms and the woods. As with Peter B. Kyne and Stewart Holbrook, Iowa-born James F. Stevens found romance and inspiration in the timberlands while working in logging camps and saw-mills. He saw service overseas in World War I as a sergeant with the 162nd infantry. Something of an adventurer and wanderer with an eye for the unusual and a delightful outlook on life, Stevens had been logger, hobo laborer, mule skinner and onetime boy evangelist; he also described himself as "sawdust savage, worshipper of Walt Whitman, axman. poet. slave, rebel, brawler, dreamer, mystic, plowman, and full-mongrel American."[5]

In the early Twenties, Stevens taught himself how to spin a yarn with typewriter and paper, and sold his first efforts to the *Saturday Evening Post*. He became a contributor to H. L. Mencken's *American Mercury* and over the years turned out well over two hundred magazine stories and articles. During his time in the woods of the Midwest and Northwest, Stevens began gathering together the many folklore tales of the legendary logger, Paul Bunyan, which he finally set down in book form. The tales grew into several volumes and brought Stevens lasting international recognition and critical acclaim, for the Paul Bunyan stories were reprinted around the world. Indeed, once Stevens wrote a tongue-in-cheek column about the way the Russians claimed to have created the lusty logger of legend under the name of "Paulski Punvanovitch." It was just a fun thing, but the great magazine, Collier's, took the matter seriously and voiced vigorous editorial outcries that the Soviets were carrying things pretty far.

Stevens was one of the most widely heralded authors of his time. But he wasn't one to rest on past laurels, for he was a writing man and so was his wife, Theresa, an ex-newspaper gal of considerable experience. Colonel Greeley was constantly on the lookout for the right man to do the right job. Stevens' lumber background caught his eye and the fact that he lived right there in Seattle was an opportunity that Greeley couldn't let slide by.

J. B. Fitzgerald of Portland was the WCLA information and publicity director for many years, coming to the association with the trade extension bureau merger. Gus Evans, also from Portland, filled in for a time. Fitzgerald who had been editor of the 4L paper and active in that movement worked closely with Greeley in setting up many of the information policies and activities.

The Depression was on and Stevens, like many a successful author, was finding it tough sledding. When the Colonel approached Stevens, the idea of helping to publicize the forests that he loved, build a new world of lumber and forestry, and work with the leading forester of the day appealed to him immensely. He signed on as public relations man for WCLA, at first on a part-time basis, and packed his staunch old Oliver typewriter down to the White-Henry-Stuart building to begin cutting a broad swath for the timber world. When Fitzgerald was hired to manage the Lumbermen's Industrial Relations Committee, Stevens filled the vacancy.

His efforts took many forms, from innumerable ideas and news releases to radio programs, including Farm and Home Hour broadcasts, speeches, home promotion, a widely circulated column called "Out of the Woods" which appeared weekly in over seventy-five Northwest newspapers and trade journals, articles for general circulation magazines and trade periodicals, answering correspondence from students working on master's and doctor's theses, and even a series of ballads and poems, the most famous of which was called "The Frozen Logger," recorded under twelve different labels.

Stevens became the most successful and effective timber promotion man of his time. Working for the Colonel was indeed an experience, since Greeley was constantly feeding Stevens good suggestions for stories. Stevens' assignment was to put together a monthly newspaper for the retail lumber trade. Soon there was industrial forestry publicity keyed to the forest fire problem and ideas for supplementing the FHA-NLMA promotion for lumber-built homes with a regional effort by WCLA. Greeley suggested, too, that something be done with "engineering in lumber" and Stevens worked up stories about the 100,000,000 board feet used for construction of Grand Coulee dam. The Colonel's mind turned to the use of publicity to bolster the West Coast lumbermen's case against reciprocal trade agreements with which the State Department was taking business from Washington and Oregon lumber ports and giving it to Canada. Stevens punched out many a story on the "vanishing ships and missing men" theme.[6]

But there were uneasy occasions, too. Stevens, like everyone in WCLA, was given a pretty free hand to operate. If his people got off the beam, the Colonel let them know it in a direct manner. In the early Forties, Greeley took under his wing a bright young forester of great promise, William D. Hagenstein. This former boss logger had the peculiar notoriety of winning a Duke University scholarship while retaining the colorful lingo of a lumberjack. Greeley tried to break him of it (he never succeeded) by fining him two-bits every time he uttered an oath in Greeley's office. But Hagenstein just couldn't quit. Once at a social gathering, Hagenstein got into a heated argument and let fly. Greeley apologized to an elderly woman standing within earshot.

"And why," she replied, "should I give a damn what kind of words he picks?"

But Hagenstein had a tremendous outgoing personality and Stevens booked him for numerous speaking engagements to talk on "Timber is a Crop—the Harvest is Homes." Greeley called Stevens into his office and pointing his long finger, declared firmly:

"Jim, I'm going to have a big plaque made, one that will cover the chest of Bill Hagenstein. And it will carry this order: 'No trespassing by the public relations department.' That is all."

Stevens saluted and walked out, hurriedly canceling the schedule of Hagenstein's speaking engagements.

Greeley once rebuked a staff member for wisecracking about the White House. He had a lasting and strong loyalty to the United States, although he could fight to the death against the things within government that he felt to be wrong. When in 1935 Colonel Greeley was severely injured by a careening truck of the Civilian Conservation Corps near Olympia and was long hospitalized, Charles Paul, WCLA legal counsel, urged that he file suit against the government for payment of the huge hospital bill.

"I will never sue the United States government," Greeley replied. Paul felt he had almost insulted the man by the suggestion.

This was how Greeley reacted to things. He had distinct loyalties and his own code of fair play, even in the face of hostility, brute force, threats and political double-talk. Greeley's loyalty to WCLA was in itself something that few could fathom. Several times when the association was hard-pressed for funds, he took a voluntary salary cut. Of course, when the trustees found out, they reinstated the full back salary. Yet he wasn't for show, driving a battered car and staying in second-class hotels to save the association money. Such things made him loved and admired during the two decades when he guided the destinies of the West Coast Lumbermen's Association and remolded the lumber world by passing from hostility to tolerance and then enthusiasm about the forests of the future.

NOTES TO CHAPTER XII

1. *From Forests and Men* by William B. Greeley.
2. Ibid.
3. *Portrait of a Forester* by George T. Morgan, Jr., *Southern Lumberman,* December 1960.
4. *Greeley Went West* by Stewart Holbrook, *American Forests,* March 1958.
5. *Seattle Times,* "Faces of the City" by John J. Reddin, March 10, 1965.
6. James F. Stevens, recollections about Colonel Greeley, *American Forests,* January 1956.

Chapter XIII

Legacy of the Lumber Code

MANY of the old-time lumbermen, and also some of the younger ones, took a dim view of the coming of Colonel Greeley. If the professional forestry world felt that Greeley had become a captive of the lumber industry, lumbermen and loggers felt the same way about WCLA.

The idea of a forester taking over and representing their industry—a federal man at that—was as distasteful to the lumbermen in 1928 as eating raw oatmeal. There was little respect for foresters who invaded the rugged timberlands. They were classed with other odd people interested in nature, such as butterfly collectors and bird watchers. The loggers and crusty sawmill men called them "bug men" and "pismire superintendents." Little heed was paid to what they said or attempted to accomplish. What few so-called industrial foresters were on the scene were either ignored or their very existence denied by rugged old-timers.

"The idea of a forester on the company payroll was unthinkable," wrote Stewart Holbrook. *"I do not exaggerate. I heard them discuss the subject with all the magnificent eloquence they had previously saved for the Wobblies."* [1]

Even so, a growing number of new generation loggers and lumbermen were college-educated graduates of forestry schools and were therefore thoroughly indoctrinated with the new ways that were coming.

The Colonel allowed critics to rant and rave without hitting back, for the important thing was to get "company foresters" into the industry and thus doctor its many ills. It was a form of infiltration, but even though they were placed on the payrolls—perhaps to keep the powerful chief of WCLA off lumbermen's backs—the lumbermen gave the newcomers a pretty rough time and often whatever advice a company forester offered to earn his check was shunted aside for the old and tried ways. He didn't stand a head rigger's damn against the logging boss when in conflict over cutting a quarter section.

Public attitude remained static against the lumbermen, classified among the damned, public enemies of the Chicago gangster type, in partnership with the Devil. Government propagandists promoting the cause of federal regulation and ownership of the forests as the only solution to the timber preservation problem capitalized fully on this attitude to further their cause. Franklin Roosevelt and Harold Ickes didn't help matters with their public outbursts against the lumbermen. In a trip through the Pacific Northwest, while traveling the Olympic Loop Highway, President Roosevelt saw an area of Douglas fir cutover land and roared: "I hope the lumberman who did that is roasting in hell." The truth was that seedlings had made a good start in the area, but then a cigarette was carelessly tossed and fire killed off the young trees. When Harold Ickes, Secretary of Interior, spoke before the Port Angeles Chamber of Commerce, he stated with great solemnity that the iron fence placed around the White House was to keep visiting lumbermen from cutting down the trees. [2]

Colonel Greeley kept his head, while many a lumberman wanted to punch somebody in the nose. Education was the answer, of the logger, the lumberman, Mr. John Q. Citizen. A way would be found through the WCLA promotion and publicity programs.

The great Depression struck the lumber industry early, ahead of much of the country and after a peak in 1928-29 in exports to Japan, China, Australia, the United Kingdom and continental Europe. Despite this peak abroad, the lumber industry was showing signs of weakness from several causes. WCLA President Edmund Hayes of the Clackamas Fir Lumber Company of Portland cited these reasons as a large increase in production without much thought of the "waning market except that the Lord will provide": large-scale competition for the consumer dollar in such things as automobiles and radios; a "tremendous increase" in other kinds of building materials about which "we did a lot of crying but nothing very constructive"; and a more critical attitude by the buying public toward manufactured goods.[3]

For three years lumbering was in a bad way, the docks and sheds groaning under the unsalable inventories, rusting stacks, and thousands of employees out of work.

"If this situation continues," said Hayes, "our industry will face a constantly restricted market for its product. Unwarranted raising in price merely brings in substitute lumber or other materials which, once they are in, are almost impossible to eliminate."

A third of the Douglas fir mills were shut down. The rest were operating at slow bell. The lumbermen had gone through other bad times, but this was far worse than anything they'd ever seen. Even the Long Beach earthquake disaster failed to give the industry any great stimulation from emergency orders.

The National Industrial Recovery Act was signed into law that June of 1933 by President Roosevelt, who hailed the passage as "the most important and far-reaching legislation ever enacted by the American Congress." Colonel Greeley and a full delegation from the West Coast Lumbermen's Association, including President Ernest W. Demarest of the Pacific National Lumber Company at Tacoma, boarded a Great Northern train for Chicago to confer with other lumber groups from the southern and northeastern regions on prospects for a Blue Eagle code system under the NRA. They were called together by the National Lumber Manufacturers Association. Under the law, "codes" of operation were to be set up for each industry, written by the members themselves as a form of self-government over the different segments of the industry. The West Coast lumbermen were indeed gloomy over prospects, especially Colonel Greeley who had fought so long and hard to keep the federal government's hands off the forests of the Pacific Northwest. But the lumbermen had their backs to the wall under the present critical conditions of the Great Depression and the stagnated industry.

During the trip east, the WCLA delegation wrote and rewrote drafts of many sections that might be a part of the NRA Lumber Code. The lumbermen drafted articles governing production, the number of hours sawmills could run, minimum wage schedules, and a list of minimum prices, all things that they expected would be asked by the New Deal administration. Then the Colonel put forth a suggestion.

"President Roosevelt is almost certain to want something in this code on forestry," he declared. "Let's beat him to the draw. It will help us get the rest."[4]

The Colonel was commissioned to draft Article X that would commit the industry to a "reasonable" program of forest conservation, which sifted down to a policy of leaving "cutover lands in good condition for reforestation." Lumbermen at Chicago began holding high hopes for the success of the NRA code; that it might bring about controls on prices and production which had been among the objectives of WCLA and other trade associations for many years. This time there was no fear of prosecution for violation of anti-trust laws. It was very strange indeed. A twenty-member emergency committee was appointed and soon became the incorporated Lumber Code Authority, with John D. Tennant of Long-Bell, a WCLA representative, as chairman. Others of WCLA on the emergency committee were President Demarest; Mark E. Reed, head of Simpson Logging Company; F. E. Weyerhaeuser as a member at large; and A. J. Morley of Saginaw Timber Company, Aberdeen, as a temporary member from the shingle industry.

Demarest returned West to report to the WCLA member-

ship, while the others continued to Washington to hammer out
the code in an acceptable form to meet the approval of General
Hugh S. Johnson, the National Recovery administrator. Final approval was made on August 19, just before the Tillamook fire
blew up. President Roosevelt beamed over Article X. There seemed
to be no fear, with lumbermen inside the White House, that
they might somehow cut down all the trees, as Ickes had wise-
cracked, and Greeley remembered that "we left the Capitol with
new halos on our heads."

Primary purpose of the code was to maintain a reasonable
balance between production and the consumption of lumber and
timber products; and to oversee this, Tennant's emergency committee was to calculate every three months the estimated consumption of the products for each timber species. There would be supervision over wages and labor, log cutting and forestry matters,
with administration to come from the boards of West Coast Lumbermen's Association, Pacific Northwest Loggers Association, Douglas Fir Plywood Manufacturers Association, Douglas Fir Door
Manufacturers Association, and the Washington and Oregon Shingle
Association.

The honeymoon was soon over as disillusionment set in regarding the NRA system and dictation from the "outside." Labor
didn't like the plan and its leaders charged that the lessening in
hours was not so much to "spread the work," as for production
control. Through the 4L, labor was able to establish the West
Coast wage at 42½ cents per hour as compared with 24 cents in
the South. A joint committee on labor was established to deal
with the problems which included handling applications for sea-
sonal classification, hearings on alleged violations arising from
field audits, and the drawing up of rules and regulations covering labor matters for employers under the committee's jurisdic-
tion. During the year 1934, the joint committee handled 360 cases
considered serious enough to come to the attention of the Lumber
Code Authority.[5]

But the crux of the trouble lay with lumbermen who rebelled against the orders of price fixing and production, and
loathed the field checks being made by outside authorities. Some
companies yelled for higher production quotas, others charged that
they were already too high. It was virtually impossible to establish and enforce the schedules for production and pricing, and
as soon as one dispute was smoothed out, another took its place.
The strong breeding of independence among American businessmen
and a balking against conformity swept through the industry. There
were heated charges of discrimination and the ruling on things
by men who knew nothing about a certain segment of the industry and its particular problems. The code took business from
one operation and gave it to another. It failed to consider mills

built for continuous operation against those that were only partial operations, and gave little attention to depreciation taxes, overhead, insurance and timber expenses. It discouraged the selling organizations.

There was mounting anger in the Northwest woods and within a year after the Lumber Code was approved, the lumbermen were openly rebelling. Violations became flagrant and widespread, and by September 1934 when the WCLA board met in Portland to review the entire matter, the lumbermen were to the boiling point. They wanted to rid the industry of the minimum price controls. J. H. Bloedel strongly warned that to do so would likely "wreck the entire code and demoralize the lumber industry." J. E. Morris, chairman of the West Coast division committee on minimum prices and trade practices, told the WCLA trustees of the necessity "for drastic action to protect the manufacturers who are observing the code — if minimum prices are to be maintained."

That blew the lid off and the sessions became as stormy as any in the history of WCLA. Telegrams from the National Control Authority asked the WCLA board to refrain from any action that would weaken the code, but instead to send a strong delegation to a forthcoming meeting in Chicago to present its recommendations for changes in the code. E. C. Stone of the Stimson Mill Company of Seattle presented a petition with 205 manufacturers' signatures as a motion that previous action taken in August in support of the price control article of the Lumber Code be rescinded. More than twenty members spoke in favor of Stone's motion and against petitions from employees of several companies asking that the minimum price provisions be retained as protection to workers in the industry and maintenance of present wage levels.

Speakers stressed that for all practical purposes, the minimum prices had been abandoned and did not now exist.

Others spoke in favor of retaining the code, pointing out that at least it was self-government and that "if it were not being complied with, it was the direct fault of members of the industry."[6] Elimination of the price rule would result in a breakdown in regulations over production, wages and hours, and in the end might bring on a code directly from the federal administration rather than one from within the realm of self-government. The session became so heated and loud that Bloedel got to his feet and rebuked his fellow lumbermen by observing that the gathering sounded more like a convention of longshoremen than one of businessmen. In the end, Stone's motion was beaten, but the WCLA trustees eight days later pledged fourteen to seven to do their utmost to gain the abandonment of "cost protection."

A month later WCLA directors made their stand even more firm in a resolution which declared that the majority of West Coast logging and lumber operators believed that the price protection parts of the Blue Eagle act were "impracticable, unworkable and unfair," and that therefore the WCLA trustees were rescinding "all previous resolutions in favor of the so-called 'cost protection' and 'fixed prices' on lumber . . . "

The strain proved too great for the WCLA leaders. President Demarest and Colonel Greeley submitted their resignations, and John Tennant soon resigned also as chairman of the Lumber Code Authority. Greeley pointed out that the trustees had completely reversed the WCLA position and placed him in a most embarrassing one, since Greeley had not only been carrying out the policies of the WCLA board, but had been a leading witness in government cases in the region's federal courts where he took "an emphatic and unequivocal position as to the necessity for cost protection prices as part of the Lumber Code and for their present maintenance." Greeley said he could not go along with the reversal of policy.

"To do so," his letter read, "would require me to retract from the position which I have taken repeatedly during the past eighteen months."

Demarest felt likewise, stating that "I cannot turn against my associates on the Lumber Code Authority or the many fine people in the government departments who have worked so hard and gone so far to give the lumber industry price protection."

The board accepted Demarest's resignation and named F. R. Titcomb of the Weyerhaeuser Timber Company to fill out the term, but Greeley was another matter. The board tabled his letter of resignation and told him to take a thirty-day vacation. Nothing more was done, apparently, and Greeley stayed with WCLA.

Yet the roaring against the hateful Lumber Code and the NRA grew louder. The minimum price business was called an economic mistake, a "subversion of justice" and "a canker sore of dishonesty in our industry."[7] A survey questionnaire sent out by WCLA and the government showed that West Coast lumbermen thoroughly disliked the regulations, and President Titcomb observed that in the pine industry, from fifty to sixty per cent of production was by-passing Lumber Code regulations. As in the days of Prohibition, the lumbermen and other frustrated manufacturers were forced into law-breaking under restrictions they could not adhere to. But it ended abruptly when the Supreme Court ruled unanimously that the NRA was unconstitutional. It was a joyous day for the lumbermen, and few if any delayed very long in removing the hated Blue Eagle from their own and WCLA letterheads.

That same month of May 1935 the lumber world was shocked by the kidnapping of nine year old George Weyerhaeuser, great grandson of the founder of the big timber company, as he walked home for lunch from school in Tacoma. It was one of a wave of celebrated kidnappings of the 1930's, among them the Lindbergh and Mattson cases.

Young George was grabbed by strangers on the street and stuffed into a car with a blanket covering him. At times he was placed in the trunk where he rode for hours as the car and his abductors eluded the road blocks. He was led blindfolded through woods, on logs across creeks where he feared the strangers would drop him in, and then came the terror of being chained and placed in holes in the ground with only a kerosene lamp for warmth . . . of being hidden for many hours in a stuffy, black closet in Spokane . . . of not knowing what they would do with him. . .

Meanwhile, authorities were combing the Pacific Northwest, indeed all the West, for the kidnappers. The days and nights dragged on, the kidnappers made their contact with George's father and $200,000 ransom was paid. Seven days later, the curly-headed boy knocked at a farmhouse door at Issaquah a few miles east of Seattle and declared to the astounded owner that he was the boy everyone was looking for. He had been turned loose during the night, given a blanket for warmth, and a one dollar bill had been stuffed in his pocket.

The kidnappers — Harmon Metz Waley, his wife Margaret, and William Dainard, alias William Mahan — were soon apprehended and most of the ransom money recovered. They were tried, convicted and sentenced to long terms at McNeil Island federal penitentiary. [8]

While the end of the NRA and the Weyerhaeuser kidnapping made sensational headlines, something else was happening to the timber world. The NRA had left a legacy, somewhat paradoxically, in what proved to be the "sleeper" of the Lumber Code. This was the Greeley-inspired Article X which called for a combined effort by the industry and the public agencies for "conservation and sustained production of forest resources." It had been shoved into the background during the hurricane happenings around wages, prices and production, forgotten by nearly everyone but Colonel Greeley, for this was near and dear to his heart.

Actually, work under Article X was begun in March 1934 when the West Coast Lumbermen's Association and the Pacific Northwest Loggers Association created a Joint Committee on Forest Conservation. C. S. Chapman of Weyerhaeuser was named chairman. Arthur K. Roberts of WCLA was named secretary. Other committee members were: C. G. Briggs, Booth-Kelly Lumber Company, Eugene; E. T. Clark, Monroe Logging Company, Everett; Carl Davis, Powers-Davis Logging Company, Marshfield; D. S. Denman, Crown-Willamette Paper Company, Seattle; G. L. Drake, Simpson Logging Company, Shelton; F. D. Hobi, North River Logging Company,

Great forest fires long plagued the timber lands. Colonel Greeley and other WCLA leaders
knew forestry advancements couldn't be made until the fire problem was licked.

Aberdeen; A. R. Watzek, Crossett Western Company, Portland; and
John B. Woods, Long-Bell Lumber Sales Corporation, Longview. [9]

The committee worked out a detailed program of conservation and betterment of conditions in the forests, covering fire
prevention and hazard reduction, cooperation over insects and
disease, conservation of young growth, restocking and reseeding,
selective logging, industrial management and sustained yield. A rule
book of forest practices was published and distributed to the industry. The committee hired Russell Mills, who was in charge of
logging engineering at the University of Washington's college of
forestry, to head up the program. Mills was to have three assistant
foresters working in the field — Kenneth M. Murdock, Eugene
district; Erwin H. Rengstorff, Portland district; and Warren G. Tilton, Seattle district. Twenty-nine Washington wardens and nineteen
Oregon wardens were brought into the program to help carry on
the inspections.

These forest practice rules went considerably beyond the existing laws in Washington and Oregon. In the early stages this
became a matter of patient education by the Joint Committee
staffers in preventing fires through hazard reduction, spark ar-
resters on locomotives and other motorized equipment, full shutdowns
during dangerous low-humidity weather, increased patrols, and other
precautions. It took some doing and a heap of temper-holding to
bring some itinerant operators into line, but this was gradually
accomplished through a momentous selling job on the part of the
Joint Committee people, and the staffs of WCLA and the Pacific
Loggers association.

In that very first summer the patrols were able to clamp down hard on maverick logging and mill operators who refused to obey the fire regulations set up under the Lumber Code. Cases were brought into federal courts for enforcement. However, it was generally felt that in the area of fire prevention, the code worked well during this initial season, proving its worth. In the first nine months, 434 operations were covered by 650 visits of foresters, 143 were checked twice or more, and the total of inspections represented fifty per cent of all the operations and eighty-five per cent of the total production.

Then the U. S. Supreme Court ended the NRA. What was to be done with the Joint Committee and the widespread and effective progress already made in the industry? Was this all to be dumped? What happened, in view of the general attitude toward the NRA, was little short of amazing. In June 1935 the industry decided to continue the committee as a permanent activity of the two associations.

Article X, expanded and reshaped, became in essence the "law of the woods." The "Forest Practice Handbook" was rewritten in the plain language of the loggers and published by the industry with government foresters serving as advisers. Director Mills and his aides continued holding meetings with loggers up and down the coast. It was a new, strange world for the rugged lumberjacks, this going to school and being "talked at" by the foresters they once hated so vigorously. Now suddenly, with great fires like the Tillamook ripping away the supply and the center of the industry shifting from the Evergreen State to Oregon, with their backs against the sea, things that the foresters were saying made sense to the lumbermen.

The average logger and sawmill man began hearing many strange new terms — industrial forestry, sustained yield, selective logging, timber as a crop, fire prevention instead of protection. Lanky young college-educated men, filled with enthusiasm and a bright vision of tomorrow, were prowling the timberlands. What's more they were likable guys who could sling the bull with the best of 'em around a stout cup of black coffee in the bunkhouse or while crouched against a fallen tree. The name "forester" didn't seem like a dirty word any longer.

And the public which had been hollering for lo these many years, was to be charged with a great responsibility and given a job to do, to make the forests safe from fire for the timber of tomorrow.

NOTES TO CHAPTER XIII

1. *American Forests Magazine,* March 1958.
2. James F. Stevens, *American Forests,* January 1956.
3. WCLA annual reports, 1936-1938.
4. *Forests and Men,* by William B. Greeley.
5. *Lumber and Labor,* by Vernon H. Jensen.
6. WCLA board of trustees' minutes, 1934-1939.
7. *Timber and Men,* the Weyerhaeuser Story.
8. Waley was paroled in 1963, while his wife who drew a twenty-year sentence was released several years earlier. Dainard, who drew a sixty-year term, was still in prison in 1965. As for George Weyerhaeuser, he was one of the few kidnapped youngsters who was returned alive. Thirty years later, on the anniversary of the crime, he granted an interview to Don Duncan, *Seattle Times* columnist. He told Duncan that while he can vividly recall being grabbed, his parents treated him so normally following his return that it left no fears or other permanent scars. He and his family today live normal lives and the incident is not a subject of discussion. A scrapbook compiled by the family after his return has remained unopened. Weyerhaeuser rose in the family company and today is executive vice president of the firm bearing his name.
9. Named to the advisory committee were: C. J. Buck, Regional Forester, U.S. Forest Service, Portland; Thornton T. Munger, director of the Pacific Northwest forest experiment station, U.S. Forest Service, Portland; T. S. Goodyear, Washington State Supervisor of Forestry; Lynn F. Cronemiller, State Forester of Oregon; C. S. Cowan, manager, Washington Forest Fire Association; R. H. Chapler, manager, Oregon Forest Fire Association.

Chapter XIV
Keep the Land Green

On a warm summer night, a passing motorist flipped a burning cigarette into the edge of a young growing forest. Small flames were soon eating at the grass and low brush. They grew larger, moving upon the first trees.

Patricia Barnes, an eleven year old school girl, spotted the sudden ominous light across the open fields and shouted to her grandfather. He grabbed a shovel and together they rushed to the scene.

The man tried corralling the flames with the shovel, while Pat scooped up dirt with her hands and beat down sparks with her shoes. But the action did little good; the fire had the advantage of a low humidity and dry brush, and it was quickly apparent that grandpa would need more force or the fire would go on the rampage.

Wheeling around, Pat raced for home a quarter mile away. She loaded a stone sled with several five gallon cans of water and gunny sacks, climbed upon a small tractor she'd never run before, backed it around, hooked onto the sled and with grandmother clinging precariously to the carrier and shouting "Girl! I think you've gone crazy!" Pat took off across ditches, fields and roads.

Reaching the fire, they found grandpa fighting a losing battle. The three of them grabbed the gunny sacks, soaked them in water, and beat down the flames. Long past midnight the fire was controlled and the forest was saved. [1]

Pat Barnes won newspaper acclaim and a citation from the Keep Oregon Green Association through the Green Guards, of which she was an enthusiastic member and where she had learned how best to fight small forest fires. Throughout the Pacific Northwest in the turbulent years of World War II and the postwar age, countless thousands of volunteer Green Guards and Junior Forest Wardens began keeping their eyes on the woods in a massive movement that had a lasting impact unlike any that foresters had ever before dreamed up. Inspired by the spirit of the kids, parents and adults generally joined the crusade in what grew into an important and lasting segment of the American way of life. Yet it was the work with youngsters, who became adults, that paid off from the very beginning.

The movement enlisting public support to keep the land green began merely as a germ of an idea, coupled with a great need. The decade of the Thirties was one of terrible holocausts in the Pacific Northwest woods. Each summer vast areas of rich timber which would last for many years went up in smoke, filling the skies with awesome terror in the face of rapidly depleting timber stands. By far the worst was the terrifying Tillamook Fire showering ashes upon metropolitan Portland as some 311,000 acres (270,000 acres in 24 hours) went up in smoke and laid waste the land. Three years later there was again great tragedy and death to twenty-three persons in the burning of the coastal town of Bandon, which originated from slashing fires in low-humidity weather and spread into highly flammable Irish furze or gorse which grew heavily around the town.

While many such fires could be traced to maverick logging operations and a damned-if-I-care attitude, there was also a reckless indifference on the part of the public. People who had nothing to do with logging and lumbering were to blame for many disasters. In Oregon the average was 1,300 man-caused fires a year; Washington's problem was of a similar nature where 150,000 acres were burned annually. The public simply couldn't find offhand any particular reason to be careful with fire in the forests, and apprehending the guilty was nigh to impossible. The careless angler who failed to extinguish his warming fire was long gone by the time all hell broke loose and probably didn't even remember that he had left a fire burning. If he did, he'd certainly never admit it, even to his wife. Yet the cold hard fact was that the Northwest forests were being rapidly depleted. In the disastrous summer of 1938 alone, fire had burned more than 250,000 acres in Washington and Oregon in 2,500 separate fires. The majority of them were man-set.[2]

But getting the message across to campers, hunters, anglers, hikers, picnickers, berry pickers, small boys and other lovers of the outdoors was a challenge that seemed insurmountable. While annual statistics told a different story of the major cause of fire, people merely shrugged their shoulders and cursed the lumber industry. Having now been thoroughly indoctrinated on the need for perpetuating forests for the future, the lumbermen were becoming weary of always being the scapegoat for setting fire to the woods. Something hardhitting, of a grass roots nature, was needed to awaken the public to its responsibility.

In British Columbia where there had been some bad fires, the Canadian Forestry Association had been successful in projecting a fire prevention program through an organization called the Junior Forest Wardens. Youngsters proved much more conscientious than their elders and through them, Mom and Dad were reached. It was working in Canada; why not in Washington and Oregon?

In 1939 Colonel Greeley, Jim Stevens and other leaders within WCLA put their heads together and created a "Junior Forest Council of the Douglas Fir Region." Stevens, in many hours at his typewriter, worked out a solid outline for such a program involving the American Legion which was actively engaged in boys' work through such things as junior baseball leagues, Boy Scout troops, and its own Sons of the American Legion. A meeting was called of industry and public forestry leaders, who were enthusiastic over the scheme. State foresters Ted Goodyear of Washington and J. W. Ferguson of Oregon were elected co-chairmen, while the two state Legion commanders, John A. Beckwith of Oregon and Harry Lawton of Washington, held prominent positions on the committee. This board of advisers included Colonel Greeley; E. T. Clark, Pacific Northwest Loggers Association; C. S. Cowan, Washington Forest Fire Association; Hugo Winkenwerder, dean, School of Forestry, University of Washington; John B. Woods, Oregon Forest Fire Association; Earl G. Mason, acting dean, School of

—Oregon State Forestry Dept.
Busses brought thousands of youngsters to denuded areas to help plant new forests. Bundles of tiny seedlings were passed out. WCLA participated in many of these planting expeditions.

Forestry, Oregon State College; and Lyle Watts, regional forester, U.S. Forest Service. In the summer, the incoming Legion commanders, Arthur J. Hutton of Washington and Neil R. Allen of Oregon, were welcomed aboard.

Working with the Legion had many advantages. It would give the organization avenues into every area of the timber belt. The Legion was known to go all-out on projects it undertook, and the endorsement and support of this huge veterans organization could also bring widespread publicity. The influence and guidance of WCLA, its offices and services were also placed behind the project, and information director Jim Stevens was kept busy pacing this new approach to fire prevention.

The over-all aim was to encourage a variety of forestry projects among young people, through their existing organizations. Yet as the program got into full swing, there was a feeling that things weren't exactly right, that this wasn't enough. The Western Forestry Conference gathered that year in Portland, and during a banquet meeting of sponsors of the Junior Forest Council, several men who had daughters as well as sons raised the question:

"Why should a program of this kind be limited just to boys? Why not get the girls and everyone into the act?"

Forester Ted Goodyear said he'd take the matter up with his boss, Governor Clarence Martin of Washington. Roderic Olzendam, the public relations man for Weyerhaeuser Timber, gave Goodyear his blessing and began building interest among newspapers to devote more prominent space to forest fires and what might be done about them.[3] At the time, a forest fire of average size, even in this timber region, was given only a few paragraphs and pushed to an inside page, or wound up in the holdover type for the following day. Only disasters of appalling size made front page headlines.

Governor Martin was won over and early in 1940 called a key group of Junior Forest Council backers and others vitally interested to Olympia for an evening meeting to discuss the possibilities of broadening the Forest Council experiment, which had been mildly successful in its first year. The program, it was agreed, should be kept simple and honest, targeted at educating all the public on forest fire prevention. A modest budget of $5,000 was adopted, half to come from the state and the balance from logging, lumbering and pulp industries. Olzendam was appointed to head a steering committee consisting of Goodyear; Jim Stevens; Don Denman, Northwest regional manager of Crown Zellerbach; J.B. Fink, state director of conservation and development; Corydon Wagner of St. Paul & Tacoma, WCLA president; Edmund Hayes of Clackamas Fir Lumber Company, Portland, public relations chairman of WCLA; Russell Peters, managing editor of the

Seattle *Post Intelligencer;* Charles Cowan, chief of the Washington Forest Fire Association; George Drake, chairman of the industry's Joint Committee on Forest Conservation; and Colonel Fred M. Fuecker, adjutant of the Washington State American Legion.

Things were rolling along well this night as it was further decided that the program would be carried on largely through the office of the state forester. Then Governor Martin threw a wrench into the head rig.

"Just who is going to do the job?" he asked pointedly, for Martin knew men and their enthusiasm. "Who is to be responsible? We've got to have someone to carry the ball."

The room grew silent as the men looked at each other, suddenly speechless. All but Jim Stevens who had anticipated such a moment and was ready, awaiting the proper time to spring his surprise. He had long had someone in mind, for which this kind of fire prevention program seemed tailor-made. Stevens drew a deep breath and threw out the name—Stewart Holbrook.

Not allowing for comment, Stevens made his pitch. Holbrook was a natural, one of the industry's own who was known and liked throughout the Northwest timber region. He was a rugged, plain speaking, barrel-chested ex-logger who understood the woods and its people, and had emerged from the tall woods to make his way as a writer with a mounting outflow of magazine articles with a timber flavor. More lately, he had created a national sensation with his book *Holy Old Mackinaw,* the best selling history of the American lumberjack. He had published a second book, *Iron Brew,* and was working on a third back east about Ethan Allen, a Revolutionary war hero of his beloved native Vermont.

Stevens grew more enthused as he talked on about his fellow journalist. Hols Holbrook had been a top sergeant in France with the American Expeditionary Force of 1918. This would make him readily acceptable to the American Legion. But currently he was living off the campus of Harvard University where he occasionally guest lectured, an event which Holbrook throughout his life boasted good humoredly, identifying himself as "the only logger ever to lecture at Harvard." It would appear that the Northwest had lost this energetic author who had become the Boswell of the timber world and was a dynamo of enthusiasm and energy whenever he sat down to his typewriter. He had stature. Could he be wooed back to the Northwest—this man of many far-flung interests?

Stevens wasn't sure, but he was firmly convinced that here was the man who could put across this new crusade against forest fires. He knew his way around the timber towns and whatever form this crusade took, newspapers and radio stations were certain to eat up his copy, for Holbrook was a seasoned professional writer who set things down in a colorful and lively fashion that no

editor in his right mind could refuse. Lastly, he had distinct loyalties and if he believed in something, he would go all out in
its favor.[4]

Stevens stopped talking and looked at the Governor. Martin
didn't hesitate:

"I'll take him."

That excited Stevens, but now Holbrook had to be sold on
the idea and that might not be easy. Stewart could be gruff
and rough at times, if something didn't strike him right.

"Who's going to tackle Holbrook?" someone asked. No one
in the room seemed anxious to do so.

"I'll take care of him," replied Stevens, unafraid. Both men
were writers, men of the woods, and understood and respected
each other.

As the meeting broke, Stevens headed for his room. He was
still wound up and decided since it was only 10:30 he'd call
Holbrook before going to bed and get the answer.

The telephone in Cambridge, Massachusetts, rang a long while
and then Holbrook's voice came on.

Stevens explained that he wanted to phone him before bedtime to tell the good news. Holbrook sputtered, never at a loss for
words in a logger's rugged vernacular.

"Bedtime hell!" he roared. "It's nigh onto two o'clock in the
morning back here."

Stevens beat a hasty retreat, having completely forgotten the
time difference. The error might well cost the movement Holbrook's
talent and services. But the logger-author simmered down and
listened attentively to what Stevens had to say. Highly flattered
at being picked, he agreed to come West to fight forest
fires with his fertile brain and his trusty typewriter. The timing was
right, for he had completed his book and was missing the Pacific
Northwest.

"Nothing could please me more," Holbrook declared.

There was also the matter of a name for this crusade. "The
Junior Forest Council of the Douglas Fir Region" certainly would-
n't do. There was a need for something simple and catchy, and
Roderic Olzendam came up with the suggestion, "Keep Washington Green." The name may or may not have been original with
Olzendam, and it doesn't really matter. It was he who suggested
it for the Washington program. Years later, Stevens and Robert
Lyman of Keep Washington Green put a tracer on the phrase,
out of curiosity. They found that in 1925 Forester E.P. Cheney
of Minnesota published a small booklet on timber taxation bearing the title "Keep Minnesota Green." The term was also used
in the timberlands of New England, among them a "Keep Vermont Green" which was Holbrook's home state. Indeed, he may
have planted the idea in the minds of others. And Jim Stevens,

too, might have sparked the notion when he penned a parody on "Green Grow the Lilacs" for Ivar Haglund, folk singer and son of a local logger, who offered to Seattle listeners of KJR: *"All nature is praying, keep our forests green . . ."*

In any case, it was Keep Washington Green that took hold of the public imagination so that it eventually spread across the entire country.

When Holbrook returned to the Northwest, Governor Martin pinned a fire warden's badge on him, a banquet was held in Olympia in his honor, and the program was officially launched on June 6, 1940. The Governor proclaimed all-out war in the Evergreen State against forest fires.

Holbrook swung immediately into action with a volume of newspaper stories and good original material for radio stations. Stevens had been right. The ideas and material stemming from Holbrook's mill were professionally tops and readily acceptable by eager editors. His stories of fires and forests weren't publicity puffs, but hardhitting factual accounts that were something new in the timber world. He wrote radio shows and went on the air himself, for Stewart was a former actor and was as clever with the spoken word as the written one. He toured the lumber communities and talked to clubs and service organizations, and to gatherings of logging and lumbering people. Because he knew the woods, the people looked up to him as one of their own kind. His words had great impact where those of another might have been met with cynicism. He spoke the language, his words unadorned and unpretentious, striking a common chord of response everywhere, doing a plain job in a plain way without window dressing and ballyhoo. . .

WCLA backed the program with a $1,000 donation, as it did throughout its existence and with a matching amount a year later for an Oregon program. Other associations gave $1,400 and logging, lumbering and railroad operators $2,200. Pulp and paper companies pledged another $2,300. WCLA, through a broadside letter from Colonel Greeley, solicited funds from Washington business interests in the name of Keep Washington Green. Greeley placed the full strength of WCLA squarely behind the crusade, and donated its services and personnel. The Colonel and other West Coast leaders went into the field as ambassadors to mills and logging operations to preach Keep Green. The publicity department of Jim Stevens helped spread the word. It wasn't long before all of the Evergreen State had heard of the movement.

The American Legion expanded its work with the Junior Forest Wardens, using a WCLA-published "Manual of Junior Forestry" compiled through Stevens' efforts. The Legion assigned organizing duties to 146 "Forest Fire Marshals" who alerted their home communities at as many local posts.

The impact and originality of Holbrook's peppery typewriter began paying dividends with the enthusiasm it instilled. Plans were made for fifty billboards and distribution of thousands of pledge cards containing a code of fire safety. Newspapers were receiving almost daily news stories and editorials on fire prevention and were publishing these handouts at the rate of 700 to 1,000 column inches per week. A total of 160 newspaper editorials on Keep Washington Green were published by mid-July.

Not content to sit at a desk, Hobrook went out on the fire lines to write graphic descriptions, accompanied by photographs, which newspaper feature sections gobbled up. On one average fire which normally would have received only a few lines, the Seattle *Post-Intelligencer* published two "spot" stories by the lumberjack journalist with pictures, editorial and cartoon, embracing a full page of space.[5]

It paid off, in aces, spades and space which aroused the public to a responsibility that had never before occurred to the people. The figures spoke for themselves. In 1939 there were 1,516 fires set by smokers, campers, berry pickers and sportsmen which burned 20,716 acres and caused a property loss of $27,252. There were more fires, 1,870 in 1940 the first summer of KWG, but the burned area was reduced to 5,726 acres and the damage loss to $1,835. The overall total acreage burned from all fires was trimmed from 103,139 in 1939 to 40,633 the following summer and the average burned acreage per fire from 68 to 21.7 acres. In 1941 the total fires was cut to 1,562 and by 1942 this was down to 842 fires. The fires were smaller, too, what with the public alerted to the dangers.

It would indeed be difficult to argue that the Keep Washington Green movement wasn't paying huge dividends, almost at once. Following Pearl Harbor, with the increased danger of forest sabotage, the importance of the crusade took on even greater significance. But it wasn't a wartime activity and therefore had a permanency that would last.

Stewart Holbrook, to whom the crusade was to some degree a personal one, continued to grind out stories and colorful material for press, radio, newsreel and other communications from his typewriter, at $2,700 salary and expenses for five months' summer services. The battle also sparked an idea which resulted in 1943 in publication of another scoring book, *Burning An Empire*, dedicated to his longtime friend and associate in this movement, Jim Stevens.

The Washington crusade hadn't long been under way when Oregon lumbermen and foresters were shouting "me too." If Washington was to be kept green, Oregon must be kept greener. Edmund Hayes, an immediate past president of WCLA, brought the plan down to Oregon that same spring of 1940. In July Hayes,

John B. Woods and Nels Rogers, the new state forester who had just succeeded J. W. Ferguson, launched a modest program along the lines of Keep Washington Green. Governor Charles A. Sprague became interested at once and the following spring called 250 leaders together to organize the Keep Oregon Green Association. Dean Johnson of the C. D. Johnson Lumber Corporation of Portland and Toledo was named chairman of an impressive board of citizens, while Ed Hayes was picked as head of the executive committee to determine policy, generate ideas and work with one fulltime employee, a director hired the following year. As with Washington, financing the Oregon program came through the industry and private and public interests. Colonel Greeley also put WCLA behind the Oregon venture.

"We should think of the KOG and the KWG campaigns as much more than summer ballyhoo," Greeley wrote WCLA members. "They should grow into permanent means of public education. They have an important part in our industry program of forest conservation."

Keep Oregon Green signed on Richard Kuehner, an outstanding 4-H leader, as its first director. But World War II was on and Kuehner was called into the service. The KOG job fell to Charles Ogle, a veteran of fire protection work who held the position until 1948 when he resigned. Albert Wiesendanger, a 39-year veteran with the U. S. Forest Service, then stepped in as executive secretary. Wiesendanger had the boundless energetic enthusiasm likened to Stewart Holbrook in Washington and became Mr. Keep Green himself. He was still going strong in 1965 and over the years has built up one of the most active Keep Green programs in the nation.[6]

Keep Oregon Green borrowed from the Washington crusade and then reshaped things to suit the Beaver state's character and needs. A friendly rivalry took many forms, but the objectives were the same. To point up the fact that the great timber states were pulling together on fire prevention, Stewart Holbrook arranged a meeting between the two governors of these commonwealths, as he referred to them, at the state boundary above the Columbia River, midway across the Interstate Bridge between Portland and Vancouver. There was quite a crowd on the bridge that day, June 11, 1943, while the governors, Arthur B. Langlie of Washington and Earl Snell of Oregon, pledged mutual assistance in a forest fire emergency, tying up traffic far into Portland and Vancouver, which greatly thrilled Holbrook who always took a delight in disrupting the common flow of the affairs of men.

When Arthur W. Priaulx was hired in 1942 to handle public relations for WCLA in the Eugene area, the Keep Green movement was getting into high gear. Priaulx took an immediate and lasting interest in the crusade, especially the Green Guards which

Dick Kuehner had just proposed as a youth auxiliary to the adult activity, and thus became the third member of the hard-working Keep Green publicity team of Holbrook and Stevens. Kuehner was insistent that the Oregon Green Guards be more than just another young people's organization, that it be an activity adaptable to Boy Scouts, Girl Scouts, Camp Fire Girls, 4-H Clubs, Future Farmers, schools, churches and community service groups in either towns or rural areas.

A carefully timed news release was prepared by Priaulx for every newspaper and radio station in Oregon. The story invited every girl and boy between eight and eighteen to join the Green Guards. Kuehner worked up a Green Guard kit to send, containing a membership card, manual, arm band, gummed poster for the youngster's home and other things which would excite most every child.

Thousands of letters poured into Salem KOG headquarters. In desperation, Kuehner phone Priaulx at his Eugene home.

"For heaven's sake," the director pleaded, "don't send any more publicity stories out on the Green Guards. We've got 20,000 applications already and at fifteen cents a head, we'll soon go broke trying to pay our way out of this deluge of requests."

Art judged that a second story might well bury KOG beneath some 50,000 applications. Therefore he held back the release he was putting through his typewriter. Some time later when Kuehner went to war, he gave Priaulx a parting word of advice:

"If you're smart, you'll keep quiet about the Green Guard activity and let the kids pass it along by word of mouth."

Priaulx took the advice; in future years the only publicity given the movement was releases inviting youngsters to enter statewide poster and essay contests about forest fire prevention.[7]

Over the years hundreds of thousands of youngsters enrolled in the youth divisions of the Oregon and Washington Keep Green movements. They reported fires, quenched abandoned camp blazes with the knowledge learned from manuals and training sessions, voluntarily patrolled the woods, jumped on adults who thoughtlessly tossed lighted cigarettes, and took a personal interest in preserving forests and wild life. An annual youth Forestry Congress, still being held, was organized by KWG at the University of Washington's Pack Forest near Rainier National Park. A yearly Shelton Forest Festival had a Keep Green theme. Between 15,000 and 20,000 posters were judged annually from submissions of first to twelfth grade youngsters, with cash awards given in the different divisions. A crisis was reached one year when the many entries stored in a third floor room of Anderson Hall of the U. of W. campus where KWG had office space were discarded by an overly eager forestry professor seeking classroom space. The posters went to the university garbage dump just before final judging.

Green Guards and Junior Wardens of the WCLA-initiated Keep Green movement learned to appreciate the forests, and to protect them. The crusade begun in Washington and Oregon is now a national institution which helped greatly to whip the fire problem.

Facing disaster, KWG Director Bob Lyman and Bill Massey, his assistant, spent two anxious days of fragrant exploration with tractor and the help of two dump attendants, together with squawking seagulls, and at last exhumed the 20,000 posters so that they could be rated a week later.

Keep Green envoys are dead serious. When a Seattle youngster was caught playing with fire, he was ordered by his parents to turn in his badge and membership card. He wrote Smokey the Bear that he was sorry, but Smokey, showing little sympathy, replied that he would have to be placed on three months' probation before being reinstated. The lad learned his lesson.

Another boy discovered a fire too large for him to handle. He flagged down car after car along the highway until he had drafted a crew of about four men to follow him into the woods a short distance to put out the fire.

But the classic of all happened one night in Portland's huge wartime shipyards. About nine o'clock five Green Guards wearing badges and arm bands appeared at the admission gate. The thirteen year old captain, displaying his credentials, demanded admission for his crew "to inspect the yards for fire hazards." The youngsters were determined, for they pointed out that they had been commissioned by the Governor of Oregon to locate all fire hazards. Only after shipyard officials had exercised considerable diplomacy and even made a call to the State Capitol was the situation eased without loss of dignity to these faithful custodians of their state and nation.[8]

—Forest Industries

Nels S. Rogers, Oregon State Forester, planted the first small tree in 1945 which symbolized beginning of the rehabilitation of the Tillamook Burn. WCLA's Art Priaulx (center) was among those participating in the historic event. The Burn became giant tree farm.

The Keep Green movement grew each passing year and took many forms. People liked the crusade because it was free from politics, profit-taking, and complicated organization. It was something anyone could do on his own. The press liked its genuine human interest qualities and its honesty. Lumbermen and foresters were enthusiastic, for the movement had markedly reduced the number and size of forest fires.

The slogans caught the public fancy to the place where a candidate to the Oregon state senate had as his only ballot slogan "Keep Oregon Green" and won without even a race. The crusade and its catch name spread to other states, for it was found applicable anywhere. Two years after Washington and Oregon became the parent organizations, Indiana started a program. By 1949 there were twenty-two states with Keep Green movements of varying degrees. The American Forest Products Industries Inc. went one step further, developing *Keep America Green* as one of its drives for public education. By 1965 the movement was in thirty-six states, each crusade independently operated from the local level, with no complex national headquarters or dictation from higher-ups.

As the matter of forest preservation and wild life conservation became a serious national problem in the 1960's, the movement grew in significance. In some states like Washington and Oregon, it became a year-round activity, with youth groups even patrolling the forest against the wasteful cutting of Christmas trees. Now familiar slogans came to the fore-Smokey the Bear . . . Keep America Green and Clean . . . Don't Be a Litterbug . . . Use Your Ashtray . . . Don't Let Your Savings Go Up in Smoke . . . Only YOU Can Prevent Forest Fires.

But it was Stewart Holbrook's show all the way, for although he departed Keep Washington Green following four hard-working summers and rose to the heights as one of the nation's great author historians, he had set the pace and the patterns for others to follow. The Keep Green movement might never have gotten off the ground in such fine style had it not been for his efforts. Jim Stevens knew what he was talking about the night he made his sales pitch before Governor Martin.

NOTES TO CHAPTER XIV

1. The story of Patricia Barnes was one of Art Priaulx's favorites in his work for WCLA with the Green Guards, in which he retained a strong and lasting interest.
2. From news release No. 1, on the Junior Forest Council, by W.R. Melton, secretary, in WCLA files.
3. *How the Keep Green Movement Got Its Start* by James F. Stevens, also an interview with Stevens by the author, June 1965.
4. Stevens later wrote, "That was the only good sales talk I ever made in my life."
5. From WCLA information department release, in bound permanent files.
6. Howard Brier succeeded Holbrook as KWG director. Others have been M.P. Lazara, Richard D. Pardo, Donald F. Flora, Barney O. Furseth and Robert W. Lyman.
7. From the writings of Arthur W. Priaulx.
8. *Keep Green Pays Off* by William B. Greeley, *American Forests*, October 1949.

Chapter XV
Timber is a Crop

S ix months before the country was shocked into numbness, then
anger by Japanese planes over Pearl Harbor, a huge overflow
crowd gathered at Montesano, Washington, in the Grays Harbor
country where Wild Man John Turnow once roamed, to dedicate
the nation's first "tree farm."

Governor Arthur B. Langlie of Washington was there to perform the rites, naming it the "Clemons Tree Farm" for the early
logger, Charles H. Clemons, who harvested much of the region's
virgin timber. In his keynote address, Roderic Olzendam of the
Weyerhaeuser Timber Company, which was a major force behind
establishing this unique experiment in forestry, declared:

"Why 'tree farm'? The moment I say 'farm' there immediately
flashes in the mind of every person here a mental picture of
his own personal idea of a farm. A farm is an area where man
grows successive crops of corn, wheat, hay, oats and vegetables. We
cooperate with farmers because they harvest the crops that feed
the nation. Well, timber is a crop, just like any other crop, except that
it takes a longer time to grow a crop of trees. So why not talk about
and have tree farms?"

Olzendam's words would have had a ring of yesteryear to
men like the late George Long, Everett Griggs and old Sol Simpson who had way back in the roaring years maintained that "timber is a crop" to be harvested and regrown again for another
generation. Now at last, here it was — the Clemons Tree Farm—
130,000 acres of land of which 62,241 were committed by the Weyerhaeuser company to growing trees plus an additional 65,000 intermingled acres set aside by other timbermen and state and county
ownerships. Within ten years, the Clemons Tree Farm was expanded
to 327,000 acres, of which 154,861 were owned by the Big W.

Like the Keep Green slogan, the term "tree farm" had a
natural appeal for the public. As Olzendam said everyone knew
what a farm was. Inside of a decade and despite the wartime up-
sets of the industry, there were 23,250,950 acres of forest land
in twenty-nine states under certified tree farm management.

Stewart Holbrook was among the first to use the term in March 1929 when writing editorially about passage of the Oregon Forest Fee and Yield Tax Act. Holbrook in this instance called the logging operator a "tree farmer."[1] Colonel Greeley picked up the phrase for a 1931 magazine article entitled, "The Tree Farmer Gets a Chance." Gifford Pinchot used it in 1935 by stating: "Wood is a crop. Forestry is tree farming." But it was Chapin Collins, editor of the local newspaper, the *Montesano Vidette*, who truly sent the term on its way. Company foresters were asking how they could gain public understanding of what was being attempted.

"Call it a tree farm," Collins answered. "Put tree farm signs all over the place. People know what a farm is. They'll understand what you have set out to do."[2]

Not long after the Montesano event, the Joint Committee on Forest Conservation, which became the Industrial Forestry Association, and a special tree farm committee of the Willamette Valley Lumbermen's Association met in Portland, October 28, 1941, to begin studying the feasibility of recruiting public support of a "tree farm movement." They asked the National Lumber Manufacturers Association to start an "American Tree Farm League" on a national scale. The Joint Committee set up a system of certification whereby owners of private taxpaying forest lands from small woodlots on up took a firm pledge for long-range forest management of their properties. Under the program, the tree farmer would give intensive fire protection, supplying additional fire equipment, guards and lookouts. The committee defined the tree farm as an area, no matter what size, dedicated "to the continuous production of forest crops." It must be protected not only from fire, but tree disease, insects and excessive grazing. The owner often appeared before the committee to satisfy it of his plans for growing trees. A committee forester inspected the farm prior to issuing a tree farm certificate.

Other things paved the way for the tree farm movement which, like Keep Green, would sweep the nation. Fire and land taxation had long discouraged the industry from retaining its cutover lands. To grow a new forest was too risky from the fire hazards alone, and too expensive in taxes. Washington and Oregon managed to ease their tax laws; Washington in 1931 when a law was passed taxing regrowing and cutover lands on a bare land assessment, coupled with a yield tax on any future crop at the time of harvesting. Oregon followed suit and this was encouragement for the lumberman and for the future of timber. There were good prospects for licking the evil above all other—fire—with better protection regulations, stricter laws and rules against logging operations. The West Coast Lumbermen's Association kept a weather eye on the barometer and hygrometer in summers to issue

warnings when conditions were critical. There were the early suc-
cesses of the Keep Green campaign. Trees would come back rapidly if given the opportunity, and fire kept out of them, in this
cool and rainy climate.

Long, Griggs, Mark Reed and other dedicated leaders of WCLA
had blazed the trails decades before. In 1909 Long founded the
Western Forestry and Conservation Association which became a
clearinghouse for all things pertaining to forest protection and practical timber growing.

"Help lumbermen with forest fires and forest taxes, and they
will find a way to regrow the timber," Long had told U.S. Congressmen. "We are exceedingly anxious to get into this reforestation game. We realize the necessity for it very keenly; and out
here where the West ends, we want to begin to grow a new
forest and will do it when we have the slightest chance of making it a profitable enterprise."[3]

Major Griggs had a lifetime pride in his industry and a concern for its future. Although among the old-timers, he never accepted the cut-out-and-get-out philosophy. He refused to default
his lands for taxes, believing wholeheartedly that the manufacture
of lumber and growing of timber were all one enterprise. Major
Griggs asked the Western Forestry and Conservation Association
to study and classify his lands; he later hired one of their men
as a company forester and with great enthusiasm tramped the
forests to study the reforesting and growth rates. He instilled this
same enthusiasm in his employees for St. Paul & Tacoma's long-
range planning, and put school boys and settlers to work planting trees. He aimed at youth activities to teach youngsters a healthy
respect for young forests. Some of this land became the Tomolla Tree
Farm for children, developed by Mary Lea Griggs. On highways and
back roads, notices were posted that "new forests are growing here."
By 1933 when Major Griggs retired, the company's original holdings
had been blocked out to 70,000 acres, constituting one of the most
productive tree farms in the Pacific Northwest.

A third man had such vision. He was Mark Reed of the
great Simpson Logging Company. A native of Olympia, Reed took
a job as foreman for the logging company under Sol Simpson and
his partner, Alfred H. Anderson. He rose to general manager of
the company's mercantile, logging and shipping interests and then
stepped into the presidency in 1916 when Anderson died. But
Reed and his predecessors held a common view in belief in the
land. They kept the cutovers and through the companies they set
up merged them into protection units.

Reed was a community builder in the development of Shelton to a fine industrial town, he and his associates presenting
the onetime rough settlement with such facilities as a hospital,

high school, library and memorial building. The pattern became clear—back of the community was the broad base of a forest industry and behind the industry a perpetual forest. Reed hired a forestry-trained engineer from the U.S. Forest Service as logging superintendent and asked him to work out a permanent forestry program. Buying land from his neighbors, Reed developed 150,000 acres to growing trees. He teamed with George Long in writing the early Forest Code of Washington and for seventeen years in the legislature worked hard to put into law the practical methods of conservation be learned in the woods.

Scattered throughout the tall timber in Washington and Oregon were others who looked behind the daily business of falling trees. Many were unknowns who failed to rise to any public notoriety as business executives or in public leadership. Rough hands of lumberjacks and lumbermen were setting out seedlings as early as 1905, experimenting with selective logging, going along with the strange ideas of the "bug men" foresters, starting "tree farms" long before there was such a term. Up in The Harbor country before World War I, the rugged Polson brothers, Alex and Robert, tried to find ways of handling logging slash that would encourage a new forest. When fire broke loose where there were little trees, their own loggers collected cones and scattered tree seed on 2,600 acres. This evolved into the 84,000 acre Polson tree farm in the historic timber area where there are more tree farms than just about anywhere else. Despite the charges by the public and politicians, many outwardly tough lumbermen and loggers had a deep love for the great woods.

The temper of the woods was changing and there were many signs of it as the tree farm movement got under way. In spring 1941 the Oregon legislature passed the nation's first forest reseeding law which Stewart Holbrook observed[4] was "not just another attempted crackdown by government on the lumber industry which often and many times has served as a whipping boy for the federal administration since 1933." The law was proposed and written by the loggers and lumbermen themselves, working closely with agricultural and ranching interests and based on longtime practical experience. Its basic aim was to control the irresponsible minority who clung to old-fashioned cut-out-and-get-out ideas; and it provided that the state would have police power over all logging operations, requiring in the Douglas fir belt that not less than five per cent of the original stand be left for seeding, and in the pine country, all trees under sixteen inches in diameter. It was significant that Oregon had enacted the first such law, for the Beaver State had now exchanged places with the Evergreen State as the nation's leader in lumber production with an annual cut of some 4,500,000,000 board feet. The center of lumbering was shifting south, for the big timber to which Henry Yesler, Nicholas Delin, George Bush, and the Popes and Talbots had first thrilled eighty years before was now a faded thing from Puget Sound.

Soon Washington too had a law. The West Coast Lumbermen's Association helped its members and non-members in the new movement and launched a program of promoting tree farms. The people of Oregon voted a $10,000,000 bond issue to erase the awful scar of the great Tillamook Burn, of which they were very conscious since it was handy to large population centers and received much publicity. The objective was to turn the Burn into a vast tree farm and outdoor forest laboratory which the industry was helping to finance. Experiments would be conducted in fire prevention, rodent eradication, snag falling, hand-planting of seedling trees, and the use of other new seeding methods, including planting by helicopter. These experiments, if successful, would be of benefit to all the timber world. But first and foremost as always, fire had to be eliminated.

In a few years the six-year fire "jinx" was broken in the Burn and small green trees, including thousands from the industry's Nisqually Nursery, were rising above the vine maple, to be exclaimed about by motorists driving to and from the beaches. By 1965, the Tillamook Burn was well on the way to being renamed the Tillamook Forest, living proof that man can indeed replenish his timber.

In September 1941, WCLA rounded out the tree farm movement by establishing, along with forest landowners, a twenty-acre industrial nursery on the Nisqually flats, eight miles north of Olympia on old Hudson's Bay Company lands and near where rugged sawmill men cut some of the first rough lumber for shipment a century ago. Corydon Wagner, WCLA president from St. Paul & Tacoma, announced that the $200,000 nursery was planned to produce at least 5,000,000 trees annually and that contracts were already on hand for 21,500,000 trees, representing over eighty per cent of the nursery's capacity for the next five years. In these beds would grow annually 5,400,000 Douglas fir seedlings, 440,000 Port Orford cedar, 60,000 Western hemlock, and 130,000 Sitka spruce. The latest scientific methods would be used to grow the trees and there would be much pioneering in the growing of young trees.

The Nisqually Nursery was the brainchild of WCLA President Wagner, who had first suggested the idea to the trustees and gained their enthusiastic approval. It was spurred forward when the Weyerhaeuser people agreed to close their own nursery at Snoqualmie Falls and buy seedling stock from the cooperative nursery. Forester W. G. Tilton, veteran conservation director of WCLA and the Pacific Northwest Loggers group, was given the appropriation and told to get the land ready, a site carefully picked from test borings which showed it to be exceedingly well suited for such a purpose. By the following January, $60,000 cash outlay had been made for the nursery.

The nursery became a prideful contribution by Major Grigg's nephew to the industry in which he also had a celebrated career. A graduate of the Yale School of Forestry, Wagner was first employed in St. Paul & Tacoma logging camps and rose to vice president and treasurer of the big lumber firm of the Griggs family. His part grew in WCLA activities, working as chairman of the trade promotion committee, trustee, treasurer and then president. He also served as a director and on the forest conservation committee of the NLMA. Forestry came to be a prime interest for him as chairman of the Joint Committee and as adviser to the American delegation to the World Forestry Congress at Helsinki, Finland, then to India and Switzerland as a delegate in later years, and vice chairman of the American delegation when the Congress came to Seattle in 1960. He became president of the National Lumber Manufacturers Association, the American Forest Products Industries, and the Western Forestry and Conservation Association, but the Nisqually Nursery, which later was named honoring the memory of Colonel Greeley, was Wagner's lasting legacy to the timberlands.

The Nisqually Nursery proved a great success, expanding within a few years to have some 8,000,000 seedlings under the watchful eye of Earl McDermitt who became superintendent, a farmer of some thirty-five years' experience growing every kind of crop. In eight years he grew some 32,000,000 seedlings for the forest industry. By 1950 the nursery had developed a "super race" of Douglas firs through a new policy of certified seed to assure superior trees by artificial reforestation.

The growth of the nursery was reflected in the enthusiasm of William D. Hagenstein, the forester protege of Colonel Greeley who guided him in his early years with WCLA. Hagenstein succeeded Tilton as forest engineer of the Joint Committee in 1948, following Tilton's death. He had worked with Tilton for many years and grew up with the tree farm movement. The lumbermen felt that his appointment was significant to the uninterrupted progress of the tree farm and industrial forestry systems. As Hagenstein took charge, the Nisqually Nursery yielded its largest crop to date—9,735,000 seedlings. Millions of trees were going out to companies and to the reforestation of the Tillamook Burn, where groups of school, church and club young people were traveling, organized through the efforts of WCLA's Art Priaulx, to plant trees on the rugged hill sections set aside for them. There was dedication, too, of an area of the Burn for the late Orville R. Miller, a leading Oregon lumberman and WCLA president, who had envisioned the day the Burn would be green again.

The Northwest tree farm movement gained with each passing year, from twenty farms of 1,620,533 acres in 1942 to 628
certified farms in 1960 for a total spread of 5,872,564 acres. The
peak single year was 1956 when one hundred new farms were
certified. One of the great bulwarks of the movement was un-
foreseen, the growth of the farm wood lot which surpassed in
total acreage the tree farms of the timber companies.

By 1950 the tree farm movement had spread to twenty-nine
states and covered 22,000,000 acres. There was a new slogan, too,
"Trees for America" which created additional public attention to
this new age in forestry. It furthered cooperation between government and private industry in the field of permanent forestry,
most notably in the sustained yield agreement under Public Law
273 between the historic Simpson Logging Company at Shelton,
Washington, and the U. S. Forest Service, which Colonel Greeley
hailed as true progress in *"the conception of cooperative forest
management by our government and its citizens, long dreamed by
forestry leaders."*

By mid-year 1965 in the forty-eight continental states, there
were 28,573 farms covering 65,615,850 acres. In the Pacific North-
wes's Douglas fir region, where there are 26,000,000 acres of well-
stocked forest land, there were 788 tree farms representing 6,801,030
acres. Largest of them all was one of over 500,000 acres near
Mount St. Helens. The smallest was one acre. In Oregon there
were 489 farms (4,836,541 acres) and in Washington 770 farms
(4,553,974 acres); 336 farms (2,995,555 acres) in western Oregon and
452 (3,805,475 acres) in western Washington. However, neither of
the two big timber states from which the tree farm movement
sprang paced the nation, although they remained high on the list.
Georgia was first with 2,240 farms representing 7,286,093 acres,
while Alabama was second with more farms, 2,463, but fewer
acres, 6,854,089. The nation's biggest single tree farm was in
Maine, a whopping spread of 1,408,000 acres, owned by the Great
Northern Paper Company. The second largest was in Florida, more
than 800,000 acres. This shows how the tree farm movement has
grown in twenty-five years. [5]

But Vermont, where there are today 133 tree farms spreading
across 265,472 acres, stole the march on the Pacific Northwest.
In June 1965 a tall handsome woman from Portland, Oregon,
joined John H. Hinman, chairman emeritus of the International
Paper Company, in the unveiling of a bronze plaque at dedication
ceremonies for a 33,000-acre Vermont tree farm. It was named
for her husband, Stewart H. Holbrook, who had died the previous
autumn in Portland, a continent away from his native homeland. Now
the memory of him was secure, not only in his many books but in
these green forest acres. It was the first time in the history of

the woods that a journalist was so honored, but it was entirely proper for this bard of the lumber world.

"It seemed appropriate," declared Hinman, "that the man who coined the phrase 'Tree Farm' be honored by the dedication of a tree farm in his name".

NOTES TO CHAPTER XV

1. James Stevens gives Holbrook full credit for coining the term, and Stevens did much research to trace its origin. George Peavy, dean of the school of forestry, Oregon State College, declared that "forestry is tree farming" in the *4 L Lumber News* in 1928. There appears to be some controversy over its origin.
2. From *Forests and Men* by William B. Greeley.
3. Colonel Greeley, writing in *American Forests*, April 1945.
4. Writing in the New York *Herald-Tribune*, April 6, 1941.
5. Report of the Industrial Forestry Association, and from John Benneth, West Coast manager, American Forest Products Industries, Portland.

Chapter XVI
Uncle Sam Changes the Rules

I n the Thirties it was great sport to attack the lumber industry by printed and spoken word. President Roosevelt set the stage with his remark on the Olympic Peninsula about the lumberman "roasting in hell." Charges were hurled from a far-flung variety of sources about the industry's hell-for-leather ways and cut-out-and-get-out philosophy — in newspapers, syndicates, national magazines, textbooks and government publications. It was part of the build-up for federal capture of private enterprise by those of the Roosevelt administration — a general attack on all business.

Jim Stevens compiled a WCLA "hell book" of the terms used to defame the industry — ruthless wreckers . . . dissipaters of wealth . . . unrestrained money-mad men . . . timber butchers . . . pseudo-conservationists . . hogs at a trough . attacking and razing the woodlands . . . devastation . . . unrestrained tree slaughter . . . scars upon the countryside . . . skeletons of abandoned mills . . . vast mounds of blackened sawdust . . . desolate clearings . . . great hordes of wretched children . . . place of ghosts . . . [1]

"It seems to be a common occurrence these days for somebody to take a verbal left hook at the lumber industry," stated the Portland *Oregon Journal*. "As a result, the plank makers have their dukes in the air most of the time, waiting for the next one."

WCLA President Wagner described the smears as a "mass of adverse material circulated by all the various media to discredit our industry with the American public."

Private enterprise as a whole was being placed on trial, and not merely in the nation's press. Early in 1939 there were rumblings that there would be a federal investigation of the practices of the lumber and building trade industries on the matter of monopoly. The Federal Trade Commission was demanding to see WCLA books and records for another investigation into the activities of the Hardwood Institute. The appointment of Thurmond Arnold as assistant attorney general of the United States, in charge of the anti-trust division of the Department of Justice, was a storm signal of more vigorous prosecution of the monopoly laws.[2]

Arnold was well fortified with a large appropriation and field staff of examiners and lawyers which began by investigating restraints on competition, allegedly causing an increase in the cost of home building. His targets were "phony building codes" which covered competitive advantages for particular industries, union labor restrictions, arranged bids, restrictive agreements between unions and contractors, plain price-fixing and other practices that would allegedly restrain competition and disrupt the recovery of building and in particular, the great and important field of low-cost housing.

"His program should clean home building of many barnacles," commented Colonel Greeley to the WCLA membership.

Greeley defended Arnold as being "thoroughly sincere; devoted to free competition as the only effective protection against extensions of government regulations and control." But Greeley realized that Arnold's investigations would do his industry no good. He described Arnold as dramatic, given to exaggeration, and extremely vocal in speeches and newspaper interviews — the kind of stuff that makes black headlines.[3]

The following January, the federal investigators showed up in Seattle to examine the WCLA files. They were allowed to do so under the watchful eye of Counselor Paul and without restrictions other than that WCLA be given duplicates of any material copied for use in a trust investigation. The FBI men reported that they could find nothing of "particular interest" on which to hang a case. However, they did show some special interest in the WCLA sales managers meetings. This appeared strange to the attorneys and WCLA officials until they learned of an indictment and "consent decree" by the federal government against the Southern Pine Association. More than half the consent decree agreement, which was something of a surrender to federal accusations or yielding without a fight to government will, concerned the pine association's grade marking activities and the necessity for separation of these functions from its trade promotion. This came as a surprise to the WCLA leaders, since nothing had been said earlier about grade marking. However, this certainly explained the interest of the federal investigators in the WCLA sales meetings. The matter came up again as the government men prowled through the records of the National Lumber Manufacturers Association and went into conference over issuing a consent decree.

Officials of WCLA began taking another look at their way of doing things, in the light of the Southern Pine decree, with the fervent hope that they could settle matters with anti-trust division representatives by conference, thus avoiding indictment and possibly a court trial. The trustees voted to set up a panel of six attorneys, so serious had the matter become.

The touchy areas seemed to be grading and inspection services, alleged price-fixing and production controls, and policies of distribution. It was assuredly a paradox, for only a few years before, under the NRA Lumber Code, the industry was forced to do these very things; now they were in danger of federal prosecution on the grounds that they were breaking the anti-trust laws. The charges would apparently be that WCLA was controlling prices through its grading and inspection system, thus shutting out non-members, although Attorney Ralph King observed that the association "has always taken an unbiased attitude between its own inspection service and the Pacific Lumber Inspection Bureau." The consistent practice of sales managers meetings was also dangerous, attorneys believed, since these meetings might unwittingly bring about some kind of price control, where one company's salesman might match the price of his competitor as a result of what was heard at a sales gathering.

The Western Pine Association and seventy-nine individual manufacturers were indicted under the federal investigation. Evidence was heard in June before the federal Grand Jury in San Francisco where there were references to "improper grading." All the while, federal men were probing the WCLA files and in September came a subpoena to produce records for a Grand Jury hearing in Los Angeles within a few days.

Paul wrote Tom C. Clark, one of the federal anti-trust division attorneys, attempting to work out an agreement that would avoid any criminal proceedings, since these lumbermen assuredly weren't "criminals" in the common definition of the word, although they would appear to be so in the public's eyes, the way the newspapers were playing the investigations. Paul suggested also that the case be turned into a civil suit and that it be removed from Los Angeles to the Pacific Northwest because a massive national defense program was on the move and the lumbermen were operating long hours trying to meet the demands of Uncle Sam. But Arnold and Clark refused, maintaining that the place for a trial was in a large lumber-consuming area. They seemed determined to make an example of the industry, writing Paul that they couldn't go along with the suggestion that settlement be made with "simply a consent decree."[4]

Out of the 220 WCLA member companies, sixty-six firms and twenty-five individuals including Colonel Greeley, all the WCLA officers and key employees were indicted by the Grand Jury on charges of anti-trust wrongdoings, especially in the matter of combining grade marking with trade promotion and the shutting out of non-members from receiving the same benefits. The charges were virtually the same for all cases as were the indictments involving other lumber trade associations: that since 1935 the lumber companies, individuals and the associations had willfully endeavored to "restrain trade through combining and conspiring," and that in concert, the organizations and individual lumbermen had violated federal anti-trust laws by fixing prices, curtailing production and adopting arbitrary rules. Arnold and his aides felt they had a good case against WCLA, one that would stick, based on their findings against the more aggressive Southern Pine people.

There was a great gathering of the indicted lumber leaders and their attorneys in Seattle, including Dr. Compton of the NLMA, to decide whether or not to go for a consent decree which would indeed appear to be an admission of guilt and place the industry under a form of government control. Some lumber leaders felt they should fight the cases down to the wire. There had to be an immediate decision, since letters from Clark said that "the government was getting impatient." A conference between the rivals in San Francisco promised that there would be only "minor fines" other than against the association, and that many of the members would not be subject to any fine at all. Attorney Paul later expressed the belief that the promises were never "fully carried out."

Several WCLA attorneys headed by Charles Paul — among them were John Ambler, Mark Mathewson and William Askren — went to Los Angeles to see about negotiating a consent decree. There were still aspects of this case that they feared might go against them, especially regarding the sales manager meetings where prices were discussed and may have innocently appeared in brief reports or filed memorandums on the meeting activities.

For another thing, a Portland lumberman — who shall go nameless here — of a pioneer sawmill company had become embittered with the association. He made accusing statements to federal investigators involving grade marking which was the kind of evidence the trust-busting attorneys were seeking, even if given as vindictive revenge against WCLA. The lumberman made these accusations before the Grand Jury and they were forceful enough, although Paul and the others never learned their content, to bring the case to trial.

Paul asked to go over the voluminous material the government had gathered as "evidence."

"As far as I know, there is not enough evidence to justify a criminal indictment," Paul told Clark.

The next four days were spent in hard-headed examination of the three drawers of papers. The government was primarily after big game with the leading lumber companies, but Paul found nothing of a serious nature among the papers of Weyerhaeuser and Long-Bell.[5] But when he turned to the files of a large northern Washington company, presently not a member of WCLA, his fears came alive. Their sales manager had gone to WCLA sales gatherings. Penciled in on the WCLA mimeographed notice of a meeting were such phrases as "agreed to go up a dollar," "down a dollar," and similar statements. This was damaging, not only against the lumber company but against WCLA.

Paul headed straight for Seattle and called a meeting of fourteen lawyers involved in the case. It appeared that while there were no set agreements at the sales meetings, the obvious intent of this particular sales manager was to learn what others were doing, then advise his company so they could undercut the figure if possible. This brought WCLA and the indicted members to the wall; the attorneys agreed to a man that, distasteful as it was, they should go for a consent decree.

Over a period of months and several drafts, the form of the consent decree was worked out, aimed at breaking down the services and system of doing business by WCLA for its members as being monopolistic. The final decree limited "the defendants (WCLA), their members, directors, officers, agents, employees, their successors, and all persons acting under, through or for the defendants or their successors, or any of them, be and they hereby are perpetually enjoined and restrained from agreeing, combining or conspiring among themselves or with any other individual, association or corporation . . . " from alleged monopolistic practices. The decree barred the association from limiting the manufacture, volume and sale of lumber; the allocation of business; the fixing or stabilizing of prices; promoting or securing raising, lowering or fixing the amount of production, or disclosing transactions of one company to a competitor; to restrict or attempt to restrict the sale or distribution of lumber to any certain group of purchasers; to gather, compile and disseminate information on production volume and shipments unless made readily available to all who might be interested; and other things which the government considered violations of anti-trust laws and which the association *had not been doing anyway!*

Key point in the decree involved the matter of grading, inspection and grade marking activities which the government contended were under the control of WCLA and closed out non-members from the benefits of a bonafide grading and inspection system, which was a guarantee of a seal of approval for lumber. The decree ordered that there could be no further trade promotion activities connected with grading. The association was directed, within six months, to set up a "West Coast Bureau of Lumber Grades" which would be under the direction of an executive committee comprised not only of WCLA members but a proportional representation from non-member mills, and that non-members could also become "inspection subscribers." In other words the bureau was to be completely separated from the association, its services and grade mark approval available without discrimination so long as the standards were met. WCLA was thus put out of the grading business.

The association was allowed to continue its weekly barometer and other summary reports, so long as these were made available to anyone at a "reasonable charge," and the Department of Justice was given access on notice to all books, ledgers, accounts, correspondence and other records to check on compliance with the decree.

The case came before the federal court April 16, 1941, and by their pleas of *nolo contendere,* the defendants including six lumber associations denied any criminal intent as set down in the allegations. But fines were imposed totaling $107,000 and ranging from $500 to $5,000.

Colonel Greeley was angered by the fines implying that individual lumbermen were intentional lawbreakers.

"These men are not criminals," he cried.

Attorney Paul explained the defendants' viewpoint to the court:

"The defendants are not conscious of any violation of the anti-trust laws. Most business men have been faced with uncertainty about the application of the anti-trust act. Persons named in this indictment, I am sure, have done their best to comply with provisions of the act. We do not admit guilt, but in view of the national crisis we feel that these matters must be settled as they are being settled now."

President Wagner stressed in a special news story the fact that acceptance of the decree "is not an admission of wrongdoing."

"It is essentially an agreement to revise business practices in accordance with new rules of the game," declared Wagner. "The Douglas fir manufacturers have followed the rules of the game as they understood them. The federal courts themselves have been confused as to what the rules are. The government's own economic policy has been uncertain. In the days of the NRA, industry was compelled to do many things — then held to be in the public interest — which are now regarded as grounds for criminal indictment. Industry has had to determine its course in the face of a good deal of uncertainty and confusion. A recent decision of the United States Supreme Court, in the Madison Oil cases, seems to extend the Sherman Act to many situations which formerly were not supposed to come under it. The Supreme Court has changed the rules of the game for industry."

Wagner pointed out that the plea *nolo contendere* was a decision simply not to contest the charges which would mean long and costly litigation in a time when the WCLA energies were needed for the national defense effort.

"We have concluded to play the game in accordance with the new rules," Wagner concluded. "We do this without any consciousness of willful violation of law. The cooperative activities of the West

"Timber is a crop," far-sighted lumber leaders of WCLA long maintained. The tree farm movement, begun in 1941 in Washington, by 1965 had spread to every state. This is a typical expanse of second growth timber on the Olympic Peninsula.

Coast lumber industry, built up around its association, have always been out in the open. Our grade marking, for example, was developed under government encouragement through the federal bureau of standards. Of course, the association had a selfish interest in promoting it — to make West Coast lumber more satisfactory to its users. This was one of the rules of the game — as everyone played it. Now the Department of Justice regards grade marking as so widespread and important to lumber users that its restriction to members of an association is monopoly. Like grade marking, our other activities have been carried out in good faith, to meet essential needs of West Coast lumber and without injury to the public. This was true of our industry meetings on trade conditions, of the efforts to keep supply and demand in reasonable balance, of the distribution of differential price lists and recommended shipping weights. We still believe that these services represented business progress; that they benefited the consumers of lumber as much as the manufacturers.

"*We shall play the new game in good faith; but we still maintain that nothing was wrong with the old one.*"[6]

Many business men and industrialists felt the same way, that the government's position after fostering the NRA system was ambiguous and *volte-face*. Later, when they had second thoughts, many lumbermen felt that they should have fought the case rather than accept the decree and pay the fines. But it might have been difficult, with the war coming on.

The six lumber associations involved were: National Lumber Manufacturers Association; WCLA and its subsidiaries; Columbia Valley Lumbermen's Association, Portland; Willamette Valley Lumbermen's Association, Eugene; Intercoastal Lumber Distributors Association, New York; and Lumber and Allied Products Institute Inc., Los Angeles.

The associations were fined $5,000 each, with a $4,000 fine suspended for the Los Angeles group. This meant $15,000 levied against WCLA and its subsidiaries, plus $9,000 against officers, trustees and employees, and $64,000 in fines against thirty association member lumber companies. Thirty-six cases against WCLA companies were dismissed or suspended, largely through efforts of WCLA representatives.

The WCLA board of trustees proposed to stockholders that the association pay not only the fines of its officers, trustees and employees, but reimburse the member companies since, President Wagner pointed out, "cooperative activities by and through the association were the cause for the government attack."

"It is wholly unjust that these companies alone should pay for the sins of the industry," Wagner wrote the WCLA stockholders.

Wagner added that it would be a "heavy load for the WCLA budget" but that it could be handled in a reasonable time. The stockholders agreed and WCLA picked up the tab. The entire affair cost the association a pretty penny, including attorneys' fees, and there were those who long regretted that the charges weren't fought. Following World War II, efforts were taken to gain some modifications of the decree, and although minor changes were made, it seemed that the decree would basically stand as it had been handed down. It caused difficulties where there should have been none; as one lumberman observed, the new rules made it "inconvenient because we couldn't talk to our competitors about things of general character which might have been helpful to everyone."

The consent decree had its lasting sting into 1965, since it still hangs over the industry. The rules of the game were indeed changed, apparently for all time.

NOTES TO CHAPTER XVI

1. Address by WCLA President Corydon Wagner at the January 1941 annual meeting at Tacoma, and also from the Lumber Industry Hell Book collection by James Stevens, WCLA annual reports, 1939-1941.

2. In relating the events and legal activities of this chapter, we relied heavily on the extended report-history of the WCLA consent decree written for WCLA in 1961 by Judge Charles H. Paul of Seattle, who was the association's legal counsel at the time.

3. Colonel Greeley, circular report to membership, July 31, 1939.

4. From the report of Judge Paul.

5. However, in *Timber and Men*, the Weyerhaeuser story, it is reported that investigators did uncover filed statements from their salesmen declaring, "We know what our competition is doing" which was taken literally by the Department of Justice, "when frequently (states the book) a salesman only *thought* he knew and the next morning was surprised to find what his competitor had really done. *Timber and Men* also says that letters were found calling a man a "chiseler" and this was taken by the FBI to imply he sold under an agreed price.

6. WCLA news release, April 1941.

Chapter XVII

The Forests Go to War

On a bright spring day of May 5, 1945, a group of young picnickers with a minister and his wife in charge hiked through the woods in the mountains above Bly, Oregon, east of Klamath Falls.

The pastor, Archie Mitchell of the Christian Alliance Church, drove the car around a road while the five youngsters and Mrs. Mitchell cut through the timber. The children spotted something hanging from a tree. They shouted to Mitchell as he drew the car to a halt. He yelled a warning, but it came seconds too late. The long arm of the enemy struck as one of the youngsters gave the object a tug. There was a violent explosion. All were killed except the pastor who rushed to the spot and stood frozen in horror until two foresters who also heard the explosion covered the bodies and led him away.

Newspaper reports under strict censorship said only that Mrs. Mitchell and five children were killed "by an explosion," but rumors flew through the countryside, spreading fear among loggers and campers. It was almost a month before Under Secretary of War Robert P. Patterson released the details and the Rev. Mitchell was allowed to tell his version to the public. The War Department wasn't anxious to let the Japanese know that their huge paper balloons carrying incendiary bombs were reaching American shores and had caused the deaths of several Americans. It would encourage them to an even greater effort.

The tragedy in Northwest timber country occurred just as hostilities were ending in Europe, resulting in the only fatalities from enemy action in the continental United States during World War II.[1]

Throughout the war the West Coast forests were under threat of attack by the Japanese who apparently placed a high premium on lumber and reasoned that to set fire to the great woods would cause a major disruption in war production. Submarines prowled the coast and shortly after Pearl Harbor the lumber freighter *Absaroka* was torpedoed only a few miles off the northern California coast. The 5,696-ton freighter had a gaping twenty-foot hole in her side, but she made it to port, her captain stating later that she would have sunk were it not for the lumber cargo.

In June 1942 a Japanese submarine attacked Fort Stevens at the mouth of the Columbia River, lobbing nine shells onto the sand dunes, but causing no damage. It was the first direct action by an enemy in over a century. Twice in September, small planes were launched from submarines offshore and dropped incendiary bombs into the woods. The first incident, September 9, occurred in broad daylight and was witnessed at Mt. Emily near Brookings by a forester who managed to extinguish the blaze and gather up fifty pounds of fragments of the one hundred fifty pound bomb. Then on September 29 at Cape Blanco, a second attempt was made to ignite the forests but it too failed.

Lookouts in their towers, loggers and forest patrols were alerted to watch for enemy planes. Then in 1945 the West Coast timberlands came under bombardment in the most bizarre experiment of the war conducted by the Japanese, the launching in their homeland of thousands of big paper incendiary balloons into the high air currents to drift across the Pacific Ocean and set fire to the American forests. The balloon barrage frightened people and officials; had they carried atomic warheads, they would have resulted in far greater anxiety. Many of the balloons didn't make the American shore, but enough of them did, coming down as far east as Michigan.

The balloons gave the men of the woods the jitters all that summer when the forests were tinderboxes, for a giant timber fire could be disastrous, not only causing a serious loss of war material, but pulling defense workers from their jobs to fight it, and soldiers from the army camps. Numerous fires were set, too, by traitors on the ground, but few got a good start; the high flying balloons were the biggest worry. That they were reaching the United states was known to authorities and many civilians, but was kept under strictest censorship. Each carried a weighty pay load of explosives and at least 225 balloons fell from Alaska to Mexico. One crossed the Pacific in a day and a half.[2]

The constant enemy threat to the forests was of concern to the leaders of the West Coast Lumbermen's Association. WCLA published instructions for dealing with incendiaries. Colonel Greeley gave public warning against the "menace of forest fire systematically planned and executed by the same sort of diabolical genius that directed the blitzkrieg in Poland and the attack on Pearl Harbor."

Long before Pearl Harbor, as the nation girded its defenses, the lumbermen felt that war would come as they listened to the deep-voiced reports "This is London" from one of their own people, Edward R. Murrow who along with his father once logged in the

woods of Washington State. A defense committee was set up by
WCLA to work with John Watzek Jr., representative of the
U. S. Defense Commission. Serving on the committee were John
D. Tennant, the Long-Bell Lumber Company; H. N. Anderson,
Olympic Hardwood Company; Everett G. Griggs II, St. Paul &
Tacoma; C. H. Ingram, Weyerhaeuser Timber; C. G. Kinney,
Clark and Wilson; C. H. Kreienbaum, Simpson Logging; W. B.
Nettleton, Nettleton Lumber; Charles Snellstrom, Snellstrom Lumber;
Orville R. Miller, Deep River Logging; and Corydon Wagner, presi-
dent of WCLA.

There were great scrap drives and it was quickly discovered
that there was a bonanza in scrap around sawmills and logging
operations. The building of cantonments was the first important
government order. The WCLA committee requested every West
Coast manufacturer to give U. S. orders priority on available and
future stocks. As the defense effort built up, it would take some
real organization on the part of the industry, similar to that accomplished by WCLA during World War I. Yet this was different,
so much vaster in potential. And among government officials and
private advisers there were expressions of doubt that lumber would
be needed in any great quantity to fight this "modern war" of
steel, iron and other metals. In two lists of twenty-nine critical and
strategic materials of the Army and Navy munitions board, lumber
did not appear and even Wilson Compton of the NLMA yielded to
the thinking, agreeing that "lumber is not a war industry."

Suddenly the picture changed as the British government placed,
early in 1940, a large order for aircraft lumber with Weyerhaeuser
Timber. There were forty-one types of British planes needing
wooden parts and Northwest mills hummed turning out the pieces
to specifications for Mosquito bombers and Hurricane fighters. As
the mobilizing continued, metal construction parts became scarcer
and the government turned to the centuries-old traditional material
of peace and war, lumber, to meet the needs. The Defense Advisory Committee announced a two billion dollar construction program. Wood-frame prefabricated buildings were introduced by the
Federal Works Agency, an achievement in design of W. W. Wurster.
Almost overnight a city of 20,000 sprang up near the Mare Island
Navy Yard at San Francisco. Wooden beams of huge size were
replacing steel as lamination came into its own. Engineers discovered anew how strong wood really was . . . Wood was
found perfectly acceptable and on a par with steel for building
hangars. warehouses, factories and housing for war workers. By the
spring of 1942. Colonel Greeley reported to WCLA members that
there were war orders totaling 800,000,000 board feet at the mills.

How anyone in his right mind believed a war could be fought
without lumber seemed beyond understanding. The Army alone
needed three hundred trains of lumber, each train over a mile long.

The demands were widespread and varied. There were the obvious needs for docks, wharves, cantonments, wagons, pontoons, bridges, ties, trench props, and the like, everything from tent poles to the walls of boot camp obstacle courses. The government placed orders for 360 cargo ships, each requiring a sizable quantity of lumber. Even the big steel and iron battle wagons of the Navy needed upward to 500,000 board feet of lumber for decking and gun mounts; steel-hulled cargo ships required 700,000 board feet of lumber and 300,000 square feet of plywood. New-type training planes were being built of thin sheets of wood veneer placed layer upon layer, impregnated with waterproof plastic glues and molded into shape under heat and pressure. Bombing planes packed for shipment by rail or water required about 15,000 board feet — the equivalent of lumber for a five-room house. The little hit-and-run mosquito boats needed 35,000 feet of Douglas fir, spruce, African mahogany and birch. The list went on and on . . . By mid-1942 the projected needs of the War Production Board as to lumber were triple the 8,500,000,000 board feet estimated for a two and one-half year period a year earlier. In all of World War I, the requirements reached only six billion board feet.

Big stuff was needed for this big war, flung across the globe. The Northwest not only had big timber but the powerful equipment to get it out. The greatest wooden structures to that time were erected, among them the "world's largest wood factory" built for Douglas Aircraft at Chicago. The 150-foot roof trusses weighed seventy tons each and the strong columns were glued laminated construction. The great building saved some 20,000 tons of critical steel and showed that wood could hold its own in the modern age. On the West Coast, other wooden structures of size were raised, among them blimp hangars at places like Tillamook, Oregon, for submarine patrols. These were 1,000 feet long, 250 feet wide and 190 feet high, covering seven acres. Old Paul Bunyan would have been mighty proud. They were an important demonstration of Douglas fir engineering, proving the strength of the great wood of the West. Then there were the huge floating dry-docks to repair stricken ships at the front in the South Pacific. These too were of the big stuff, but there were more billions of board feet going into things of quantity not so dramatic — shipping crates for aircraft motors . . . army trucks with wood bodies . . . structural lumber for advance hospitals and other quickly erected installations . . . casings for everything from aircraft parts to pistol cartridges . . . hand rails for stretchers . . . tanks for storage of gasoline of Douglas fir and with rubber fabric linings . . . even dummy cannons and planes to fool the enemy . . .

A fleet of new-type escort aircraft carriers was being secretly built at the Kaiser-Vancouver shipyards by 30,000 men and women laboring along the five ways. WCLA publicist Art Priaulx de-

scribed the carriers as "floating islands of Douglas fir lumber."
Teak wood was used in all early carriers, but now teak wood
wasn't available in quantity. Douglas fir, after many tests, filled
the bill for the all-important carrier decking.

Escort carrier production proved one of the things that turned
the war, giving air power protection in driving Hitler's and the
Japanese submarines from the seas. Navy engineers worked out the
difficult cutting items and experts from the West Coast Lumber
Inspection Bureau began training a small army of lumber graders
and inspectors in the requirements for these new aircraft carriers.
The sawmill men had to be specially trained, too, to get the
maximum in perfect decking from every log. It meant slower work,
more pains with sawyers, resawyers, edgermen, trimmer men and
other key personnel. But it was done, somehow, so that the production was continuous to meet the shipyard needs on time.[3]

Nerve center for the industry's war effort was the WCLA
headquarters in Seattle. Here were screened the day-by-day problems
and needs of the industry, the government, the lumbermen and the
loggers. The staff was short and the work was voluminous; Colonel
Greeley himself was putting in ninety hours a week. Steno-
graphic help wasn't to be had. Boeing Aircraft was taking the
bulk of Seattle-Tacoma labor in great swarms, and despite the demand for lumber for the war, lumbermen and loggers weren't
considered directly engaged in a war industry!

The war hit the lumber industry in unique ways, often un-
anticipated even by defense officials. When the Japanese attacked
Pearl Harbor, the West Coast was blacked out, for it was feared
an enemy invasion force might be hovering just off the coast. Air
raid wardens were horrified to find the region's hundreds of sawmill waste burners shining like beacons to guide in the planes.
They went around every mill town dousing the burner fires. There
were five hundred or more burners and when the blackout was
lifted, at least for the moment, it took twenty-five barrels of crude
oil to get each burner going again.

The burner problem was a critical one to which no one had
given any thought. Ralph D. Brown, assistant secretary-manager
of WCLA, sent out a survey letter pleading that a quick solution
be found for blacking out the burners during air raid alarms.

"This is something that will challenge the mechanical and in-
ventive genius of the industry," Brown declared.

The objective was not to kill the fire with an excessive dousing
of water that would make it difficult to rekindle. A heavy volume
of water could damage the hot brick linings or other parts of the
structure. There was need for something efficient and economical.
Four companies came up with ideas — Forcia and Larsen, Long-
Bell, Westfir and Weyerhaeuser. These were incorporated into a

set of detailed plans by WCLA which was sent out to every mill. Essentially, the plans called for a simple nozzle spraying system some twenty feet above the base of the fire cone and pointed upward. When turned on, the nozzles would create a fine mist or fog in the superheated air of the upper part of the wigwam. As this settled down upon the fire, the flame was eliminated in the brief time of about two minutes. The spray could then be cut off without soaking the burner and if the blackout were a long one could be turned back on when necessary. When the blackout was over, the coals remained and the full fire could easily be built up again.

Colonel Greeley was teamed up with two great wartime WCLA presidents, Orville R. Miller of the Wauna Lumber and Deep River Timber companies, and Dean Johnson of the C. D. Johnson Lumber Corporation. Both men had an intensive drive and organizational ability which went far in bringing about the astounding wartime production record for the WCLA mills. Like Greeley, Miller was a forestry product of the University of California, graduating the year the first world war come to an end. He signed on with the California Barrel Company, owned by the Koster brothers, and was assigned to helping Charles Koster develop a spruce tract for the Army near Astoria. There were plans for a huge wood packaging plant by the Kosters at Vancouver, including sawmill, veneer plant, cooperage works and box factory. Miller was to have charge, but things went down the drain in a postwar depression. He liked the Northwest, however, and took to logging under the banners of Koster Products Company and the Deep River Timber Company. He also engaged later in extensive salvage logging in the Tillamook Burn.

Miller became intensely interested in the sustained yield program and in greater wood utilization, and was a prime mover in establishing the plant at Springfield, Oregon, which was the first nationally devoted to the large-scale extraction of ethyl alcohol from wood waste. He served on numerous WCLA committees and was a vigorous proponent of forest research. Miller also liked to keep the land green and growing, and thus pioneered the roadside plantings in the Tillamook Burn where once he stopped his car and personally dug a protective fire line around a replanted area of young trees.[4] He was president of the Pacific Logging Congress in 1934 and turned later from logging to lumber manufacturing, rising to president of the Wauna Company, secretary of the Mt. Jefferson Lumber Company, and having mills at Glenwood and Lyons. Then Miller moved to the WCLA head rig for two strenuous wartime terms which may have shortened his life, and also served in a position of responsibility on the lumber industry's advisory committee to the War Production Board. For years, he was on the board of the National Lumber Manufacturers Association and became a vice president.

Johnson had an equally celebrated career in lumbering, following the earning of a mechanical engineering degree at Cornell University. He came to Oregon to join his father in the large C. D. Johnson Lumber Corporation mill at Toledo, after service in World War I with the Greeley forestry engineers in France. His experience ran from small gyppo mills to those of larger size, first in southeastern Missouri and later in Oregon. He was a firm supporter of the industrial forestry movement, active in WCLA committees for many years, and among the original sponsors of the Nisqually nursery. For two years he served as vice chairman of the NLMA and was a director of the National Association of Manufacturers which was also close to his heart. Johnson became interested in prefabricated wood, and during World War II his mill not only turned out lumber but built prefabricated houses, barges and patrol boats. Thus, Johnson was fully involved in the war effort before he took over the WCLA presidency from Miller.[5]

The association also had a very capable anchor man in Washington, D.C., in H. V. "Hal" Simpson, of whom we shall hear more later. Simpson was appointed WCLA's permanent representative there late in 1942 when the war work load grew too heavy to be handled by H. W. Murphy, operating director of the bureau of grades, and R. T. Titus, director of trade extension. Simpson's regular detailed reports to the WCLA leaders and members kept them abreast of the needs and problems of conducting this world-wide war from the nation's capital, and helped to coordinate things on the forest fighting front, from lumber auctions to the Office of Price Administration.

Simpson found there were plenty of problems: manpower shortages — 40,000 were needed for the woods — lumber shipments, poor grub for loggers and mill hands who had to have solid stuff that stuck to the ribs, wage difficulties, strickes, the breakdown of equipment and the wearing out of everything from gears to truck tires without immediately available parts, getting out the logs and cutting to the correct specifications to meet the orders on time.

Simpson's reports were not always heartening. Lumber found itself in a crazy wartime paradox, finally designated a most critical material and needing rugged men to bring in the logs and run the sawmills, yet the government was reluctant to defer any of its husky fighting strength to work in the woods. The selective service would grant loggers only a ninety-day extension from the draft.

Then rough and tumble lumberjacking got the worst shakeup in its long and leathery history as women invaded the mills and woods, for the mills were twenty per cent short on crews, the

H. V. "Hal" Simpson was WCLA's wartime anchorman in Washington, D.C., later succeeded Colonel Greeley.

logging operations thirty per cent, and Hal Simpson reported that efforts to furlough 5,000 soldiers to the Western logging camps were refused by the War Department. So they came, as they had to the shipyards, the lipstick brigade in blue jeans and plaid shirts, their hair tied up in tight rolls, and the old-timers nearly choked on their snoose at the sight, for women other than the frumps of the skid roads and a smattering of cooks and waitresses had never dared set foot in the woods or sawmills. The old men had little to say other than to spit in disgust and remark that the guts had sure gone out of the bold and brawny industry.

The women proved best at light mill tasks, working with tallying and grading, running small cutoff saws, handling and piling lumber, driving cars and trucks, and running panel controls of live roll sets where lumber is shunted from the fast-moving head rigs. But doing these jobs relieved the men for the heavier tasks in the 48-hour work week that had been set up to get the lumber to war.

Still the manpower shortage remained serious and in the critical year of 1943, the War Manpower Commission made a special effort to put 4,000 more loggers into the woods by combing shipyards and other war industries to locate men with timber experience and convince them to return to the woods and sawmills. The WCLA information bureau and its representatives gave a hand and, through news stories and feature material, tried to stress to the public that the war fighting front at home was in the forests, not only just with keeping out the forest fires, but in every way their help was needed. A survey of eighty-three sawmills showed that average hourly production had dropped 12.5 per cent, largely from inexperienced labor. The mills required 40,000 workers for a "full crew," the logging operations needed some 30,000 loggers.

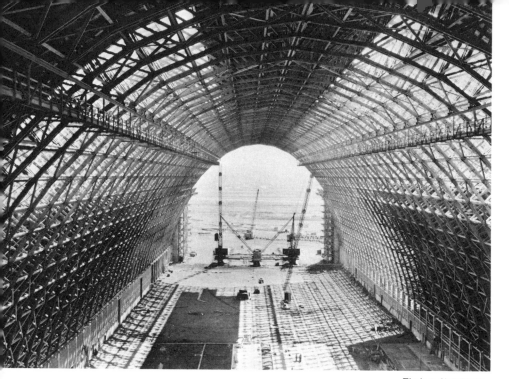

—Timber Structures

Lumber was in critical demand during World War II and demonstrated its strength and adaptability, replacing steel in such big projects as this blimp base at Tillamook, Oregon. Japanese knew the value of wood for war and tried to burn the Pacific Northwest forests.

The mills were short 2,800 hands, or seven per cent; the logging camps down 6,000 men. Only through employment of women and inexperienced men were the mills able to keep crews, but they suffered terribly from a big labor turnover.

Machinery wore out and spare parts were hard to come by, especially for trucks and caterpillar tractors. Many trucks were idle for days and weeks waiting for replacements. It was tough getting priorities and in convincing government officials that fleet log truck operators needed stockpiles of spare parts in the inaccessible locations where they operated. Red tape denied the right of truck operators to have such stockpiles. A breakdown could lay up a truck for a long while, holding logs in the woods instead of getting them down to splash. WCLA officials headed by Simpson fought to get the truck operators the replacements they needed. The log trucks had to be kept rolling at all cost, including that whopper up on Puget Sound called the "Big Blue Ox," the granddaddy of them all, eighty-five feet long with twenty-eight wheels, eight forward speeds, and able to tote 150 tons of logs at a single crack.

By straining every muscle, the Northwest loggers got out 100,000,000 board feet of airplane logs, "aeros," the cream of the West Coast forests, fine straight grained the entire length. The Forest Service rafted at high cost 40,000,000 feet of top-grade

Sitka spruce logs from Alaska to Puget Sound, measuring thirty-six feet in length and three feet across at the small end. The aeros were treated with tender loving care, and some West Coast mills installed special "pony bands" for resawing clear sections from their logs. Every likely clear cant was inspected and resawed, turned and resawed again to gain even a single piece of "aero."

Many lumber firms were awarded the coveted "Army and Navy E" for their records in wartime production. WCLA received the Navy's "Certificate of Achievement" for the coordinating work that the association did. But despite the technical advancements, the citations and all the rest, the timberlands were as badly battle scarred as were the cities of Europe. Colonel Greeley termed World War I a "love pat" by comparison with the shock of World War II. In six years the United States consumed an astounding 215 billion board feet of lumber, representing at least ten million acres of American forests. The timberlands knew they had been in a war and the President knew it, too, for when Harry Truman announced the explosion of the first atomic bomb over Hiroshima, he wore a Paul Bunyan necktie.

NOTES TO CHAPTER XVII

1. The balloon landed on forest property of the Weyerhaeuser Timber Company, which in 1950 established the place as a "patriotic shrine" known as the Mitchell Recreation Area, and erected a historical marker reading "America's only World War II loss of lives on home soil." Besides Mrs. Mitchell, the children who died were: Sherman Shoemaker 12, Jay Gifford 12, Eddie Enger 13, Joan Patzke 11, and Dick Patzke 13.

2. The *Oregonian*, July 21, 1950.

3. *"Fir Floors for Shangri La"* by Arthur W. Priaulx, *Oregon Journal*, November 21, 1943.

4. A memorial forest area of the Tillamook Burn bears the name of Orville R. Miller, who died in 1948.

5. In August 1951 the C.D. Johnson Lumber Corporation and the industry suffered a triple tragedy when Dean Johnson and his brother, Ernest E. Johnson, also active in WCLA affairs, were killed in the crash of an airliner' approaching the landing at Oakland, California. Four days later during the funeral services at Portland, the resident manager of their Toledo sawmill operations, Robert P. Richardson, suffered a heart attack and died moments later.

Chapter XVIII

Beating the Log Drums

Long before the A-bombs were dropped on Japan and people danced in the streets and swam nude in the fountains of San Francisco, the West Coast lumber industry was laying plans for the postwar age.

The big demand would be for homes for returning GI's, the boys coming back to wives and girl friends, boys who had a belly full of war and seeing foreign lands and now wanted only to get some education, settle into a good job and establish a home in the city suburbs or the small towns.

Looking to the future, Colonel Greeley in 1943 wrote the WCLA members:

"The more rapidly we can create peacetime demands for labor and industrial products, the easier the adjustment will be. I view it as a challenge to American business and our vaunted system of private enterprise. It is certain that if American business does not work it out, the Government will attempt to do so with all manner of federal programs, pump priming, socialized housing, and so on."[1]

"Homecoming Homes for GI's" became the theme, with WCLA sending out literature and informational material to the Homecoming Home clubs throughout the land. A Home Planning Institute was developed in cooperation with the Western Retail Lumbermen's Association, the National Lumber Manufacturers Association, other forest products groups, and the Equitable Savings and Loan Association of Portland. Ralph Cake, a local banker, represented the Savings and Loan League as its president in this experimental institute, for which WCLA underwrote $7,500 of the $10,000 cost.

The general idea was to encourage people to save for a new postwar home through the purchase of U. S. Savings Bonds, and at the same time both to stimulate their interest and to help educate them by a series of lecture programs on the mechanics of home planning and building for individual tastes and needs.

The "pilot" run in Portland took off like a rocket. It was meant to educate the sponsors as well as the enrollees and to take the bugs out of the institute. There were 900 inquiries and 200 signed up for the initial classes. The overflow necessitated expanding the lecture program to accommodate all who wanted to attend. Most of the attendees were wives and sweethearts of men in the war, all dreaming of the day that peace would come again. WCLA staffers worked up a portfolio "kit of tools" on home planning, available at cost to the retail lumber dealers, savings and loan associations, groups of realtors, and companies and civic organizations interested in forming home planning institutes in their communities.[2]

Now was the time, President Johnson stressed, to get people thinking about wood as the versatile product. A widespread publicity campaign must be initiated to "popularize wood as a building material." Such a program could cost WCLA some $300,000 annually; this can be compared with $20,000 subscribed for national advertising in 1913 by the WCLA members.

There was little doubt that the lumber industry was in serious jeopardy, for new competitors were cropping out on all sides. Other materials promised to make critical inroads on lumber usage in the postwar period — glass, steel, aluminum, composition boards, concrete — and not only did these have great public appeal but the backing of powerful trade and merchandising associations. To deal with the problem, a special WCLA committee of twenty-six members was appointed, headed by an executive committee of eight: Dean Johnson, chairman; G. E. Karlen, vice chairman, Karlen-Davis Lumber Company, Tacoma; E. H. Houston, Long-Bell Lumber Company, Longview; J. E. Morris, Weyerhaeuser Sales Company, Tacoma; P. C. Stevens, National American Wholesale Lumber Association, Portland; William Swindells, Willamette Valley Lumber Company, Portland; J. R. Titcomb, Weyerhaeuser Timber Company, Springfield, Oregon; and C. L. Wheeler, Pope & Talbot, Inc., San Francisco. The advertising firm of Mac Wilkins, Cole & Weber was signed on as an advertising counsel, with George Weber himself sitting in on the meetings.

It was decided that advertising and trade extension for this gigantic effort should be under a single captain, so the association hired Paul E. Kendall of Chicago, experienced in lumber advertising and promotion, as manager of the new merchandising group called "West Coast Woods." Kendall had a sound background in this work as former advertising manager for fifteen years with Long-Bell, secretary-manager of the National Door Manufacturers Association, head of farm sales for the Johns-Manville Sales Company, and an executive with the merchandising institute of the National Retail Lumber Dealers Association. A broad soliciting program was undertaken, within and outside the association, to raise at least $500,000;

and 125 lumber manufacturers, loggers and timber owners, treating companies, wholesalers and one trade publication pledged funds as sponsors. It proved to be one of the most ambitious under-takings in WCLA history.

By the day when the Japanese signed the surrender aboard the *USS Missouri,* the West Coast industry was ready. Colonel Greeley reported the advertising fund in excess of $700,000 from seventy-five subscribers and that an effort would be made to gain the additional support to reach the goal of $1,000,000.

"It means that the industry will move aggressively to control its own future and maintain its progress," Greeley said. "This plan represents real postwar planning."

With the war done, the aging military forester decided to muster himself out, to retire at the age of sixty-six to his beloved thirty-seven acre tree farm at historic Port Gamble. He retired, it was soon found, in name only, for the Colonel remained a vice president in WCLA and active in forestry through the last decade of his life. He became chairman of the American Forest Products Industries, Inc., devoting his energies to a national campaign to "Grow Trees for America." He continued to be a forceful voice in the timberlands and did much writing for national publications and two books, *Forests and Men* and *Forest Policy.* He was in great demand as a speaker nationally, and during the last two years of his life devoted his energies to the Yale University en-dowment program. At home he contributed much time and thought to the Kitsap County forestry program. The *Oregon Journal* pointed out that *"he has now come so far that he is without question America's No. 1 forester."*

At a great testimonial banquet for him in Portland, attended by hard-driving and picturesque lumbermen from across the nation, Greeley declared:

"In the next ten to fifteen years, I can very clearly see taking shape, new ideas, new industrial processes, new uses of wood. We are going to see a great alchemy of forestry of utilization of new products based upon the marvelous growing power of the Douglas fir forest. I expect to live to see West Coast forestry become the outstanding example of forest economy in all these aspects."[3]

Perhaps Colonel Greeley had the future in mind when he hired Hal Simpson to take on the grueling responsibility of managing the Washington, D. C. office in wartime. If Hal Simpson didn't have the stuff it took, the wartime job would bring it out.

Now again, the picture in the lumber industry had shifted, for the need was that of marketing and trade extension to meet the onslaught of the new materials developed during the war years. Simpson wasn't a forester; he was a business executive, a sharp and calculating trade promoter, a hard-driving lumberman up from the timberlands of the Oregon country, who knew the lumber business all over the world. One of his fellow employees said that he always thought of Hal Simpson as a "super-salesman."

President Dean Johnson, himself a go-getter, emphasized the need in the postwar era of a man of Simpson's calibre in making the announcement at a trustees meeting at Gearhart, Oregon, in September 1945.

"Hal Simpson is powered and trained to head a drive to maintain West Coast lumber against the competition of other building materials and foreign forest industries," Johnson declared.

Simpson had the fragrance of sawdust in his nostrils and the ring of the head rig in his ears from a very early age. He was born in an important sawmill area, at Ashland on July 18, 1897. This was his home until called to the service in World War I. Simpson found himself suddenly half a world away from his beloved southern Oregon with the field artillery in France. Upon discharge, he entered the University of Oregon and in 1923 marched down the long aisle in cap and gown as president of his senior class to receive a degree in business administration. At that point, he may have been torn between two loves, business and journalism, for he was active in his college years on campus publications and had association with enthusiastic young classmates who would rise to the heights in the field of letters during that golden age of professional authors. Among them were Palmer Hoyt, who became publisher of *The Oregonian* and later the *Denver Post,* and Ernest Haycox, one of the greatest Western novelists of them all.

Instead, Simpson turned to lumbering. He worked for a few years in sawmills, learning the business from the ground up, and then went into the selling of lumber on the intensely tough New York market. He entered the export field, expending his energies and talents for some years in the United Kingdom and South Africa, and as secretary and assistant manager of the Seaboard Lumber Sales Company, Ltd., of Vancouver, British Columbia. He also was in the lumber business in Seattle. When World War II came and WCLA was girding itself, Greeley hired him for the Washington office. To many, the step up into Greeley's chair seemed a natural advancement for Hal Simpson.

Other changes, some long anticipated, were culminated with the retirement of Colonel Greeley. Simpson's title was to be "executive vice president" and the old title of secretary-manager was dropped. Ralph Brown, the longtime and loyal assistant secretary-manager, remained in charge of the Seattle branch office until his retirement. Harris E. Smith, who joined WCLA in 1928 in the merger with the trade extension bureau, moved to Portland as secretary. Smith had come West five years earlier to work as auditor for Long-Bell at Longview and then in 1928 he was asked by John D. Tennant, the Long-Bell general manager, to take over the financial and membership work of the West Coast Trade Extension Bureau. When WCLA was reorganized, Smith was given the job of auditor and financial manager. He protested to Tennant that he wanted to quit to go into private business as a certified public accountant. Tennant replied that the job was "only temporary." Thirty-one years later when he retired, Smith remarked that "now the temporary job is over," and within the year opened his long-dreamed-of office as a CPA. He would have plenty of business, for Smith had become an authority on lumber accounting, having authored a number of publications on lumber cost accounting and developing sound, accurate and useful cost accounting and statistical systems for sawmills and wood products plants.

Another startling development was announcement that the headquarters of the West Coast Lumbermen's Association were being moved to Portland. It was a sign of the times and a necessity, for the center of lumbering had shifted south from the Evergreen State. Since 1938 Oregon had led the nation in lumber production, upwards to seven billion board feet, while Washington leveled off in a trend toward a stabilized cut under a sustained yield program. There were 134 WCLA lumber companies south of Portland and 78 to the north, in all representing eighty per cent of the region's cut and approximately one-third of the nation's annual lumber output. There were big, brawling camps of the Columbia River and huge mills were turning out the planks, including the great Oregon-American plant at Vernonia. Portland was already the center for many private and governmental timber groups, and therefore the move by WCLA seemed both wise and logical. For a long while the association had maintained a branch office in Portland's Yeon Building and also in Eugene. Now, to accommodate the headquarters, the office was moved to the sprawling eighth floor of the Neighbors of Woodcraft Hall at Southwest Fourteenth and Morrison, where it would remain until the association reached the end of the sawdust trails two decades hence.

The move brought about other changes in WCLA personnel, faces that had become familiar through the many years. One was that of Jim Stevens who balked at giving up his beautiful hillside home of many years overlooking Lake Washington. WCLA officials certainly understood, but didn't want to lose Stevens entirely, so kept him on a part-time basis as adviser and consultant. But a full-time man of ability was needed for publicity and public relations in the Portland office.

Art Priaulx was doing an outstanding job down at Eugene, with a continual flow of words and ideas from his typewriter, and numerous by-lined wartime features in *The Oregonian* Sunday magazine section and in other Northwest papers, as well as many magazines. A big, friendly sort, Priaulx knew his way around the industry and had long been an active newspaperman, once rated as the "youngest chain newspaper publisher in America" with five weeklies in his string. The California-born Priaulx (at Pasadena in 1903) migrated to Oregon at an early age, attending both the University of Oregon and Oregon State College for work in journalism, political science and economics. He started out his newspaper career at Drain, later acquired the other publications and boldly entered the field at Eugene, publishing the *Eugene Daily News* for four years before selling out to the powerful *Register-Guard*. It was then that he joined WCLA to work the branch office under Jim Stevens and Colonel Greeley.

Hal Simpson also signed on Robert E. Mahaffay, a freelance writer and a staff member with the *Seattle Times* to assist Priaulx. It wasn't long before Simpson observed that Mahaffay had a talent for advertising and promotion, and was shifted to that department where he became trade promotion director upon the retirement in 1953 of Paul Kendall. Mahaffay soon found himself up to his eyeballs in advertising work. In the eight years following the end of the war, Mahaffay supervised the development and distribution of over seven million pieces of literature, established a WCLA motion picture, television and slide series, and implemented the industry's promotion of low-grade lumber. He also found time to produce other cleverly original pieces of writing. One which won high acclaim was an illustrated lumber booklet for children called *Happy Little Handsaw* done at the request of schools and people in education, and distributed by WCLA in 100,000 printings.

The department not only handled a voluminous amount of work on the national level in conjunction with the advertising agency of Cole & Weber, but won many national honors, among them two first-place awards in a field of 446 entries from throughout the United States and Canada for both its advertising and promotion literature, sponsored by the National Advertising Network; and in 1962 the "Premier Award" against 284 entries in a creative awards competition for displays in architectural and builder magazines.

All means of communications were used. Many services were provided the schools through Arthur K. Roberts, the WCLA education director. A number of educational films were produced and distributed to schools and other institutions, and to motion picture houses and television stations. Among the early ones were "The Magic of Lumber" and "Lumber for Homes"; the latter which portrayed the use of West Coast lumber in house construction was one of six selected by the U.S. State Department for a builders tour of Russia for showing in the Soviet Union. Bob Mahaffay, who supervised the production, had managed the full-color sequences to be so clearly illustrated that the State Department didn't feel it was necessary to provide a sound track in the Russian language.

A sixty-six frame film strip, "The Story of West Coast Lumber," was made in cooperation with the Society for Visual Education in Chicago and presented outright to some 5,000 schools. Three thousand additional film strips were needed to meet the demand. Some 7,000 slides on fire prevention and tree harvesting were also distributed to the schools. The film strips were an outstanding success of the education department and the distribution came to total 25,000 sent on request to elementary and high schools and some colleges.

The first objective of the WCLA postwar advertising drive was to convince the American people that, contrary to federal propaganda, there was an ample timber supply and that if they wished wood for their homes and other construction, it was available. The great *Saturday Evening Post* advertisements were milestones in public relations, setting the pace for similarly-styled displays of today for not only the trade groups but private timber companies.

"Enough West Coast wood to rebuild every home in America" cried the costly full page ads. "There are 14.5 million acres of saw timber in Oregon and Washington alone." Advertising told the wood story to 10,000,000 readers each week of the great national magazine of 3,350,000 circulation.

Not all lumbermen cheered the promotion, for in this transformation from war to peace, lumber products were still short.

"Don't you think it a bit premature?" asked a Columbus, Ohio, retailer. "Won't you please tell us where this lumber is?"

That was the general complaint. Others were more favorable, and the *Mississippi Valley Lumberman,* hailing the WCLA effort as a great forward step, commented that the program "if continued permanently can prove to be the best investment its sponsors ever have made. Other great industries have fallen by the wayside through lack of foresight. Lumber could well go the same way. It is high time for lumber to look ahead."

Mats of advertisements were supplied lumber dealers who wished to advertise in their local newspapers. More space was taken in the second six months in other publications, among them *American Home, Better Homes and Gardens,* the *Farm Journal* and the *Country Gentleman.* The lumbermen went after the farm market. A "Farm Book" was developed and distributed by the many thousands during the first month following publication. Promotion emphasized the use of low-grade lumber and the economy grades — "the right lumber for the right use."

The Simpson-guided promotion and merchandising program took varied forms and the growth was next to fantastic. At the end of the war, the association budget for literature was only $7,500, with the annual distribution around 45,000 pieces. By 1948 WCLA was sending out 425,000 pieces, 846,000 in 1949, 1,316,000 in 1950, and over 3,000,000 pieces in 1951 at a cost of $125,000. Some ninety separate pieces of literature were kept constantly in print by WCLA, good, sound factual information done up in attractive and well-illustrated forms, and produced by some of the best talent the association could find among artists, writers, photographers, layout and production people. There were more than a dozen fetching full-color lumber booklets and brochures, plus a lengthy list of how-to-do-it booklets, technical books such as the fine *Douglas Fir Use Book*, farm building books, lumber painting books and miscellaneous publications. The 300-page *Douglas Fir Use Book* was virtually a bible for the use of Douglas fir by all lumber specifying groups, and won many awards and honors. It was originated by Chester J. Hogue, the veteran WCLA technical engineer, and in this postwar era revised by T.K. May and R.G. Kimbell Jr., to win first prize in competition of the Producers Council, an affiliate of the American Institute of Architects. Aptly nicknamed "Tank," May influenced standards for West Coast lumber in his 28 years with WCLA to a degree in keeping with his own imposing size. He started under Hogue, who devoted nearly 30 years of pioneering work in wood technology, earning international note. When Hogue retired in 1945, May became technical chief. He played a key role in developing standards for glued laminated lumber. Moving solidly toward full acceptance as WCLA was striking its tents was May's "load sharing" concept for framing lumber. He argued that the codes had long required more wood than necessary in construction, and that recognition for the plain fact that all the pieces in a roof system, for example, help each other, was to mean the saving of millions of dollars in future constructions costs.

The West Coast Woods national advertising program, supplemented by local dealers, stimulated mounting interest. Response to single advertisements was phenomenal, with 10,000 replies received over a single weekend. In each instance, prospective lumber customers wrote in for free literature and would receive handsome full-color booklets and pamphlets suggesting lumber for homes, schools, churches, commercial and business structures. Requests for one early booklet reached 58,000 in the first month and 175,000 copies were distributed during the peak month.[4] Another example: Bob Mahaffay reported that in the first six months of 1951, the trade promotion department of WCLA distributed 1,603,000 pieces of literature, an increase of almost 300,000 over the entire previous year. A single month's requests for newspaper advertising mats reached 10,455 from 1,258 dealers, resulting from a monthly dealer publication called "West Coast Woods" which also brought with a single issue requests for 100,000 copies of a brochure "Beautiful Homes" and an equal number for "How to Build Farm Buildings," plus the sale at cost to 20,000 lumber retailers of advertising mats, blotters with the names printed on them, farm books, display racks, posters and billboard paper. WCLA President D. W. Gossard of the White River branch of Weyerhaeuser at Enumclaw reported in 1949-50 that in fifteen months, there were 104,000 requests from every state in the Union for 900,000 pieces of promotional literature in two, three and four colors, resulting from advertising in twenty national magazines, aimed primarily at pushing the lower grades of lumber. A new publication "Be Sure When You Build" would have an initial press run of 250,000, said Gossard, and a new 21-minute sound film, "Lumber for Homes," was ready for release.

Simpson now took another daring step forward by ordering costly full-color advertisements in the big national magazines. Simpson wanted to show the people lumber in all its full glory and beauty to gain the greatest attention and to get the most mileage from every advertising dollar. Color photography and advertising became an important facet of the WCLA program; it was found to be very effective.

Meanwhile, the publicity and public relations department under Art Priaulx's direction kept a run of feature material, articles, editorial suggestions, ideas and general information on the many activities of the timber world going to newspapers, syndicates, trade publications and national magazines. Priaulx and his assistants pounced upon just about anything that might have a timber and lumbering "angle" to help create a better-balanced image of the much assailed industry which was once again under attack in the dying throes of legends about the uncivilized, thick-headed, greedy timber barons and reckless loggers who had wasted the people's domain.

Priaulx's own volume of stories was tremendous and he kept in close touch with freelance writers, authors and editors, not only of his own region but throughout the country. He was a friend of young, struggling freelancers who found a warm informality at his office, a man generous not only with ideas but paying markets where articles might go (often he sacrificed markets that he might have filled himself), and a huge file of free WCLA photographs which could illustrate just about any kind of article on forestry and lumbering. Writers learned there was always an able and willing hand in the WCLA publicity office to solve their problems, answer their questions, and provide instant facts and figures about the industry.

When Author Ernest Haycox wanted background for one of his Western novels concerning pioneer sawmilling, he turned to his old friend, Art Priaulx; when magazine writers John and Ward Hawkins sought material for a serial for the *Saturday Evening Post* and later a television show, they turned to friend Art. Priaulx grew in stature as a writer as well as a publicist. He became president of the Oregon Freelance Club, a Portland professional group, and long served on its board of directors. He was the best known lumber publicist in all the West.

Like Jim Stevens and Stewart Holbrook, Priaulx struck his own lasting marks in the tall timber. In his enthusiasm for the Keep Oregon Green movement and the planting of trees in scarred areas like the Tillamook Burn, Priaulx knew no peers. He organized, through WCLA channels with Hal Simpson's approval, many a tree-planting outing by school youngsters into the big burn. When it became apparent that the nation's woods were becoming garbage dumps, it was Priaulx who came up with the now familiar words "litterbugs" and "woods hooligans."

Illustrated home features to help the public with its building problems originated from this department. In later years, Priaulx added two more capable staff members, Jocelyn Schilling Cox, a bright young graduate of Whitman College, and Merlin Blais, a veteran newspaperman and for many years business editor of *The Oregonian*. Blais later took over Priaulx's duties when he turned to the first work on this book. An entire series of home idea features was syndicated widely throughout the United States. An illustrated newspaper feature, "Home Individuality," came to be used by 750 large daily newspapers. An illustrated television service was distributed to some two hundred stations, and a radio version of the same series to nine hundred stations. Millions of readers, viewers and listeners were exposed to this material which made the names of West Coast woods familiar household terms.[5]

Priaulx was liked and respected around the newsrooms, considered basic for any publicist. He believed firmly that gaining good will came not merely from providing clean and lively copy for the editors, but being on top of things. The way to win friends among the hard-working gentlemen and ladies of the press was to be one of them — which he most certainly was — and to throw an occasional party for them, educating them on timber matters along the way. Priaulx sold Simpson and the WCLA public relations committee on this approach, and as a result the lumber association got behind many a shindig to entertain visiting groups of editors and writers with all-day trips into the tree farms, followed by outdoor barbecues, cocktail parties and feeds, and special activities for conventions. Art saw the Northwest woods as a proud showplace for displaying to out-of-staters, especially those from back east who had never trod the fragrant woodlands.

Perhaps the most bizarre of all his parties occurred in June 1956 when editors John Armstrong of *The Oregonian* and Ed O'Meara of the *Oregon Journal*, convention co-chairmen, contacted Art about entertaining a national gathering of the American Association of Sunday and Feature Editors in Portland. This was "a natural"

WCLA's pretty grading girls made the grade as a national sensation. The fetching quartette, in cleverly designed costumes, called attention to name changes in popular lumber grades to assist the public in postwar do-it-yourself projects.

for WCLA, since its publicity and promotion department worked closely with many of these editors. But Priaulx wasn't about to coddle them by throwing a formal banquet; instead he welled up the idea of a wild-life feed which would give eastern editors a true taste of the tall timber.

Priaulx and his assistants worked out a tentative menu for this Forest Buffet, to be preceded by a cocktail party sponsored by the Douglas Fir Plywood people. Heading the list was crow, for as Art put it, "all editors eat crow." For five days the WCLA publicity man cruised the timberlands in search of wild game, running up some five hundred miles on his car. He brought back quite an assortment, including cougar, bear, antelope, elk, venison, crow, bobcat, raccoon, wildcat, moose, porcupine and salmon. Many of the items came directly from the woods, but those out-of-season were taken from hunters' food lockers. The most difficult to bag was cougar; they were scarce, but hunter Cliff Rolinson and his hounds tracked one down in Lincoln County. Other trimmings included grasshopper, crab, shrimp and Tillamook cheese hors d'oeuvres to be added to the array that took Chef James Dimitriadis several days to prepare, using a lot of spice, wine, lemons and vinegar; and Priaulx himself brought in fresh eagle's eggs for a concoction call Pseudotsuga taxifolia resin chiffon. The invitations were printed on thin pieces of veneer, creating quite a stir when they reached eastern editorial offices and more than one hundred guests showed up at the feed which became the sensation of the convention.

"Many thanks," Stanleigh Arnold of the *San Francisco Chronicle* wrote Priaulx. "I don't hanker especially for any more grasshoppers, but I could go some more crow. You did a good job that memorable night—and you gained a lot of good will for WCLA from all us hungry Sunday editors."

Such ideas were characteristic of Priaulx who made them work to the advantage of WCLA. Another classic occasion arose in 1956 when it was decided to overhaul the grades and give them names instead of numbers, in hopes that it would help the how-to-do-it customer and Mrs. Housewife better understand the varieties of lumber at the yards. Nothing could be duller, from the point of view of a publicist, than try to "sell" this to an editor. Priaulx was confronted with perhaps the stickiest problem of his successful career.

Art knew his newspaper friends. Editors everywhere were suckers for photographs of leggy and shapely girls in skimpy attire. Many newspapers had a standing policy of running at least one ankle-to-thigh photo each day on their picture pages, and no magazine was complete without its cheesecake shots. But pretty girls and lumber grades seemed about as far apart as you could get in this old world. Art and his assistants cogitated over the problem for a good many cups of coffee and stronger stuff, and finally came up with the scheme to dress the models, but briefly, in costumes depicting the various grades, with banners across their curvy chests naming each according to grade as in a beauty pageant.

Costumes were designed and made, even to pert hats. Miss Economy was dressed in Scotch kilts, Miss Utility in an abbreviated set of blue overalls, Miss Standard in traditional skirt and sweater, and Miss Construction, the glamor grade of them all, in satin and silk, elbow-length gloves, dangling earrings, and huge picture hat. The two blondes and two brunettes each also carried a sign about the grades, and when they traipsed into a local yard for the photograph session, the lumber stacks came tumbling down. The boys had seen nothing like it, not even in the days of the camp followers. What was this lumber business coming to, anyway? The models were posed gaily with stacks of lumber and lift trucks. The array of fetching photgraphs went out over the country to be used not only by the trade publications (Crow's *Lumber Digest* carried it on the cover) but played big by newspapers, syndicates, feature sections and magazines. *Parade Magazine,* with a huge circulation, published the picture full page. In a relatively short time the grade name change was brought to the attention of millions of people.

Simpson's crew showed you could really sell lumber. Under his dynamic guidance in these great years, WCLA became one of the foremost trade associations in the world, and a household byword. Its various departments were an integral part of the operational plans of member mills, and it was a force within and without the industry. Traffic, national affairs, technical engineering, building codes, statistics, public relations, education, promotion, forestry, grading and countless other services were handled every day for the members.

"The fight to keep traditional markets for lumber and win new customers was part of the daily job for WCLA employees," wrote Art Priaulx. "Pressure from competitors who manufacture substitutes for lumber is constant and must be answered every day. The fight against high freight rates, against unfair building codes that would exclude lumber from many cities, against unfair legislation that would penalize lumber, all find WCLA on the firing line. Those associated through the years with WCLA in its work for the lumber industry are proud and zealous of its accomplishments. They are proud that they are up-dated, yes, even advanced in their thinking . . . Believing that is what it takes to make a success, they still think they can lick the world."[6]

NOTES TO CHAPTER XVIII
1. Report of Colonel Greeley, WCLA news release, 1943.
2. From WCLA minutes of trustees meeting, 1943.
3. Colonel Greeley died of cancer in 1955. Yale University in 1959 named its new forest research laboratory in his memory.
4. From the WCLA advertising committee minutes.
5. From the writings of Arthur W. Priaulx.
6. From "Cooperation Licks the World," by Arthur W. Priaulx, *Weyerhaeuser News,* October, 1953.

Chapter XIX
End of an Era

During these high-ball years of merchandising, the West Coast Lumbermen's Association took another bold step, reaching out aggressively to the far corners of the shrinking world to sell the products manufactured from the woods of the Pacific shore.

Where once the windjammers and the steam schooners came seeking the great raw timber, West Coast lumbermen were now reversing the cards, going afar to learn the needs and the conditions of marketing abroad on an expanding scale. The WCLA trustees with considerable industrial backing sponsored two trade missions to eight foreign countries.

The missions to Europe, Japan and Australia were tours of good will, to demonstrate the interest of the West Coast lumbermen in those lands. The missions would enable American shippers to learn more about competition facing them, the various trade practices and trends in the use of wood products, to exchange views on timber construction techniques, and most important, to emphasize the fact to those countries that they could look to the West Coast as a dependable source of lumber.

G. Cleaveland Edget, the new executive vice president of WCLA, headed up these ambitious trade missions and it seemed most natural that he should do so, since Edgett had much experience abroad in lumber merchandising. Hal Simpson was ailing from a heart condition and when it was obvious that the great merchandiser would be forced into semi-retirement, Edgett was hired in 1961 as his assistant. That was October and nine months later, Simpson retired early and Edgett succeeded him officially, the youngest and last of a celebrated line of high ranking leaders who not only carried the weight of the association through critical periods, but in a different and characteristic way helped to civilize and mold the great industry.

"Hal was a pioneer at heart," editorialized the *Lumber Letter* of the National Lumber Manufacturers Association upon Simpson's death in November 1962. "He earned the right to succeed Colonel Greeley in 1946 entirely on the investment of his own genius for productive labor. The pioneering instincts continued during his time at WCLA."

All were pioneers in one way or another—Griggs for founding and guiding the early years of the trade association; Babcock for his early promotional efforts; Greeley for bringing the new era of industrial forestry; Simpson for creating a great selling and promotion program when it was direly needed. Long . . . Bloedel . . . Burnside . . . Dixon. . . Tennant. . . Wagner . . . . Brown . . . Miller Johnson . . . Stevens . . . all the rest who had in countless ways contributed to the robust character and world-wide fame of WCLA throughout the years. Edgett too was a pioneer at heart, this time on the international marketing scene. His career to the age of forty-one, launched upon graduation in 1948 from the University of Washington in industrial and public relations, was an impressive one. He had fourteen years of association lumber business behind him on this continent and abroad, having resided both in Canada and England. He'd traveled extensively in Europe and South Africa; like the windjammer skippers of old, he knew his way about the lumber world.

The WCLA board of trustees had demonstrated for decades a certain genius for selecting the right man at the right time. It appeared that the new executive vice president could not only keep pace with the policies established by Greeley and Simpson, but would add significant programs of his own. It was all important that WCLA continue to move forward, representing as it did a membership producing over four billion board feet annually in a region cutting twenty-eight per cent of the nation's yearly softwood lumber supply.

But a storm was boiling in from the horizon. The industry was going through a period of vast technological change. A battle was shaping up over the controversial grade standardization program that would make the previous fight over the thirty-second of an inch look like a tempest in a teapot. Domestic market conditions were poor and cheaper Canadian lumber imports were taking an increasing share of the market. To make matters worse, WCLA and the West Coast Lumber Inspection Bureau adopted entirely different policies on the complex question of relating dry and green lumber sizes.

When Hal Simpson turned over the reins of office to Edgett, he made a dire prediction.

"Cleve," he said, "you are faced with a situation that cannot be resolved on a rational basis. I know this industry and its people intimately, and I cannot see how the differences that lie beneath the surface can be restrained. It appears to me that the industry and the membership of WCLA will split right down the middle in the months ahead."

One plus factor that Edgett inherited from the previous administration was a group of dedicated employees. These he proceeded to mold into a cohesive team. Gone were the days when a single individual dominated the affairs of the association. Responsibilities were reshuffled. Increased latitude was given department heads. Aggressive programs and policies were developed and presented to the board of trustees for ratification. Truly, a new era was born even though it did have its labor pains.

Faced with a revolt over a do-nothing attitude on Canadian imports, Edgett pressed for a statement of policy that was realistic and that would mollify the divergent groups. This in itself developed into a paradoxical situation because the then president of the association, Bill Garnett, St. Regis Paper Co., joined former president Wagner in the acquisition of Canadian lumber interests. Meanwhile, Edgett, with his long connection with the Canadian industry, found himself on the opposite side of the fence. Personal differences were set aside in the interest of industry harmony, and Garnett and Edgett together hammered out a program that was endorsed not only by the membership of WCLA but the other federated associations of NLMA and by western Congressmen.

One of the obligations that WCLA assumed in its struggle to achieve parity between American and Canadian producers was a sincere effort to develop markets abroad. The Kennedy vision of reducing trade barriers throughout the world was rampant in Washington and the WCLA proposal to organize a government-approved, industry-sponsored trade mission program fell on receptive ears. Ken C. Batchelder, the WCLA traffic manager who was about to retire, arranged the schedule for a 1963 junket to the United Kingdom, the Netherlands, West Germany, Belgium, France and Italy. Then in the spring of 1965, the second mission was organized and Harry Fimmel, former industry relations director of WCLA, was sent to Japan and Australia to set up the detailed itinerary.

Between these projects the battle on grade standardization grew in intensity. At industry meetings, Edgett found himself wearing two hats; one as executive vice president of West Coast Lumbermen's Association and one as manager of West Coast Lumber Inspection Bureau. To make matters more intriguing, the new president of WCLA was Nils Hult and the newly elected chairman of WCLIB was Hult's brother-in-law, Aaron Jones, both of Eugene. Hult and Jones were powerful personalities, leading sharply differing elements of the industry. But both men contributed to the progress and maturing of the lumber industry. As this final chapter was being written, it appeared that the industry was resolving its differences on the size standard, thus brightening prospects for the lumber industry of the Western states.

G. Cleveland Edgett, last of WCLA's executive officers, succeeded Hal Simpson in 1962. Edgett posed for photo at a Japanese lumber auction when he led two association trade missions to Europe and the Far East.

The forests have changed so vastly that an old-time lumberman would scarcely recognize them. The logging camps are gone from the woods; now the lumberjacks live in modern towns and suburbs, in carpeted houses filled with appliances, and travel daily in their sleek automobiles over good roads to the timber operations. Primitive logging is a thing of the past, as is primitive sawmilling. The chain saw has taken the brawn out of the falling and bucking. Powerful bulldozers and loaders get out the logs and load them on huge diesel trucks to be hauled swiftly to the sawmills, the wood pulp plants and to the river log dumps where they are boomed up in the traditional way. Holy old mackinaw! It's even hard to find a high climber any more; those new fangled portable telescopic spar poles have replaced the spar tree. And at Bohemia near Cottage Grove L. L. "Stub" Stewart found a sky hook at last, the thing loggers always dreamed about, in great balloons floating above the logging operations, from which the lead lines are hung and the logs moved through the air with the greatest of ease.

Helicopters are used to string lines, to plant, fertilize and patrol the tree farms, as smoke spotters, and to carry crews of parachuting foresters trained and well armed to fight fires. These brave smoke-jumping forces hit fires before they can go on the rampage. Many of the old forest lookouts are being abandoned in favor of plane patrols. Networks of good roads are cut through the back country so ground forces may also reach fires quickly. The widespread Keep Green programs are winning permanent results and it appears that Colonel Greeley's lifetime dream of eliminating fire from the forests is coming true. The Keep Green movements have made lasting impressions on several generations of people now, in urban as well as rural areas, and it can only be hoped that similar campaigns to save wild life and against turning the hard-pressed forests into garbage dumps can pay off equally as well.

More and more you hear the terms "wood products" and "wood utilization." The world's first forest products laboratory established in 1910 at Madison, Wisconsin, was far ahead of its time. Some universities began doing limited research, but few if any lumbermen bothered to enter experimentation for their lower grades and waste materials. The lumbermen looked upon laboratory foresters with the same jaundiced eye that they turned upon the field foresters. Still, there were men like Sol Simpson and Major Griggs, and those tough loggers of the Polson Brothers who were sent into the woods to plant trees . . .

Other things happened that were to have dramatic impact upon all the industry. Two world wars spurred them forward. One was glue lamination and jointing techniques which paved the way for technical achievements in huge gymnasiums and warehouses that put wood on a par with other materials for great building projects.

The important Oregon Forest Products Laboratory, opened in 1941 at Oregon State College, became involved in a growing list of probings into the mysteries of wood and wood fiber, and improved utilization of low-grade lumber. Many other university laboratories are continually making contributions to the frontiers of forest products research. Among the modern pioneers is Dr. Bror L. Grondal, a longtime member of the University of Washington faculty, whose many patient and imaginative studies led to scores of useful applications in forest products markets.

Plywood...veneer...wood fiber...pulp...adhesives...packing materials...bark products...a growing host of wood chemicals...these are the things that you hear about today. Among the latest is a wonder drug called DMSO, a chemical by-product of the paper industry which in 1965 was holding great promise of bringing relief to sufferers of arthritis, bursitus, rheumatism, and other painful and crippling disorders. There seem to be no surprises and only a boundless frontier to come from the wonderful world of wood, now that the scientists are probing the log and its fiber and chemicals for their remaining secrets.

Not all the research is concerned with getting the most from a log. The test tube invaded the forests and tree farms to uncover better ways to grow healthier trees more rapidly, to reforest more effectively, to cope with forest diseases with greater efficiency. Things were advanced by 1965 so far up the road that the forest scientists from the Oregon State laboratory, under the leadership of Dr. Julius A. Rudinsky, were interfering with the sex life of bark beetles. The female, it seems, sends out a perfume which draws the males, thus breeding more destructive beetles within the trees. So the scientists were considering sterilizing the males by atomic radiation. A second tactic was to develop a perfume similar to that of the female, spread it around the woods, and completely confuse and frustrate the romantic intentions of the love-lorn males. That's how far the forest laboratory has gone.

The modern lumberman really isn't a lumberman anymore in the strictest sense. He is a skilled manufacturer of frame components, beautiful panelings, sidings, attractive overhead beams, and shiny wall materials which bring out unique and wonderful grain patterns of the woods. Artistic and decorative uses for thousands of wood items have been uncovered, along with the finishings and preservatives which enhance their great natural beauty as never before. Wood is now cut, fitted and molded for countless special uses, and architects seem to be trying to outdo each other in finding new ways to display woods in modern homes, offices and public buildings. Outstanding examples of what can be done are found in two tourist showplaces, the Village Green built by W.A. Woodard, a veteran WCLA lumberman, at Cottage Grove, Oregon, and Salishan on the middle Oregon coast. New uses catch the eye of the consumer for home, farm and industry as the world of wood keeps pace with rapidly changing times.

Full utilization . . . this is the watchword now . . . the goal and utopia of the wood world. And the public, except the most ignorant, can hardly rant any more about wanton lumbermen. Certainly lumber is still around in large quantities and is a basic material for construction, but the sawmills too are different from head rig to planer. They are becoming automated and in 1965 a great push-button mill was being built by the historic Simpson company at Shelton, Washington. Pulp plants have sprung up all around the land and chip bins are replacing the old wigwam burners in scores of places, for lumbermen find value now in their leftovers. Wood chips are the blue chips of today, and even portable chippers reminiscent of the old-time portable mills have invaded the woods, gobbling up the former waste on the spot so that one day the log truck itself, like the logging railroad before it, may become old-fashioned.

A most significant milestone of the times came early in 1965 when the Crown Zellerbach Corporation announced that it was breaking ground at Wauna, the old lumber center on the lower Columbia River, for a plant for the processing of chips, sawdust and pulp for its paper and packaging operations, first portion of an eventual $90,000,000 complex. The huge new development will employ some 1,000 men and was the largest industrial undertaking in the Pacific Northwest in some years. It promised booming things for the lower Columbia and was reminiscent of the glory days when the huge sawmills were established on Puget Sound, Grays Harbor, the Columbia and the Willamette . . .

Yet despite all the advances, similar strides were being made by the producers of competing building materials. The wood products industries found themselves hard pressed to meet the challenge. Long ago, Major Griggs browbeat a bunch of stubborn lumbermen into pulling together. In 1963 associations were thinking in the same direction, of merging instead of duplicating their efforts, in order to promote their products and wrestle their problems jointly, agreeing that there was more competition now from without than within, and that they should hang together or they might jolly well hang separately.

Somehow the word "lumber" didn't cover the field any more. So they met to smoke the peace pipe. Led by Chiefs Nils Hult of WCLA and John Richards of the Western Pine Association, the idea of becoming a single tribe and perhaps bringing in other wood and timber groups to make a powerful trade force of a dozen western states gained support. It took many months, but the consolidation was accomplished in the summer of 1964, creating by far the largest single lumber trade organization in the world, with an annual cut of some ten billion board feet. This group would be headquartered in Portland, and the name itself signified the new era: *Western Wood Products Association.*

On the evening of July 31, 1964, the many WCLA lumbermen and their ladies, in white dinner jackets and formal gowns, gathered in the huge ballroom of Portland's Multnomah Hotel, itself fading into the past, for the final social event of the old association and to herald a new one. If there was any sadness, it wasn't shown here. Instead, it was what the neswpapers described as a "lively wake," presided over by Nils Hult, the last president of WCLA. Hult had served several times as a vice president and there was considerable funpoking over the fact that he was now chief of an all-but-dead organization.

There was much reminiscing by past presidents and veteran staff members, the reading of telegrams and letters expressing both regret and praise for this great association and the people who did so much for the lumber industry, a rollicking skit telling the colorful story of WCLA, and the announcement that as a swan song, a book would be written putting into the permanent record the story of WCLA and the part it played in the history of the West, and of all America.

At the stroke of midnight, WCLA ceased to function as an active trade association, nearly 53 years after that August day in 1911 when the hardy lumbermen gathered at Raymond. As they filed from the hotel, it was hard for old-timers to believe that

the West Coast Lumbermen's Association was all but finished—
reduced to a corporate shell that would remain to fulfill a few
final obligations to the industry. But most were aware, too, that
a new era was just beginning, one of a powerful new alignment
of lumbermen throughout twelve western states with an identical
interest in progress for their industry through organization. The
future to them appeared just as exciting and full of challenge
as the past had been.

Major Griggs, the old patriarch of the trade associations, had
said it well a long while ago:

Slab light, reduce the saw kerf, and keep your eye on the burner...

It was a simple commandment, the key to it all, and good advice for all future time.

THE END

Acknowledgments

It is always difficult to fill a good man's shoes. That is the position in which I find myself in the writing of this book. Originally, it was to be Art Priaulx's project and Priaulx was no small shucks as a writer, especially when it came to the tall timber. He possessed a sweeping background of the lumber industry and its people, acquired through personal observation and long association with it. Priaulx's roots were deep in the world of timber; no amount of reading and listening to people can equal such first-hand knowledge.

Thus, this is no doubt a far different book than he would have written, although I have followed the outline that my friend left behind as he set it down, as to subject matter. But for those who are looking for his words in the wonderful free-wheeling manner that he employed, I can only say that they will be disappointed. Art's time was too short to get very far beyond the initial stages of organizing and roughing out some of the early chapters. He would have been the first to admit it. Fortunately, he made an excellent beginning which I have most gladly retained as he wrote it. I have also drawn heavily upon his past writings and noted the sources. Beyond this, I found it necessary to build upon my own style and my own approach to telling this story.

What I have strived to do in this informal history is to present a broad and detailed portrait of the West Coast lumber industry, from its rough and tumble beginnings down to the present day. Two strong personalities are predominant throughout, the lumberman and his great organization, the West Coast Lumbermen's Association. They revolve around a single hub — the sawmill. The faces and settings change, but these personalities remain constant. This then is a "biography" of the lumberman and WCLA, and how they lived and struggled and achieved lasting things along the Pacific shore.

The story of the logger, because of its obvious color and rugged action, has been told many times. Much has also been written on forestry. The lumberman has been generally neglected in the saga of the West, partly because of his own reluctance to "talk." Now the West Coast Lumbermen's Association, in bowing out of existence, has "talked." I have been most fortunate in having free and unrestricted access to WCLA's private files, records and correspondence compiled during more than half a century. This is rich and exciting material, enough for a dozen books, for WCLA saved everything for the attic. I am informed that much of it will go to the University of Oregon library where it will be available to others interested in studying this fascinating industry in detail. In this regard, I hope that this book will serve through its footnotes and references as a guide for future projects.

To cut through such a vast amount of very detailed material in the time allotted would have been impossible without the incomparable services of Ann Nordstrom, a longtime staff member of WCLA. No few words can suffice in lauding her contribution to this work and her assistance to this author. Her vast personal knowledge of WCLA, the lumber industry, and the people pulled me from many a knothole, solved many a problem, added touches in the right places, and pinned down countless details. There were such sticky things as names spelled incorrectly by WCLA's own secretaries in early record books. Miss Nordstrom knew them to be wrong and set me straight. With both patience and diligence, she chopped our way through the thick timber and the heavy undergrowth like a wilderness scout wielding a machete, and I followed along until at last daylight fell in the swamps . . .

I found invaluable the works of James F. Stevens and Stewart Holbrook. Mr. Stevens wrote a number of letters making suggestions of lines to explore, supplied material from his own files to fill in the chinks, and gave me a rewarding afternoon at his Seattle home.

Countless others were most generous and kind to me, Miss Nordstrom and the late Mr. Priaulx. Among them were a number of past staff members of WCLA. Thorpe Babcock of Los Angeles, California, sent up a lengthy manuscript of his own reminiscences which proved very useful. Ralph D. Brown of Seattle did likewise. Much of the color and anecdotes in the chapter on Grays Harbor must be credited to the excellent research job done by Harold B. Olson of Portland, a onetime newspaper editor at The Harbor. Olson also supplied the author with special newspaper sections from his own files which were exceedingly helpful, while William D. Hagenstein of the Industrial Forestry Association spent hours seeking out some special material on Grays Harbor tree farms.

O. R. Hartwig of Portland, consulting safety engineer for the Crown Zellerbach Corporation, gave generously of his time to reminisce on the early days of sawmilling and labor activities. Harris E. Smith of Portland recalled another period in WCLA, while Judge Charles H. Paul of Seattle explained problems of the NRA and the consent decree, and related some wonderful anecdotes about Colonel Greeley. There were memorable talks with Harry E. Jenkins, an old-time sawmill man of the Jones Lumber Company, who provided much color on early lumbering in Oregon. L. A. Nelson of West Slope was helpful regarding grading rules, while J. G. Manning of Western Wood Products Association explained the problems of lumber traffic.

Our thanks go to Dean F. Sherman and the Miller Freeman Publications who generously opened their library for extensive research in their back files. Staffs were also most helpful at the Henry Suzzalo Library, University of Washington; the Seattle Public Library, especially those of the periodical department; the Portland Public Library; the Oregon Historical Society; *The Oregonian* library; and the Aberdeen and Hoquiam public libraries.

E. G. Griggs II of Tacoma furnished much material about his uncle, Major Everett G. Griggs, the early leader of WCLA. Mrs. Edgar F. Piper of Portland supplied information on her father, Ralph H. Burnside, and on the Willapa Harbor of yesteryear; Mrs. William H. Parks of Newnan, Georgia, sent facts about her father, John D. Tennant; Prentice Bloedel of Bainbridge Island, Washington, about his father, J. H. Bloedel, and supplied a company history; N. M. Larsen, Junction City, data on his father, T. V. Larsen; and Ben H. Gardner, Jr., regarding his father-in-law, Walter B. Nettleton. Carwin A. Woolley supplied data on the Pacific Logging Congress. Many lumber companies provided facts and anecdotes, and there were countless letters from lumber people offering their assistance, and making contributions.

Merlin Blais, Jocelyn Cox and Cleve Edgett of WCLA were most helpful in their comments and suggestions from the chore of reading the manuscript in typewritten form. Walter Foelker of Hillsboro High School who knows his Northwest history was kind enough to read some of the early material and give his comments.

Last, I must salute some longtime friends and associates in my writing career, Mrs. E. B. "Pat" Cunningham who read both copy and proof with a practiced eye; Phil Dana who guided the book through the stages of production; and George Hoerner, Portland artist, who made numerous and worth-while suggestions. I am also most grateful to Mrs. Priaulx for her words of understanding and encouragement.

ELLIS LUCIA
Portland, Oregon, 1965

Bibliography

BOOKS:

Abdill, George B., *This Was Railroading*. Superior Publishing Co., 1958.

Andrews, Ralph W., *This Was Sawmilling*. Superior Publishing Co., 1958.

Binns, Archie, *Sea in the Forest*. Doubleday & Company, 1953.

——— *The Roaring Land*. Robt. M. McBride & Company, 1942.

Clark, Donald H., *18 Men and a Horse*. Metropolitan Press, 1949.

Coman, Edwin T. and Gibbs, Helen M., *Time, Tide and Timber: A Century of Pope & Talbot*. Stanford University Press, 1949.

Corning, Howard McKinley, *Dictionary of Oregon History*. Binfords and Mort, 1956.

Cour, Robert M., *The Plywood Age*. Binfords and Mort, 1955.

Fuller, George W., *A History of the Pacific Northwest*. Alfred A. Knopf, 1945.

Greeley, William B., *Forests and Men*. Doubleday & Company, 1956.

Guthrie, John A. and Armstrong, George R., *Western Forest Industry*. Johns Hopkins, 1961.

Hidy, Ralph W., Hill, Frank Ernest and Nevins, Allan, *Timber and Men, The Weyerhaeuser Story*. Macmillan Company, 1963.

Holbrook, Stewart H., *Green Commonwealth*, Simpson Logging Company. Dogwood Press, 1945.

———, *Tall Timber*, Macmillan Company, 1941.

———, *The Columbia*. Rinehart & Company, 1956.

———, *Far Corner, A Personal View of the Pacific Northwest*. Macmillan Company, 1952.

———, *Burning an Empire*. Macmillan Company, 1943.

———, *Half Century in the Timber*, Schafer Logging Company. Dogwood Press, 1945.

Horn, Stanley F., *This Fascinating Lumber Business*. Bobbs-Merrill Company, 1943.

Hosmer, Paul, *Now We're Loggin'*. Binfords and Mort, 1930.

Jensen, Vernon H., *Lumber and Labor*: Labor in Twentieth Century America. Farrar and Rinehart, Inc., 1945.

Johansen, Dorothy O. and Gates, Charles M., *Empire of the Columbia*. Harper and Brothers, 1957.

Johnson, Jalmar, *Builders of the Northwest*. Dodd, Mead & Company, 1963.

Lavender, David, *Land of Giants*. Doubleday & Company, 1958.

Lucia, Ellis, *Tough Men, Tough Country*. Prentice-Hall, Inc., 1963.

Morgan, George T., Jr., *William B. Greeley, A Practical Forester*. Forest History Society, 1961.

Morgan, Murray, *The Last Wilderness*. Viking Press, 1955.

——— *The Northwest Corner*. Viking Press, 1962.

——— *Skid Road, An Infomal Portrait of Seattle*. Viking Press, 1960.

O'Connor, Harvey, *Revolution in Seattle*. Monthly Review Press, 1964.

Pollard, Lancaster, *History of the State of Washington*. American Historical Society, 1937.

Spencer, Betty Goodwin, *The Big Blowup*. The Caxton Printers, 1956.

Stevens, James F., *Green Power, The Story of Public Law 273*. Superior Publishing Company, 1958.

NEWSPAPERS AND PERIODICALS:

American Forests Magazine (various issues)
Collier's Magazine
Columbia River and Oregon Timberman
Crow's Forest Products Digest
Daily World, Aberdeen, Washington
Forest Industries
News-Tribune, Tacoma, Washington
Oregon Historical Quarterly (various issues)
Oregon Journal, Portland, Oregon
Post-Intelligencer, Seattle, Washington
Reader's Digest
Register-Guard, Eugene, Oregon
Saturday Evening Post
The Oregonian, Portland, Oregon
The Seattle Times, Seattle, Washington
The Timberman

SPECIAL REPORTS AND ARTICLES:

Cox, John H., *Trade Associations in the Lumber Industry of the Pacific Northwest, 1899-1914.* Pacific Northwest Quarterly, University of Washington. October 1950.

Holbrook, Stewart H., *Shanghai Nights in Oregon.* True Magazine, August 1947.

Hult, Ruby El, *The Saga of George W. Bush.* Negro Digest, September 1962.

Priaulx, Arthur W., *Cooperation Licks the World.* Weyerhaeuser News, October 1953.

Roberts, Arthur K., *The West Coast Lumbermen's Association — Its Purposes, History and Activities.* Speech at the College of Forestry, University of Washington, Seattle. 1949.

Stevens, James F., *Out of the Woods* columns, distributed to Northwest newspapers. Bound files, WCLA.

Vinnedge, R. W., *Genesis of the Pacific Northwest Lumber Industry.* Yale School of Forestry lecture, December 18, 1923.

Presidents and Executives

West Coast Lumbermen's Association

PRESIDENTS

TERM	NAME	COMPANY
1911-1912	Everett G. Griggs	St. Paul & Tacoma Lumber Company Tacoma, Washington
1913-1914	Walter B. Mackay	North Pacific Lumber Company Portland, Oregon
1915-1916	Julius H. Bloedel	Bloedel Donovan Lumber Mills Bellingham, Washington
1917	Arthur L. Paine	National Lumber & Manufacturing Co. Hoquiam, Washington
1918	Ralph H. Burnside	Willapa Lumber Company Raymond, Washington
1919	Robert S. Shaw	Hammond Lumber Company Astoria, Oregon
1920-1921	R. Webb Vinnedge	North Bend Lumber Company North Bend, Washington
1922-1923	A. C. Dixon	The Booth-Kelly Lumber Company Eugene, Oregon
1924	Ernest Dolge	Ernest Dolge, Inc. Tacoma, Washington
1925	E. D. Kingsley	West Oregon Lumber Company Linnton, Oregon
1926	C. D. Johnson	Pacific Spruce Corporation Portland, Oregon
1927	Roy F. Morse	Long-Bell Lumber Company Longview, Washington
1928-1932	John D. Tennant	Long-Bell Lumber Company Longview, Washington
1933-1934	Ernest W. Demarest	Pacific National Lumber Company Tacoma, Washington (resigned 11/22/34)
1934	F. R. Titcomb	Weyerhaeuser Timber Company Tacoma, Washington (remainder of term)
1935	Walter B. Nettleton	Nettleton Lumber Company Seattle, Washington
1936-1937	T. V. (Vic) Larsen	Forcia & Larsen Noti, Oregon
1938-1939	Edmund Hayes	Clackamas Fir Lumber Company Portland, Oregon
1940-1941	Corydon Wagner	St. Paul & Tacoma Lumber Company Tacoma, Washington
1942-1943	Orville R. Miller	Wauna Lumber Company Portland, Oregon
1944-1945	Dean Johnson	C. D. Johnson Lumber Corporation Portland, Oregon
1946	C. (Chris) H. Kreienbaum	Simpson Logging Company Shelton, Washington
1947-1948	Charles Ward Ingham	Fisher Lumber Company Marcola, Oregon

1949-1950	D. W. (Bill) Gossard	White River Lumber Company Enumclaw, Washington
1951-1952	Hillman Lueddemann	Pope & Talbot, Inc. Portland, Oregon
1953-1954	G. E. (Fred) Karlen	Eatonville Lumber Company Tacoma, Washington
1955-1956	N. (Nat) B. Giustina	Guistina Bros. Lumber Company Eugene, Oregon
1957	Robert M. Ingram	E. C. Miller Cedar Lumber Co. Aberdeen, Washington
1958	Jack Fairhurst	Fairhurst Mill Company Eureka, California
1959-1960	Eliot H. Jenkins	The Booth-Kelly Lumber Company Eugene, Oregon
1961-1962	W. (Bill) R. Garnett	St. Regis Paper Co. Tacoma, Washington
1963-1964	Nils B. Hult	Hult Lumber & Plywood Company Junction City, Oregon

WCLA SECRETARY-MANAGERS OR EXECUTIVE VICE PRESIDENTS

TERM	NAME	OFFICE
1911-1914	W. C. Miles	Manager
1911-1917	Thorpe Babcock	Secretary
1917-1928	Robert B. Allen	Secretary-Manager
1928-1945	William B. Greeley	Secretary-Manager
1945-1955	William B. Greeley	Vice President
1945-1962	H. (Hal) V. Simpson	Secretary-Manager Executive Vice President
1962-1964	G. C. (Cleve) Edgett	Executive Vice President
1917-1946	Ralph D. Brown	Assistant Secretary Assistant Secretary-Manager
1928-1946	Harris E. Smith	Auditor
1946-1958	Harris E. Smith	Secretary
1963-1964	Gordon J. Brown	Secretary